Audrey + Jim —

As Rick [?] end of Casablanca,
"I think this is the beginning of a beautiful friendship."
Best fishes,
Doug Kelly

Florida's Fishing Legends and Pioneers

WILD FLORIDA

UNIVERSITY PRESS OF FLORIDA

Florida A&M University, Tallahassee
Florida Atlantic University, Boca Raton
Florida Gulf Coast University, Ft. Myers
Florida International University, Miami
Florida State University, Tallahassee
New College of Florida, Sarasota
University of Central Florida, Orlando
University of Florida, Gainesville
University of North Florida, Jacksonville
University of South Florida, Tampa
University of West Florida, Pensacola

Florida's Fishing Legends and Pioneers

Doug Kelly

FOREWORD BY M. TIMOTHY O'KEEFE

University Press of Florida

Gainesville · Tallahassee · Tampa · Boca Raton
Pensacola · Orlando · Miami · Jacksonville · Ft. Myers · Sarasota

Library of Congress Cataloging-in-Publication Data
Kelly, Doug
Florida's fishing legends and pioneers /
Doug Kelly ; foreword by M. Timothy O'Keefe.
p. cm. — (Wild Florida)
Includes bibliographical references and index.
ISBN 978-0-8130-3576-5 (alk. paper)
1. Fishers—Florida—Biography. 2. Fishing—Florida History. I. Title.
SH483.K45 2011
799.1092'2759—dc22
[B]
2010040993

The University Press of Florida is the scholarly publishing agency for the
State University System of Florida, comprising Florida A&M University,
Florida Atlantic University, Florida Gulf Coast University, Florida Interna-
tional University, Florida State University, New College of Florida, Univer-
sity of Central Florida, University of Florida, University of North Florida,
University of South Florida, and University of West Florida.

University Press of Florida
15 Northwest 15th Street
Gainesville, FL 32611-2079
http://www.upf.com

To those whose hearts beat faster the closer they get to the dock.

Just remember, *these* are the good old days of tomorrow.

STU APTE

Contents

Foreword

The previous 10 volumes in the University Press of Florida's broad-ranging series Wild Florida have concentrated on the numerous activities still possible in the vast remaining natural areas of the Florida outdoors. These have included hiking, walking and beach-access handbooks as well as instructive how-to guides.

Florida's Fishing Legends and Pioneers is the first Wild Florida book to take a historical perspective by describing many of the anglers, guides and outdoor writers responsible for building Florida into the world's most popular fishing destination.

It takes someone with in-depth knowledge and extensive contacts to attempt a work of this type. I vaguely recall running into Doug Kelly for the first time in 1991 while I was serving as president of the Florida Outdoor Writers Association (FOWA). Doug and I were attending FOWA's Tallahassee conference, where the marquee speaker was internationally known fly fisherman Lefty Kreh. Lefty's presentation on photography techniques still resonates with both of us today. Not surprisingly, Lefty and his many contributions to Florida angling are featured in one of this book's chapters.

Since our first meeting, Doug has amassed an impressive set of credentials. He has served as executive director of FOWA, managing editor of *Florida Sportsman* magazine and editor of *Sport Fishing* magazine; produced award-winning videos and TV shows; hosted radio programs; and written for newspapers, magazines and blogs. His work has taken him the length of Florida's coastlines and to its inner lakes, allowing him to meet just about everyone who is involved with the state's recreational fishing industry. Without question, Doug has the qualifications to write this kind of historical compendium detailing Florida's remarkable sport-fishing heritage.

The prodigious amount of work required to painstakingly research and glue together the myriad shards of facts, myths, legends and records probably accounts for why a book of this caliber and depth has never before been published.

Organized by year of birth, the chapters cover anglers living from the late 1800s to the present. Each chapter of *Florida's Fishing Legends and Pioneers* is written like a separate short story, engrossing us with insights, anecdotes, reflections and rare photographs about a remarkable group of characters and personalities. Some of the names may surprise you. Ted Smallwood, Ernest Hemingway, Ted Williams, Curt Gowdy and Guy Harvey are all better known for accomplishments other than fishing.

Several of the chapters deal with individuals I have known and worked with, such as Karl Wickstrom, who founded *Florida Sportsman* magazine, and Vic Dunaway and Lefty Kreh, who did editorial chores on many of my manuscripts for the magazine over the course of 23 years. Karl was one who took his passion for fishing and turned it into unbelievable success, starting *Florida Sportsman* in 1969.

Like the section on Karl, each of the book's 36 chapters adds a new plank to the wharf representing the state's different eras, making for a spirited walk down Florida's fishing history. *Florida's Fishing Legends and Pioneers* unquestionably will enrich every reader's historical perspective and should be on the bookshelf of every angler who has ever cast a lure into Florida waters.

M. Timothy O'Keefe, Series Editor

Introduction

I surmise you're reading this because fishing means more to you than just cranking in a fish or eating fillets. Like passionate football fans who become familiar with the names of former gridiron greats, you'd appreciate a similar recognition of those who have made contributions to the popularity of fishing in Florida's bountiful waters.

Many unknown legends and pioneers in Florida remain so simply because of the lack of available written sources or photographs. The earliest records of fishing in Florida can be found in mid- to late-1800s books, newspapers and magazines. These publications at times mention Florida guides and anglers of yesteryear, but just one source's experience on a chosen trip does not a legend or a pioneer make. Often names of guides appear in print only because they happened to be at the dock during an author's trip.

Some of those depicted in the upcoming chapters were born in the 1800s, but most began their fishing exploits during the twentieth century. As Florida started to draw national attention for its weather and unexplored resources, so too did the population greatly increase. Communities sprang up, newspapers were born and stories and pictures involving fishing feats became better known. People still fished to eat, but soon the services of someone who knew the local waters and best fishing techniques took on new importance for sporting enthusiasts thirsting for rod-bending duels. Novice anglers with dedication and passion advanced to the expert category. Journalists progressed from mere reporters to eager participants.

Many of the earlier writings about Florida fishing entailed a curiosity about tarpon, or "tarpum" as they were often called in the years follow-ing the Civil War. Articles and books broadened on target species to include everything from bonefish to billfish. As the century progressed, so too did an interest in fly fishing the flats for blitzing bonefish and—at first considered impossible—even blue marlin and other offshore species on the long rods.

As you might appreciate, the reward of choosing a list of "bests" in any sporting category is like volunteering to be the target at a pie-throwing contest—you're going to end up with meringue on your face. Despite the limits of one book and devout dedication to due diligence, it is my hope that few, if any, deserving names have been overlooked.

Rest assured that I delved into Florida's recreational fishing history with the panache of Zorro. I interviewed hundreds of sources and ex-changed countless e-mails, visited libraries and bookstores around the state, queried scores of local historians and read articles containing profiles on various personalities until my jumbled mind more closely resembled Don Quixote's than the Z-man's.

The final roster of *Florida's Fishing Legends and Pioneers* evolved from a starting point of over 800 potentials. I'd hoped the ultimate subjects of the chapters would not only live in the state at least part of the time but also break down into residents of equal segment of Florida. Unfor-tunately, too great a dependence on geography would have eliminated too many worthy candidates. I therefore picked those I considered the top Florida legends and pioneers regardless of where they docked their boats. As it turned out, the book does touch upon most portions of the state.

The chapters are ordered chronologically by year of birth. That gives a more accurate perspective on how recreational fishing in Florida evolved and its formative eras. Some of the legends and pioneers con-tributed to fishing lore by demonstrating fantastic angling skills. Oth-ers made the list due to their artful journalistic abilities or promotional prowess. The common thread is that each put the spotlight on the sport in a remarkable way and helped to popularize it.

This project, like the building of a matchstick house, began as a thou-sand scattered pieces and it gradually evolved into an exciting ride for me through Florida's angling history and lore. I hope you feel the same way after reading *Florida's Fishing Legends and Pioneers*. If you'd like to comment on my selections or anything else regarding the book, visit www.FloridasFishingLegends.com.

1

$\approx\approx\approx\approx$

Jesse Linzy, 1872–1955

PONCE INLET

Many notable charter captains took northerners on coastal and off-shore fishing trips from Ponce Park and Mosquito Inlet beginning in the 1940s. Just north of New Smyrna Beach, Mosquito Inlet is now known as "The Town of Ponce Inlet." The surrounding area sprouted boat rentals and charters such as Timmons Fish Camp and Myers Fish Camp along the Halifax River, Mosquito Inlet and the Atlantic Ocean. Capt. William Redwood Wharton was the area's best-known skipper from 1944 until 1999 aboard his famed *Gay Wind*.

Preceding Wharton and, for that matter, most other guides in Florida outside of Key West was a fellow named John Gardner. First using simple rowboats, Gardner started his guiding business in 1871. For the next 30 years he familiarized himself with all the harbors and inlets on Florida's east coast. As a result, visiting anglers and yachtsmen sought out Gardner to take them fishing or captain their vessels on longer trips.

Between the eras of Wharton and Gardner arrived someone even more intriguing. This is the curious case of Jesse Linzy, fishing guide. Not many guides or charter captains even nowadays are black, let alone back in the early 1900s. The Civil War ended only seven years after Linzy's birth, leaving a still-divided country when it came to matters of race. That a black man broke into a profession that depended on white people to hire him and to do as he instructed can be considered no minor achievement.

It indeed required incredible talent as a guide in order for word of Linzy's reputation to spread from satisfied charter clients to other (white) anglers. After all, to even fish in the company of a black man all day and to be in his charge wasn't commonly acceptable. That so many inevitably did entrust their care and safety to Linzy is all the more amazing when eyes first witnessed his physical stature.

Linzy, known in later years as the "Giant of Ponce Park," reportedly stood around six feet, eight inches tall. In his prime he was solid muscle, and though in later years Linzy gained a bit of a paunch, no one ever doubted his extraordinary strength.

Linzy's hands were enormous and his feet so large that even the biggest shoes available required the top ends cut off so his toes would fit. His feats of brawn and stamina were the subject of awed chitchat all over the region. One of the more widely known legends involves Linzy taking guests offshore in a heavy wooden boat that he single-handedly rowed through the always-choppy inlet, often doing so against the tide on both the trip out and back. He picked up 100-pound bags of cement mix with ease and carried several at a time while co-workers struggled just pushing one in wheelbarrows on sand or dirt roads.

As strong as he was, Linzy never provoked anyone, and his intimidating size ensured that no one tempted fate by tugging on Superman's cape. A non-drinker with few activities other than an honest day's work and fishing, trouble did not follow the man around.

When I originally sent out notices about the book to historians and museums around Florida, this response came quickly from Ellen Henry, curator of the Ponce Inlet Lighthouse:

"I'm told that you are writing about Florida fishing legends. Well, if you don't include Jesse Linzy, you'll be missing out on a good story. Jesse was one of the few African American residents of Ponce Park at the turn of the century. He came here around 1909 to work at the lighthouse and stayed for the rest of his life. He was rarely seen without a fishing pole."

From what records exist and the fragments of history that can be pieced together, it seems that Jesse Linzy came into the world on August 7, 1872, to Bill and Matilda Linzy. At the age of 27, Jesse left the family behind in Savannah, Georgia, and headed down the coast to find work. No one had any jobs to fill or seemed willing to give him a chance until he arrived in Mosquito Inlet.

Linzy heard about a project requiring the construction of a sidewalk from the Mosquito Inlet Lighthouse to the river. The existing wooden boardwalk, crumbling and in disrepair, needed a concrete replacement. With a background in construction and his physical talents obvious, Linzy got the assignment. He did such a thorough job (the sidewalk is still there today) that it led to additional work. Linzy went on to build a solid concrete apron surrounding the tower base and to design and make cisterns for the keepers' residences.

The lighthouse would play prominently in Linzy's future employment. A fellow named Bartola Pacetti had sold the land for the lighthouse to the U.S. government, giving Pacetti funds to build the Pacetti Hotel nearby. Pacetti knew firsthand the quality of work Linzy rendered and that the man had an inexhaustible work ethic. It's not known whether Pacetti asked Linzy first or Linzy popped the question, but in any case, Jesse Linzy started employment at the hotel as a handyman when it opened.

With few lodging competitors between Jacksonville and Cape Canaveral, guests began to crowd the Pacetti Hotel. Some would inevitably query about the fishing possibilities or would arrive already knowing about them. At first Linzy provided tips and suggestions or at times even led them to productive locations. This came easily for Linzy because he'd learned to fish not long after he could walk—every extra cane pole in the water meant more food for the family. He was astounded by Mosquito Inlet's resources and by his ability to catch fish at whim all day or night.

When Linzy approached Pacetti and told him about the ever-increasing interest in guiding services, the businessman immediately recognized the opportunity. Instead of just providing another amenity to guests, the availability of a guide of Linzy's caliber would actually create new hotel traffic and another income stream.

Hardworking people usually excel at whatever they do, and this proved true for Linzy and guiding. He quickly became known as someone who didn't rest until his anglers caught fish, a man who knew the right places to be at the right times no matter the conditions. It didn't take long for anglers to seek him out after hearing stories about

A little leisurely dock fishing. Note the cut-out toes of the shoes. Photo courtesy of the Ponce de Leon Inlet Lighthouse Preservation Association.

the incredible fishing in Florida in general and about Jesse Linzy and Mosquito Inlet specifically.

Local novelist Robert Wilder included Linzy in some of his writings. In *The Sea and the Stars,* he refers to Linzy as "Ogeechee Jesse" since Linzy was born near Savannah's Ogeechee River. According to old-timers who knew Linzy, Wilder's descriptions were right on the money:

The uncertain popping of a single-cylinder outboard motor caught their attention. They watched as a heavy, flat-bottomed rowboat nosed toward a rickety dock below. A huge Negro, bare of chest and in patched and washed-out dungarees, towered in the stern, his weight lifting the bow to a steep angle.

"That's Jesse." Tod reached for her hand. He led her down the slope, heavily carpeted with the oaks' oval leaves and browning acorns. "Jesse's been around here for as long as anyone can remember. If his stories are true he must be a hundred years old, but he looks and acts like a young buck."

They picked their way along the rough ground with its outcropping of bleached coquina rock. "This part of the river is posted by the Government as a waterfowl preserve. There's a sign out there which says 'U.S. Waters.' Jesse's very proud of it. He calls the area 'us waters,' meaning it has been set aside for him and a few of those privileged to call him friend."

Jesse was the blue-black of the Ogeechee River Negro. His poll was gray, deep wrinkles were carved into the dark satin around his eyes. When he lifted himself from boat to dock his movements were as lithe as a boy's. He regarded most white men with a friendly tolerance and made a fine living guiding fishing parties. He took no nonsense from the winter tourists, though. When he accepted a client it was with a warning: "Don' you be late gittin' heah en th' mornin.' Don' be stayin' up ahl naight drinkin en wrestlin' wid wimmen. You late we don' git no fish. Dat don' do my reputation no good." A tardy angler was quite likely to find Jesse asleep in a hammock and no amount of explanation would rouse him. He would merely grunt his impatience and set the hammock to swinging lightly.

Another catch for dinner from the plentiful Mosquito Inlet. Photo courtesy of the Ponce de Leon Inlet Lighthouse Preservation Association.

Employment as a handyman and guide at the Pacetti Hotel wasn't to be the only benefit of Jesse Linzy's relationship with Bart Pacetti. In 1908, William Taft was elected president and he continued a program generated by his predecessor Theodore Roosevelt to do something about hunters wiping out plumed birds in order to obtain feathers for ladies' hats. Mosquito Inlet thus became one of the regions declared as a Federal Bird Reservation. Bert Pacetti, one of Bart's sons, decided to get involved, and he became a federal bird reservation inspector. By this time, Linzy's loyalty and service to Bart Pacetti was fully appreciated by his family members. Accordingly, after Bert became a full-fledged game warden, he deputized Jesse Linzy and brought him along on many trips throughout U.S. states and territories, including Alaska and Hawaii. Bert Pacetti must have figured that plume hunters, poachers and other roughnecks might think twice about serving up any trouble with the big man standing with him.

A view of the Pacetti Hotel, circa 1900, where Linzy spent most of his years working and guiding. Photo courtesy of the Ponce de Leon Inlet Lighthouse Preservation Association.

Linzy continued to prosper through the end of the magical 1920s, his legend spreading on the tongues of tourists leaving Mosquito Inlet. After the Great Depression, however, the Pacetti Hotel was sold to Olivia Gamble, herself a vacationer at the hotel as a child. She adored the place and also Jesse Linzy, whom she considered a tourist attraction unto himself.

That suited Linzy just fine, because he had no desire to live anywhere else or to do anything differently. Linzy and Miss Ida, his wife, continued to dwell in the hotel and to keep the place in top working order. He could fix anything, his loyalty was beyond question and few unsavory characters chanced an unpleasant confrontation with Linzy on the hotel property or anywhere else for that matter.

As mentioned, in later years the area's name changed from Mosquito Inlet to Ponce Inlet, most likely for marketing reasons—the word "mosquito" had too many repellant connotations, pun intended. But Linzy aged gracefully and always seemed many years younger than he was. He died in nearby Ponce Park in 1955, a lifetime spanning the onset of new generations of specialized charter captains, newer boats and engines, improved fishing gear and an ever-increasing appreciation by traveling anglers of the area's resources and appeal.

A Daytona newspaper was among the publications carrying the news of Jesse Linzy's death. Though Linzy lived his entire life after the Emancipation Proclamation, even the obituary for him that follows contained references that showed the prevailing verbiage when it came to black Americans:

Jesse Knew Birds and Was A Fine Fisherman

Service for Jesse Linzy, 83, well known Negro resident of the Gambie place in Ponce Park for more than 45 years before his death at home last Thursday, will be at 2 p.m. tomorrow at Gainous Funeral Home. Burial will be in Mount Ararat.

Linzy, a deputy U.S. game warden from about 1908 to the middle 1920s, had traveled to all bird reservations in the U.S. with U.S. Game Warden Bert J. Pacetti, Mrs. John E. Hebel recalled last night.

"He was affectionately known not only as the Mayor but also as the giant of Ponce Park," she added. "He was also known from north to south as the best fisherman along the Florida coast."

Born in Savannah, Linzy is survived by his wife Ida, and a daughter, Mrs. Marion Goodwin, Philadelphia.

It must have been quite a remarkable experience in those days—and it would be today as well—to climb aboard the boat for a day's fishing with the big, big man, Jesse Linzy. I wish I could have been there.

2

Charlie Thompson, 1873–1946

MIAMI

If you happen upon a 40-foot shark weighing about 13 tons, the smart money says to get the heck out of there, quickly. But if the shark appears to be stranding itself and is moving about in uncharacteristically shallow water, many of us might—*might*—move in for a closer look.

Not Capt. Charlie Thompson. He immediately recognized a juicy promotional opportunity and pounced upon it like a skyrocketing kingfish.

Born near the Cape Florida Lighthouse on Key Biscayne, Thompson became an outstanding charter-boat captain. He also turned into a local celebrity who—thanks to providence and a Madison Avenue promotional mind—took center stage on the national level as well. His father had been involved in the burgeoning carnival-amusements-fair business in the mid-1800s, no doubt a lineage instilled in Charlie that would serve him well as an attention-getter. But before you write him off as vain and egotistical, realize that that was only his PR hat. Friends knew his exuberance to be of a friendly nature and all considered him a very enjoyable person to be around.

His worldly travels and esoteric hunts for sea serpents notwithstanding, Thompson will remain immortalized for his part in a momentous quirk of fate that occurred in 1912. The short of it is that he captured a 38-foot whale shark off Marathon weighing an estimated 26,594 pounds, had it skinned and preserved, and toured the nation for several years with the massive "monster" atop a railroad car and flatbed truck. He charged a fee to see it, much like a sideshow in a carnival. Indeed, Charlie Thompson would have made P. T. Barnum quite proud.

Dispatching the giant whale shark in 1912 gave rise to celebration and this redoubtable pose. Photo courtesy of the Florida State Archives.

The telling of the saga certainly invites sorrow and amazement, for with today's greater consciousness about gentle creatures, few would even want to duplicate the pitiless slaughter. Some Web sites and bloggers still insist the chronicle of what happened that day is a fairy tale or litany of misinformation. However, too many eyewitnesses attested to what occurred for it to be labeled fiction, not to mention that numerous photographs were taken despite the fact that nearly 100 years ago only a few people toted around cameras. So, too, could thousands ultimately testify to the genuine sight and feel of the beast as they gazed under the tarp at the massive hulk of the marine alien.

The drama unfolded at 9 a.m. on a crisp day in 1912 off Knight's Key near Marathon, Florida. Capt. Thompson's fishing schooner *Samoa* lay anchored about half a mile from one of Henry Flagler's railroad docks. Thompson, his eyes fixed northward, spied a huge submerged dark object moving close to the dock trestle. He asked his charter customer, Charles Brooks of Cleveland, Ohio, for permission to delay the start of their fishing day to check out this strange anomaly, and Brooks agreed. Off they went with mate Bob Denney in the launch.

Thompson shut down directly atop the spotted creature and soon realized it must be some sort of shark judging by its tail and shape. It seemed listless, possibly sick, and it likely had swum into shallow water on a suicide mission. Trouble was, the paying customer on board wanted to fish, and Thompson didn't have time to wait possibly days or even a week for the beast to go belly up.

Thompson lifted a harpoon and sunk it just behind the head—the big animal didn't even flinch. Startled at the lack of response, Thompson shouted to several fishermen in a nearby boat to lend a hand and, sensing an uncommon adventure unfolding, they readily agreed. Thompson had along a .30-30 rifle that he kept aboard the *Samoa* to take the starch out of struggling big fish at boat side, and he fired several shots into the back of the shark.

Nothing, no reaction.

During the balance of the day he delivered about 50 more rounds of lead into the beast and none of them provoked any response. Either the shark didn't feel them or didn't care. Even a shotgun blast did little

News of the capture had already reached Miami and drawn a crowd by the time a construction crane transferred the animal to a railroad car. Photo courtesy of Al Pflueger Jr.

more than produce a round exterior wound on the hide. Thompson felt like he was trying to kill an elephant with a pellet gun.

At times their quarry would drift half a mile or so from the railroad trestle to signal it might be heading to the deep Gulf Stream waters, but the giant fish would circle right back to where it started. By now five harpoons hung from its bullet-riddled body like hors d'oeuvre toothpicks, and yet its tail calmly swayed to and fro in the shallow green water as if nothing unusual were going on.

Hours went by before, at last, the shark began to show signs of wear and tear, its tiny silver dollar–size eyes starting to glaze. Just before dusk they prodded the giant with a boat hook, goosing it toward a sand bank where it gladly stranded itself. The men scurried to secure the fish with lines and stakes. Thompson attempted to kill it once and for all by thrusting a knife into its brain. When the blade encountered several inches of thick skin and leathery tissue, Thompson confirmed why the harpoons and gun fire barely affected the Greyhound bus of a fish.

They finally dispatched the shark—or more likely, the shark died of natural causes—and the bloody corpse was rigged with tow ropes behind the *Samoa* so it could be dragged to Miami. Thompson was certain that sharks would take their toll on the carcass as they trolled it throughout the night, but his luck held. He docked at the marine railway depot, where one of the cargo cranes broke down trying to lift the shark. Workers summoned their largest heavy-duty construction crane to finally hoist the immense sea creature from the water and onto an eight-wheeled open railroad car.

The incredible hulk immediately attracted exactly what Thompson had hoped it would. Crowds crushed against each other to behold the sea monster; researchers from Washington, D.C., arrived within a week to inspect it. Length and girth measurements were taken to reveal a shark 38 feet long with a weight of 26,594 pounds. Interested ichthyologists would later consider the "official" weight estimate a precarious figure, claiming that the on-site scientists who'd rushed to the scene had neither inspected a whale shark before nor any sea creature of that proportion. Thompson knew a window of opportunity when he saw one, and forever after insisted his fish was actually 45 feet in length and weighed "over" 30,000 pounds.

At least the unmistakable shape and coloration of the animal allowed for an undisputed proclamation to be made that it was, indeed, a whale shark. Although the animal's thousands of teeth and shark-like appearance at first suggested that it might be a dangerous man-eater—as Thompson hoped—the marine biologists assured everyone that this species only fed on small schools of bait fish via water-suctioning. That did not quite jive, however, when its huge stomach was slit open and out popped a 200-pound goliath grouper, a large octopus of a species not previously known and a 250-pound chunk of live coral. If it could eat objects that large, Thompson reasoned, it surely could swallow a diver or luckless swimmer who happened to be in the wrong place at the wrong time.

Thompson didn't have much wiggle room in trying to further embellish his prized catch, however. Witnesses included his client; his mate; railroad employees such as Carlton Corliss, Henry Hyman and James Dunaway; and fishermen and onlookers beholding the whole episode near the bridge. Pictures were taken as the captors frolicked inside the mouth of the slain monster when its head was winched out of the water against the hull of the *Samoa*.

How he caught the whale shark and its actual weight didn't really matter anyway. It was a spectacle of spectacles, a King Kong of the sea, a real *monster*, for heaven's sake, and Thompson somehow pulled off the logistical challenge of extricating one of the ocean's largest creatures onto an open railroad car where people could see and touch it. But another big challenge loomed—making it more than a local Miami attraction. Thompson, the deal-making charter skipper, struck an agreement with the railroad to keep the shark aboard the flat car. He even partnered with them to transport it from city to city. In this way both Thompson and the railroad would share the limelight.

It took weeks to remove the four-inch-thick skin and scrape off over half a ton of sinew and muscle tissue so that the giant skin mount could be placed over a frame to make it look reasonably lifelike. Its body extended past the front and back of the railroad car—just enough to counterbalance while also making it appear even more massive. Thompson transferred the conglomeration—much lighter as mainly skin and frame—to a larger flatbed that could be towed by a truck. Thompson paraded the shark mostly along the eastern coast with occasional forays west, a tarp covering most of it so the curious could only be gratified for a cost of 10 cents; for another five cents you could pose with your head in its open maw. Lines were at times enormous, and Thompson hired a traveling photographer to create another revenue stream. He sold thousands of postcards displaying a picture of the sea beast. No one could deny that Thompson's impulse to act when a bankable opportunity presented itself had made him famous and a good piece of change.

No one's absolutely certain as to how the whale shark later vanished. Most reports say it accidentally went up in flames in 1922. According to one of Thompson's daughters, Barbara Kelly, it wasn't an accident at all and probably occurred well before 1922.

"The skin began to stink like high heavens, partly due to the Miami heat and humidity," she said.

"Everyone started complaining, and it got worse to the point of

Charlie Thompson made a name for himself—and considerable money—parading the "sea monster" to various cities for those willing to pay 10 cents for a close-up look. Photo courtesy of the Florida State Archives.

paying customers gagging and holding their noses. Dad finally doused it with gas when no one was around and burned it up—it had served its purpose and then some."

Even prior to the great whale shark caper, Charlie Thompson was hardly a newcomer to controversy. In 1908, a couple who'd been out fishing in Biscayne Bay returned to the dock wild-eyed, declaring they'd just observed a 30-foot sea serpent with a long neck. Only one man was suited to investigate a claim fraught with such lunacy: Capt. Charlie Thompson. "He knew the serpent claim was a farce and suspected the couple had downed a few rums too many," Barbara Kelly told me. "But he saw it as a chance to grab a few headlines."

The *Miami Metropolis* gave him just that, running a story stating that Thompson was the man for the job when it came to digging up the truth and that if anything of monstrous proportions indeed plied local waters, Charlie Thompson would—as Agent Smith in *The Matrix* would put it—"find and destroy them."

Needless to say, no evidence of sea serpents ever materialized. But fact or fiction didn't really matter. Being an opportunist expanded

Thompson's demand by rich men wanting adventures at sea. His charter schedule remained full, and his guest book over the years would include Warren Harding and three other presidents, John Jacob Astor and Frederick William Vanderbilt. Concerning the latter railroad heir, in 1928 and '29, Thompson, his wife and their two daughters accompanied Mr. and Mrs. Vanderbilt on a world cruise to collect specimens for Vanderbilt's museum. Thompson added many of the photographs he took to his album *A Pioneer's Exciting Life.*

Much is always said about the intriguing life of Charlie Thompson, but the south Florida fishing community—as small as it was when he began chartering in the 1890s—embraced him as one of the best guides in the world. Just before he happened upon the whale shark in 1912, Thompson was trying to figure out how to keep sailfish on the hook. The species' airborne twists combined with their lack of reluctance in taking baits only compounded the frustration of luckless hook-ups by charter customers.

Thompson experimented and found a better success rate when he created line slack that allowed the sailfish time to "kill" the bait with its bill and turn the bait headfirst to swallow. Other captains at his dock—Elser's Pier on Miami's waterfront that would later become the famed 5th Street Pier—didn't target sailfish because it was far easier for their novice anglers to best willing kingfish and dolphin rather than to attempt the more skillful technique of drop-back fishing.

One captain who did take notice of Thompson's sailfish tinkering was Bill Hatch. Though credited with coming up with the drop-back technique for sailfishing, he actually just picked up where Thompson left off and fine-tuned it. Whereas Thompson kept slack in the line, Hatch opened the bail and let the sail run before setting the hook; whereas Thompson always used mullet for bait, Hatch found greater success with bonito. Sailfish could bat and mouth bonito without it coming off the hook as easily as mullet did. From there Hatch went on to cutting bonito strips because they also attracted kingfish and most everything else. Thompson stumbled upon the technique and Hatch perfected it, but it reveals that Thompson's imagination was not limited to hucksterism.

It's only due diligence for me to relate that of all the chapters in this book, the one I most looked forward to researching was this one. I'm related—sort of—to Charlie Thompson. He'd passed on before I was born, but my father's oldest brother (Don) married one of Thompson's daughters (Barbara). It's her recollections via tales directly from her father and mother that provided additional insights into Charlie's character.

My aunt, uncle and their children, Frank and John, lived in an old stucco home on Abaco Avenue in Miami. In the 1960s it was a walk of only a couple of blocks to Gordon's Bait & Tackle at the northeast corner of U.S. 1 and S.W. 27 Avenue—and across the street from that was a Royal Castle. I clearly recall my dad speaking of Barbara's famous father. On several occasions the topic of Charlie's exploits came up during family gatherings. Barbara, extremely gregarious and outgoing, volunteered many details about the background information as well as her opinions regarding well-publicized stories involving her father—and some amazing tales that didn't make it to print.

In addition, my Aunt Barbara's mother—Charlie Thompson's wife— lived in Boone, North Carolina, at a cottage on a grassy knoll she'd nicknamed the "Oh-So-Cozy." Known simply as "Mrs. T," she lived comfortably with frequent visits from relatives and well wishers. Not far away, Don and Barbara owned a summer cabin in the hills of Boone near Grandfather Mountain, which I visited often.

One nuance, according to Aunt Barbara, is that Charlie Thompson didn't use sunglasses, saying that his doctor warned that use of such newfangled things would eventually ruin his eyesight. As a charter boat captain, Thompson couldn't take the chance of that happening. That his eyesight failed later in life is probably no coincidence.

Charlie Thompson will always be linked to his whale shark escapade, and that's as it should be. Everything he went through to exhibit the incredible spectacle to the world and the fact that the shark appeared sickly and determined to beach itself anyway worked in Thompson's favor. The P. T. Barnum of sport fishing made a colorful impression in life and enjoyed every moment of it.

What more could any fisherman want?

3

Ted Smallwood, 1879–1951

CHOKOLOSKEE

Some consider the southwest portion of Florida from Everglades City south to be the least disturbed and most primitive in the state. I've been there many times, and that's my opinion too.

Indeed, the splinters of islets dotting the region called the Ten Thousand Islands are barely visited, much less inhabited. Outside of park ranger stations and rickety remnants of old piers here and there, much of Collier County comprises swamps like the Big Cypress National Preserve and Everglades National Park. Outside the populous cities of Naples and Marco Island, you're more likely to run into an alligator or water moccasin than a two-legged creature.

That wildness is precisely what appealed to Charles S. "Ted" Smallwood when he arrived before the turn of the twentieth century. He sought a peaceful life amid Seminole Indians and farmers. He would build a store in his new hometown of Chokoloskee that would become absolutely crucial to the ability of anglers to access and explore these rich mangrove-fringed waters and rivers chock-full of snook, tarpon, redfish, trout and dozens of other species.

Lynn McMillin is her mother's youngest daughter, meaning she never met her famous grandfather before he died in 1951. Nonetheless, as a family member and resident of a small town like Chokoloskee, she's heard plenty of stories from relatives and friends who knew Ted Smallwood.

"You can see his personality in his descendants," said McMillin, who reopened the Smallwood store as a museum, providing a fascinating time capsule of the area. "The way he did business made him one-of-a-kind, his wry sense of humor is something that people enjoyed."

Smallwood's mother died when he was a baby, and he didn't get along with his father's new wife. Fed up with all the drama, he ran away from home at age 10 to work on a mail "run" boat delivering supplies. Smallwood bounced around Ybor City near Tampa for a while, visited Cuba and the Bahamas, and decided none of them quite suited his fancy. He also lived for a time in a small settlement in north Florida called Fort White—but we'll come back to that later in his story.

In 1891 he hopped aboard a small ferry from Everglades City. Five miles to the south he stepped onto the island of Chokoloskee, an Indian term for "old home." At the time a small settlement—and it still is, really—Chokoloskee lies near the mouth of the Turner River with Chokoloskee Bay and the Gulf of Mexico to the west. Turner River meanders northeast into the Florida interior for about nine miles before terminating at what's now U.S. 41—the famed Tamiami Trail that connects Miami to Naples.

Below the delta-like soil, vegetation and trees of Chokoloskee is a base of shell mound composed of discarded crustaceans from many hundreds of years of Calusa Indian dining. It was common for Indians to carry canoe loads of the remains of oyster, crab and conch shells to a designated island for disposal. Chokoloskee sprang up as a cluster of settlers in 1874—17 years before Smallwood's arrival—but a lack of any commerce meant slim pickings when it came to jobs for newcomers.

A resident named C. G. McKinney settled in Chokoloskee in 1886. He opened a post office in 1891 as well as a small schoolhouse for the smattering of children present. Otherwise, the handful of hearty locals survived simply as hunters of bird plumes for ladies' hats, alligator hides, furs, turtles and fish.

Smallwood hired on as a farm hand up the Turner River for the House family. He toiled in the fields throughout most of his teenage years, getting to know not only all the locals very well but also Mr. House's daughter, Mamie, in the process. In 1897 he married Mamie and they moved to Chokolosee. Smallwood busied himself in the same fashion as other residents by hunting, fishing and farming. He also agreed to pick up and deliver mail for McKinney, covering Chokoloskee

Smallwood's fairness won the respect of Charlie Tigertail of the Seminole tribe. Both are pictured here in Chokoloskee in 1928. Photo courtesy of the Florida State Archives.

to Ft. Myers and points in between. Smallwood blew into a conch shell to notify residents of each small community of his arrival. The slow sailboat run paid him $1 a day—good money back then—but Smallwood's heart just wasn't in it.

In 1906 he and Mamie opened a store in Chokoloskee that would partially encompass the post office. By this time Smallwood had taken over as postmaster—a position he would occupy until his retirement in 1941. All went comfortably well for years until a hurricane flattened the store. The Smallwoods immediately rebuilt it, knowing that their base of customers would return.

They were right, and the store became even more in demand as a "must stop" for both boat travelers and residents of the nearby settlements that were slowly increasing in population. Without any competitors in the region, it would have been easy for Smallwood to gouge prices. However, he didn't do so because he knew the value of repeat business and word of mouth. Visiting boat traffic steadily increased thanks to the population boom up the coast. The fact that the Smallwood store could be found and accessed easily didn't hurt either.

As a local, Smallwood knew exactly what items were needed by residents of the area and boating transients. The store stocked building supplies, home goods, cooking utensils, fishing gear and bait, boat parts and other possibles not available except at distant mercantile locations. Navigational charts began noting the Chokoloskee store's location for the benefit of mariners, enabling smaller vessels to ply the wild southwest Florida coastline and schedule convenient pit stops at the Smallwood digs.

With that background established, it's time to turn the spotlight more directly on Ted Smallwood. Lynn McMillin said her grandfather dropped out of school and wasn't educated, but he had a photographic memory.

"You could mention any word and my grandfather would provide not only the exact definition in his dictionary but the page it appeared on," she said.

"People came into the store with a long list of things they needed, and he'd be staring out the window as if disinterested while they read it off," McMillin continued.

"When they'd finish, he'd walk around the store and bring every item to them without forgetting a thing. That amazed and amused everyone."

Smallwood fished whenever he could sneak off to wet a line. Then again, everyone did that, living in an area with such an abundance of sea life. It was nothing to collect at whim a seafood platter of conch, crab and fish. Plenty of deer, alligator and manatee steaks provided all the red meat fare they desired, and many residents like the Smallwoods farmed their own veggie gardens. No one ever went hungry around Chokoloskee.

Bob Wells, a resident of Chokoloskee who owns a real estate company, has talked to a lot of people over the years who knew Smallwood and were familiar with his way of doing business.

"He'd always use a negative approach, but in a wry, entertaining way," said Wells.

He explained that no matter what gadget someone might pick up to buy, Smallwood would say something like, "It doesn't work all that great, but I'll sell it to you anyway." After hearing that familiar disclaimer each time they came into the store, customers got to the point where they were disappointed if Smallwood didn't recite it.

His manner became so well known that at times people who knew Ted would drop by the store and sit a spell just to listen to him handle trade and talk with customers. It became a source of local entertainment right up until Smallwood's retirement around the start of World War II.

Smallwood, not book smart but intelligent—he spoke three languages and was very articulate—realized from the beginning of his retail career that if you give people more, they'll come back for more. He'd always add an additional handful of this or a pinch of that to a bag no matter what people bought. Buyers got value, and Smallwood reaped the rewards of repeat business.

He also bent over backwards to be fair, something the Seminole Indians appreciated and respected. Although the Seminole wars ended before Smallwood arrived in Chokoloskee, his goodwill and honesty in dealing with the tribe went a long way toward keeping things peaceful between the Indians and all those in the local white settlements.

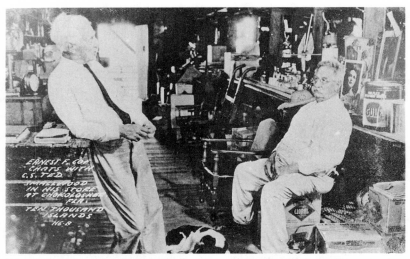

Friends like Ernest Coe (standing) often dropped by the Smallwood store to chat or listen to Smallwood's unique trading style. Photo courtesy of the Florida State Archives.

Smallwood took a keen interest in issues and politics. Though stuck way out in the sticks in Chokoloskee, he maintained a full awareness of national and international goings-on. He listened to his shortwave radio and read every newspaper coming into the store. An example of this occurred in the late 1930s.

A scrap dealer came into Chokoloskee and noticed under the dock a bunch of defunct engines Smallwood had put there to buttress the seawall. The dealer wanted to buy all of them.

Smallwood wanted to know who his buyer would be. "I'm going to sell them to Japan," the man said.

Smallwood refused. The befuddled dealer left without the engines, not realizing that Smallwood perceived long before Pearl Harbor the signs of impending trouble for the U.S. in the Pacific.

I don't know the veracity of the following story about Smallwood, but it might be true, considering how his wife Mamie was supposedly the Victorian prim-and-proper type. It seems Ted Smallwood wasn't shy about anything, and particularly not about the scent of a woman. He once took a good-looking gal fishing, unaware that she'd had more than casual tutoring in karate. Ted put the moves on her, and she flung his considerable carcass completely out of the boat. After drying off, darn if he didn't make another play for her. She upped and tossed his butt right back into the bay. After the second dunking, he got the message and switched his sights to catching fish the rest of the day.

Another humorous tale—likely more true than the last—involved Smallwood's penchant during idle times for perching himself on the porch atop the stairs of his store. He'd catch a breeze and muse about whatever activity might be going on at ground level. On one such occasion, he observed a man stirring some loggerhead meat in a pot he'd found under the store. Smallwood laughed with great gusto, distracting everyone nearby. Between bouts of laughter, he loudly notified the poor fellow that his wife Mamie used the pot as a portable toilet on their boat excursions. Horrified and embarrassed, the man launched his boat and fled posthaste amid derisive howls and hoots from the shoreline.

A far more serious scene occurred just outside the Smallwood store in October of 1910 that would be the stuff of endless articles, books and controversy ever after. An outlaw named Edgar "Ed" Watson had settled south of Chokoloskee at Chatham Bend. He'd formerly resided at Fort White in north Florida—perhaps not coincidentally, so had Ted Smallwood and C. G. McKinney. Whether or not they met up at one time or another in Fort White, at the least they had mutual acquaintances and a locale in common.

That might explain why the three men got along well. Considering Watson's reputation, that was no small assurance of one's continuing good health, as it wasn't a good idea to get on Watson's bad side. It's rumored he killed western sharpshooter and prostitute Belle Starr in Arkansas, though he beat the rap when put on trial for it due to lack of enough evidence. Workers employed on Watson's property at Chatham Bend would suddenly up and disappear. Watson would also get into the sauce and be overheard threatening to snuff out this person or that, and sure enough, shortly thereafter the very same would vanish from among the breathing.

While visiting Key West to sell a load of chopped wood, Watson became embroiled in a brouhaha with Adolphus Santini, one of Chokoloskee's original settlers. Watson cut his throat with a knife—the scar from which the otherwise fortunate Santini forevermore displayed. In Arcadia, Watson allegedly killed a fellow named Quinn Bass after a shootout. And when a man named Tucker and his nephew decided to squat on land Watson had purchased while at the same time refusing his direct request to leave, you can guess what became of them.

Suffice it to say that Watson's resume was a violent one, and people around Chokoloskee were fed up with living in constant fear of him. And so it was that when a group headed by the House family—including Smallwood's father-in-law—heard Watson was coming to town, its members decided to give him a shotgun welcome. Watson's boat was heard chugging down the pass and as he stepped off his boat, the lead started flying. Watson lay splattered and his body was hastily buried on a nearby key. Good riddance, said all the lynchers.

Whether Ted Smallwood shared their lack of condolence is still speculation. Smallwood heard the fracas take place, glanced out his window after the gun blasts had ended and saw the crumpled and bloody body of Ed Watson. He didn't take part in the murder and wanted no part in it. In fact, it's written that at one point, when Watson brought back part of a load of cane syrup he hadn't been able to sell in Tampa, he found Smallwood amenable to accepting the unsold syrup to sell on consignment at his store. That seemed to merit Smallwood a good-health pass from the tempestuous Watson.

What Smallwood did or didn't know about Watson's murderous history and predilections continues to be a subject of debate. I can't conceive that he wouldn't have gotten that word. But the fact that, as mentioned, they may have crossed paths when both lived in the tiny settlement of Fort White adds to the intrigue. From the back window of the Smallwood museum, you can see right where the killing of Watson took place.

Even today, Chokoloskee has submitted to modernization only slightly. It wasn't until 1956 that an extension of State Road 29 provided direct access. It's still a very small, tight-knit community of about 400 sprinkled over a 15-acre island. The Gulf breezes gently cool the island and the fishing is stupendous, just like it was in Ted Smallwood's day and many centuries before that.

Ted and Mamie's son, Ted Jr., became an outstanding fishing guide

The presence of the supply store in Chokoloskee opened the way for greater fishing opportunities in the Ten Thousand Islands. Photo courtesy of the Florida State Archives.

in the area. He even designed lures that became popular in the 1950s for taking snook, redfish and other battlers. Lynn McMillin's son Cory is now a professional guide as well.

I've often fished the Ten Thousand Islands area from Everglades City to Flamingo, particularly rivers jutting from the interior of the Everglades like Turner, Harney, Lostmans and Shark. The oyster bars, mud banks, island points, mangrove edges and seemingly endless other casting opportunities offer a special setting unlike anywhere else in Florida. Throw in the riot of birds, alligators, raccoons and other wildlife with the strange exhilaration that comes from knowing that help in the event of an emergency isn't close at hand and you get at least an imaginative taste of how extraordinary it is here for anglers.

Without Ted Smallwood and his historic trading post in Chokoloskee, the quality of life—and fishing—around southwest Florida in the early to mid-1900s wouldn't have been enjoyed even "remotely" as well.

4

Tommy Gifford, 1896–1970

MIAMI

Before the popularity of light-tackle angling increased in the 1950s and beyond, most public impressions of saltwater fishing comprised images of Ernest Hemingway and others battling huge fish aboard offshore charter boats. The pictures in the newspapers of anglers standing next to behemoth fish said it all.

Even with the advent of flats fishing, the drama and style of big-game fishing will always be a huge draw to the man-versus-beast crowd. Fishing with 80-pound test against a blue marlin compared to four-pound fly tippet for trout is like a heavyweight boxing fight versus a flyweight bout. Which style one prefers is entirely personal.

The skippers of the early big-game era in Florida were largely content to prowl familiar waters with converted merchant or commercial vessels, slowly puttering around deep waters for wahoo, dolphin and kingfish in their region. One of those skippers, however, was among the few to plow new fields, to devise new methods, to go beyond the expected and the typical.

Enter Tommy Gifford in 1920 as a charter boat captain at the self-proclaimed age of 23—although he was really only 20. The fishing industry off south Florida would forevermore be changed by Gifford, and in fact, the same would be the case anywhere offshore fishing guides plied their craft.

Born in Long Branch, New Jersey, Gifford caught his first fish, a 16-pound striped bass, at age six. The boy nearly drowned in the process when he wrapped the line around his body to stop the fish's frantic run. At age nine he hid in a rope locker in an attempt to stow away. This

Gifford with Phyllis Bass, who he said was gifted with great reflexes. Unlike many others of his day, Gifford believed that women were fully capable of landing even the biggest of fish, such as this bluefin tuna. Photo courtesy of the International Game Fish Association.

didn't make him popular with the family, and it became obvious early on that Gifford would only be content to go his own way. He tried his hand at commercial fishing in California at 17, and three years later decided that charter fishing would instead be his career.

Gifford's mainstay boat for many years, the *Stormy Petrel,* measured only 26 feet, sported a tuna tower and three fighting chairs and moved along with one engine at a plodding 12-knot cruising speed. Like Gifford himself, the boat was short and stocky, built for utility rather than comfort. In later years he owned a succession of boats named *Stormy Petrel,* including a 31-foot Bertram, but in his successful earlier chartering years he ran a boat back and forth between Miami and the Bahamas called the *Lady Grace.*

Gifford's reputation, at first egged on by curiosity more than anything else, grew instantly among the other captains in Miami. His boat started piling up the charter bookings. In his first year or two, Gifford wasn't returning to the dock with a greater number of fish or larger specimens than the rest of the fleet at Miami's Pier 5. So they wondered: what gives?

The other captains soon noticed that Gifford's catches and his quotes kept ending up in local newspapers like the *Miami Metropolis.* As it so happened, Gifford was feeding newsmen details of his fishing trips, expounding on the more remarkable catches, ensuring that the names of his customers were spelled correctly and offering "inside information" on what was going to be biting. Not only did Gifford welcome reporters visiting Pier 5 with open arms while most other captains disdained them, but he actually sought them out.

Smart man. Gifford easily visualized the value of a high profile. He also didn't depend upon mere chance for meetings at the dock. Gifford befriended some of the reporters. He learned who was writing what for the newspapers and invited those charged with penning articles about the outdoors to ride along on charters. At times he took their families on free trips aboard his boat. Not only did Gifford divulge all of these things to his colleagues, he encouraged them to do likewise for the good of all. For whatever reasons, however, most didn't feel compelled to follow suit, and a few even considered publicity-seeking to be a social disgrace.

Gifford went a step further. In order to spread his acclaim more quickly, Gifford offered free trips to movers and shakers he felt could do him some good, such as Michael and Helen Lerner—of the Lerner clothing chain—and Ernest Hemingway. Gifford knew he'd never get far without recognition both from the press and those high in the fishing industry circles, so he accordingly spread the gospel about himself and did it quite successfully. His plan worked, and his boat slip was usually empty every day of the year.

Gifford disdained ruts and routines. The "same ol', same ol'" grind other captains fell into just never resonated with him. Gifford instead wondered how he could catch more fish, grab more headlines, make more money. One way was to keep his finger on the pulse of fishing outside of Miami. With news reaching him that kites were being successfully employed by the venerable anglers of the Tuna Club of Catalina and elsewhere, Gifford jumped on the act off Miami. Almost immediately he was catching more fish than the other boats by dangling offerings of live baits at the water's surface, where fish could more easily see them. It wasn't long before the other charter skippers had to get in on the act too, as is often the case for those behind trailblazers.

Gifford wasn't the only captain coming up with innovative ideas, and he didn't fail to cash in when others hit on something good. Another colleague of Gifford's who chartered out of Pier 5, Bill Hatch, devised the drop-back method for taking sailfish. Gifford, not a bit shy about "borrowing" successful techniques, expanded his repertoire exponentially. If it worked, Gifford incorporated and even improved on it.

Tommy Gifford's learning curve was a short arc. He watched what others were doing, remembered what others said and made use of his talent for recalling the tiniest details. He thus became an expert on every species that could end up on the opposite side of a fishing rod. With a reputation as a known source and resource, Gifford found his quotes ending up in the *New York Times, Sports Illustrated* and other prominent publications. That kind of publicity feeds on itself, and sure enough, he was soon sought out by visiting captains, by more newspaper reporters from other regions and by curious anglers with money to spend who were intrigued by the provocative stories about this sensational Miami skipper.

Gifford, left, and an angler in the late 1920s with a swordfish. Both are wearing formal attire typical of that era. Photo courtesy of the International Game Fish Association.

While based out of Pier 5 and in later years at the Ocean Reef Club, Gifford's renown earned him lucrative requests to run private fishing vessels in the Bahamas. That turned out to be most fortuitous, because the relatively virginal waters of the Bahamas—especially Bimini and Cat Cay—would become familiar stomping grounds to Gifford and his clients. Other captains, such as Bill Fagen, had already discovered the bounty of those waters, but not many Floridians took advantage. In fact, it was Fagen who first encouraged Gifford to spend at least some of his time in the islands, and after his first couple of drawn-out, knock-down fights with bluefin tuna, Gifford needed little further encouragement.

The subsequent techniques refined off Miami and Key Largo by Gifford boosted his success in the Bahamas; the techniques refined off the Bahamas boosted his success off Miami. Every day, Gifford sought to become a better charter boat captain, and at that he unquestionably excelled.

It makes one wonder why more south Florida skippers in need of more charters didn't at first follow in Gifford's long-distance footsteps. Most captains no doubt recognized the potential of fishing waters across the Gulf Stream, but it wasn't all that practical—without important contacts and ready clients, the big wallets weren't as yet plentiful enough in the Bahamas. That attitude was to slowly change as Gifford's successes and acclaim mounted and other Miamian skippers like Fagen, Bob Luedemann and the Cass brothers kept spreading the word.

While Gifford's fondness for the Bahamas grew, his bread and butter remained the charter business off south Florida. In the 1920s, '30s and even through the '60s, the visiting season shut down around April. It just grew too hot and sticky for northerners to brave the sweltering tropical summer heat before the advent of air-conditioned salons and hotels, not to mention faster boats. Besides, blue marlin, swordfish and hefty yellowfins kept big-game anglers on the U.S. side of the Gulf Stream busy enough. Gifford usually headed north each summer to fish waters off Montauk, New York and Nova Scotia while also expanding his connections with anglers wintering in Florida.

Richard Stanczyk, owner of Bud N' Mary's Marina and before that a dock-rat kid doing chores for the charter fleet at Pier 5, heard the legendary stories about Tommy Gifford long after the storied captain split the scene to retire to the Virgin Islands.

"Tommy was an icon, and his memory lives on," said Stanczyk. "His adapting the use of kites and his invention of outriggers completely revolutionized the sport. His fishing knowledge was seemingly limitless."

Miamian Al Pflueger Jr., who with his father pioneered the taxidermy business, added: "Gifford perfected the use of flying gaffs, constructed the first self-adjusting fighting chair, worked on the prototype for Fin-Nor reels and developed star drags. So much of what we do today is based on his contributions not only with techniques but the gear used."

As might be expected, Gifford's client list became one of the most impressive in the world. Everyone wanted to fish with him, including the top anglers, celebrities and business leaders of the day. Gifford didn't horde the big names for himself, either, as often the best captains at Pier 5 would ping-pong customers. Someone might charter Gifford for a day or two and then do the same with Bill Hatch, Archie Cass, Bill Fagen or one of the other top-notch skippers. While nobody was getting rich as a charter captain, the reputation of Pier 5 and of guides like Gifford kept business brisk.

Gifford relished setting new records and proving that the ability to find fish is as important or more so than the quality of the angler in the fighting chair. It wasn't that Gifford disdained great anglers, as he often chartered outstanding fish-fighters such as surf-casting master Van Campen Heilner, offshore expert Kip Farrington and the aforementioned Lerners. Instead, he felt that inexperienced anglers could be taught the rudiments of how to fight even the biggest bruisers offshore as long as they did exactly what he said.

It was during an outing with Farrington in 1936 that such a debate ensued. Farrington, a New Jersey native who became a noted writer while establishing new records on a wide variety of game fish, confidently made the statement that a woman simply could not handle a powerful fish such as a bluefin tuna. He even joked that any female who tried to do so would be "taken back to Miami in a box," meaning such a fight would kill her.

The 26-foot *Stormy Petrel* displaying the famous outriggers and an A-frame behind the bridge for hoisting the big ones. Photo courtesy of the International Game Fish Association.

That's all Gifford had to hear. Two years later, Gifford guided Helen Lerner—a slight woman, to be sure, and an expert angler in her own right—to not one but 11 catches of the giant bluefin. To prove that Helen was no fluke, Gifford got the job done with another woman with very little previous experience. While Gifford fished out of Cat Cay on the cruiser *Kaybara*, his angler Mrs. James Shand of Lancaster, Pennsylvania, bested a 441-pound bluefin tuna. Farrington could say no more, and in fact gracefully ate his words.

As to Gifford's inventions, the outrigger remains the most noteworthy still associated with his name. Some boats out of West Palm Beach sported poles on the ends of masts as early as 1926, but those devices displayed nothing compared to the utility of what Gifford designed. He first envisioned how they might work, drew up some plans and then set about constructing them. He obtained two long bamboo poles and hinged them to the sides of *Lady Grace*. Gifford added pulleys to vary the degree of angles with the poles, and a ring at the outer ends allowed the fishing line to run from the rods in the boat's cockpit.

Clothespins on each outrigger secured the lines after they were run behind the boat to the desired distance. The line could be hoisted up and down, just as is done when running a flag up a pole. Hung at the 10 o'clock position, the baits would skip and jump with the boat as it rocks with the waves and the movement of the flexible bamboo outriggers. It was a huge improvement over trolling straight from the rod tips to the baits just above boat level.

From there Gifford refined the process. He repositioned some of the trolling rods so the ones on the outriggers flared out slightly to decrease the friction on the lines from the rod tips. Trolled lures and baits on the 'riggers needed to be adapted more precisely so they'd stand up to the added pressure as they skipped above the surface and constantly plowed back into it. Gifford experimented with trolling speeds in various wind and sea conditions so lines wouldn't tangle as often when making even steep turns.

The initial use of the outriggers came about during a trip that began on January 19, 1933. Gifford departed Pier 5 for a 90-day charter at Cat Cay on the *Lady Grace*. His benefactor for the trip was Louis Wasey, the owner of Cat Cay. Wasey, whose resources were plentiful, heard about Gifford's plans to construct outriggers and he wanted to have a hand in it. He received the blueprints for the outriggers from Gifford, and he constructed two sets of 'riggers—one for Gifford and one for himself. Gifford and Wasey deployed the outriggers and immediately recognized how they would revolutionize ocean trolling forevermore.

When other skippers at Pier 5 saw Gifford's outrigger set-up, they laughed and spewed forth numerous reasons as to why that would never work. As we now know, Gifford quickly proved them wrong—the outriggers separated trolled lines and helped deter tangling while still allowing flat lines to be deployed. Every boat that heads offshore now sports outriggers or can easily accommodate a pair, including smaller boats.

Of the many who fished with Gifford, it was his exploits with Farrington that became the most legendary. This included trips with huge

In more informal attire than in previous years and pictures, Gifford (right) admires Michael Lerner's blue marlin. Photo courtesy of the International Game Fish Association.

500-pound-plus bluefins caught on gear such as 54-thread Ashaway line, Hardy rods and 16/0 vom Hofe reels. By the early 1930s Gifford had deciphered the code for catching blue marlin, and in 1933 the payoff resulted in victorious blue battles by Farrington, Louis Wasey (whose picture with a 187-pounder found its way into the *Miami Herald* on March 1, 1933) and even guests of Wasey's.

However, the bluefin catches could not be considered pure. Something bad always happened: The rod would snap or someone else would have to tag-team the fish or a shark chomped off a bite or two—all maladies taking them out of the running for a world record or even a sanctioned catch according to accepted rules of the day.

Nonetheless, when Gifford returned to Pier 5 with a 502-pound blue marlin that angler Ann Moore bested while out of Cat Cay—a drawn-out battle during which she passed the rod to Wasey—the enormous size of the marlin caused an absolute uproar. The immensity of that fish completely blew everyone's mind, from sightseers to anglers to captains.

It should be mentioned that in Gifford's day, standards eventually adopted by the International Game Fishing Association did not exist. Instead, captains gauged the validity of potential records using standards established at the time by the Tuna Club of Catalina based at Catalina Island off California. But let your mind drift back 80-odd years ago to when rods frequently broke under the stress of long battles with large fish, of fishing lines made of linen or silk that didn't stretch and often snapped from the pressure, of inferior rod guides unable to handle the friction, of reel drags literally burning up during long battles. Think back as well to the frequent bane of all: sharks making short work of tired tunas and marlin.

In May 1933 one of Gifford's anglers finally conquered a blue marlin without a rod breaking, without passing off the rod to someone else, without a shark ending the affair in a bloody mess. It was not accomplished by Kip Farrington or another man, but instead by Mrs. Marie Chadbourne. She worked the fish to the *Lady Grace* unaided and unscathed, doing exactly what Capt. Gifford told her to do during the battle.

That Gifford and other capable big-game captains were able to find fish, get them to strike, hope the angler was up to snuff, pray that the gear would hold up and keep fingers crossed that a shark didn't happen upon the scene was a gauntlet begging disaster. That Gifford became more and more adept in achieving clean catches of giant gamesters during that era is no small testament to his talents.

On Gifford's boat, you did it his way or that would be your last trip with him. He wrote an autobiography called *Anglers and Muscleheads,* wherein he deplored anglers over-tackling fish and not following directions.

"Big-game fishing is knowing how hard you can pull on the line without breaking it," he often said. "Over a long fight, the greatest danger is impatience." Gifford also felt that a short pump-and-wind technique keeps a fish's head up and thereby ends the fight faster.

Of the many luminaries who stepped forward in the early and formative years of offshore charter boat fishing, Thomas M. Gifford unquestionably stood among the head of the class. He still does.

5

~~~~~~

Webster "Doc" and Helen Robinson, 1896–1966 and 1900–1989

KEY WEST

This book is filled with originators, discoverers and explorers who succeeded in devising new and better ways to fish. You might say that these hearty souls became the pioneers with the arrows in their backs, their experiments and ideas often failing until, ergo, all the slots lined up.

It's inevitable for such individuals to come forward in every generation. Ever since man first tried to catch fish with something more complicated than gigging a sharp stick, people have constantly been thinking of better techniques and more useful gear—and that evolution never stops. Contributions from trailblazers make it that much easier for the rest of us to be successful, to better enjoy what we all love doing: catching fish and—in most cases—releasing them unharmed.

Such is the story of a remarkable husband and wife team. In 1962, Dr. Webster "Doc" Robinson became the first to best a sailfish on fly, a 74 ½-pounder at Pinas Bay, Panama, aboard Capt. Louis Schmidt's boat *Caiman*. The bigger story, however, is how the angler and crew succeeded in doing so. Even non–fly fishers can appreciate the near impossibility of getting flies anywhere close to the striking zone of deep-running spindle beaks.

The Robinsons worked closely with their longtime skipper, Lefty Reagan, and their combined research on the behaviors of big-game fish left no doubt that billfish and other species readily rise to the surface when they need to feed. Marine predators know that they can use the water's surface to trap sardines, ballyhoo and other fleeing bait fish. Of

Big trophy for Doc and Helen, whose record-setting escapades began when they were in their sixties. Photo courtesy of the International Game Fish Association.

course, anglers had long since established successful trolling spreads or the drifting of live or dead baits near the top of the water column, but even before hard-and-fast rules were drawn up in the mid-1960s it was against the spirit of fly fishing to troll or add any bait to the hook.

The Robinsons and Reagan—with input from mate Bob Marvin—came up with the solution: teasing. It's simple to explain, but the method requires practice and precise teamwork to be successful. Basically, someone in the cockpit like the mate entices a fish close to the stern so the fly angler can cast to it. How that "enticement" works is the devil in the details, and there's more to come on that. But what's truly remarkable is that Doc and Helen didn't even become serious fishermen until they were in their sixties. At that age most people slow down a little or a lot, eschewing all-night fishing trips, nixing the idea of going out in rough seas, or decidedly not subjecting themselves to the arduous punishment of drawn-out battles with big fish.

Those notions went right out the window when it came to the Robinsons. Webster was a successful New York doctor and investor, someone who knew how to invest a cash flow in ways that would multiply money. However, fate would deal him a life-altering blow. While driving home on what he thought would be just another day, he became involved in an auto accident so severe it totaled his car and nearly killed him. The essence of the prognosis from his doctor: "The good news is that you're going to pull through with a bit of recuperation; the bad news is that you need to move to a warm-weather climate so your joints will stop aching." He'd earned more than enough money to retire, but where to go?

An ardent reader of works by Ernest Hemingway, Philip Wylie and Zane Grey, Doc felt an affinity to the characters in their books who loved battling giant bluefin tuna, sailfish and marlin. Interviews and articles from and about those authors frequently mentioned the time they spent in the Florida Keys. Grey, for instance, made extended visits to the Long Key Fishing Club in the early part of the twentieth century, while Hemingway's residence in Key West, an island for which he had great affection, was well known. For his part, Wylie lived in Miami part of the time and often could be seen bobbing the waters off Key Largo and Islamorada. At that point in time in the late 1950s, Hemingway and Wylie were still very much alive, so Doc related even more closely to their writings and favorite haunts.

The Robinsons flew to Miami and drove to Key West. They hung out for two weeks just to get a feel for the place, noting the colorful coterie of characters and porch-style Conch houses. The city's Bohemian tendencies didn't faze these big-city transplants, and they immediately grasped the area's coming of age as a fishing Mecca. Vic Dunaway of the *Miami Herald* visited here often, and his exploits soon lit up Key West like a Broadway marquee. Magazine articles appearing in *Outdoor Life* and *Field & Stream* spotlighted the reefs, the blue water, the flats and the channels, and soon readers believed you could point the bow in just about any direction and haul in fish after fish—and they weren't far from wrong.

Doc and Helen bought a cute dream house with blue clapboard shutters, a wraparound wooden porch and a gabled second floor. It wasn't as big or lush as their place in New York, but it was a hell's measure more charming. With Keys disease now in their blood, they quickly concluded that this, indeed, would be their island icon, an improbable place in the sun. If before the accident Doc Robinson had even dreamed of actually living the Crusoe life, he'd have laughed it off.

At first the couple seemed content exploring the flats for bonefish, permit and tarpon, but the call of deep-sea fishing ingrained in their hearts and minds from the Wylie and Hemingway novels kept prodding them. Hemingway's shadow still hung in the Key West air. They fished offshore in the blue water several times and discovered that Doc had literally become rejuvenated. The salt air, warm sunshine and more relaxed living had virtually recharged his batteries. His strength fully recovered long before expected, Doc felt well enough that their daydreams shifted from confrontations with schoolie dolphin and blackfins to marlin and big yellowfins.

And so it was in 1959 with Doc at age 63 and Helen about to turn 60 that they made plans to fish off Panama's Pacific coast in Pinas Bay. They'd been hearing marvelous stories about huge numbers of marlin and especially sailfish being caught there. That Pacific sails averaged about twice the size of their Atlantic brethren was music to their ears. The Panama trips turned out to be so successful that they returned for the next several years and also expanded their voyages to relatively virgin waters off Ecuador, Peru and Chile. If Doc's body showed any wear and tear from the accident, he wasn't showing it. What with all those trips in the early 1960s, Doc and Helen racked up frequent flyer miles long before it became popular, with a travel regimen that would exhaust most people half their age. Doc alone caught an astonishing 115 black marlin—far more than anyone had ever previously caught off Central and South America.

Helen was no slouch herself. The reason her name heads this chapter with husband Doc is simple—she was a phenomenon behind the big rod and a key element in their teasing discovery. Born in Colorado, Helen moved with Doc to Key West and later lived out the rest of her life in Miami. While Doc took his turns at the fighting chair for Pacific billfish, so did Helen. She captured the women's 80-pound-class world record for a 796-pound black marlin and also notched new records for both men and women in the 50-pound category with a 584-pound black marlin. Years later in 1969, Helen also became the first angler to ever achieve world-record catches in all six of the International Game Fish Association's (IGFA) line classes.

Doc and Helen Robinson jumped into the minutiae of offshore fishing like kids excitedly attaching one Lego after another. They read everything available on marlin and sailfish as well as analyzed what offshore charter captains were doing off Palm Beach, Miami, Key West, Hawaii, the Bahamas, Cuba, Australia and Bermuda. They wondered how some of these tactics could be applied to fly fishing and whether, if a way could be found, they could disprove the legion of Doubting Thomases saying that bruisers like blue and black marlin were simply too big to take on fly gear.

Only days after being ensconced in their new home, Doc and Helen became regular onlookers at the charter docks of Key West. They not only viewed what was caught, they also asked lots of questions of those willing to share their experiences. One such skipper was a stout fellow named Lefty Reagan. The Robinsons took an immediate liking to him. Tough and skillful behind the wheel, Reagan was also unencumbered, which meshed nicely with their own plans to travel and one day conquer big fish on fly gear. Their trips outside the United States clearly revealed that most of the charter crews in Central and South America were subpar, and the creaky boats for hire ran the gamut from barely acceptable to totally unacceptable. Few captains and even fewer mates—many of whom were merely children—knew how to coordinate with fly anglers.

The Robinsons also knew all too well that if an emergency were to occur on one of these vessels off a remote coastline, they likely wouldn't remain among the breathing. What, then, if the Robinsons could sponsor Lefty Reagan—already a talented and experienced captain—to run

The Robinsons initially followed rules established by the Miami Beach Rod & Reel Club, which honored them with this "10 to 1 Club" award. Photo courtesy of the International Game Fish Association.

their own boat? They'd have total control over the gear and safety aspects, meaning they'd be able to make modifications suitable for fly fishing and, more importantly, be able to ensure consistency in the quality of the boat skippering, mating and fishing procedures.

"I knew a good suggestion when I heard it," Reagan later said of his reaction to Doc's proposal. "The arrangement allowed me to fish charters when not scheduled with Helen and Doc. I liked both of them and I could tell they wanted to till new fields, but at first I wondered if they still had the strength and stamina to do what they envisioned. Most people don't know how draining it can be to stand in that tropical heat and pull against a fish weighing hundreds of pounds. I've seen the toughest of men give up on it in the midst of battle, and trying to get 'em on fly had me pretty skeptical at first."

However, charters off Key West in sometimes rough conditions proved to Reagan that the Robinsons had what it took. "So, we shook hands on it," Reagan said.

With decent shots at times for billfish right in their own backyard—the Gulf Stream, around walls and seamounts off the Keys—the team had plenty of prolific waters to perfect what is now commonly known as teasing. The principles of fly fishing disallowed trolling a fly or using bait on the hook, and the cast had to be made without the boat in gear. Many fly anglers over the decades had presented flies to big fish that suddenly appeared on the surface, but it was done incidentally, without real forethought. When the big guys didn't stick around long enough to show any interest in a streamer, popper or anything else not reeking of fish scent, fly anglers reported such attempts to be an exercise in futility.

How wrong they were. Doc's first sailfish as well as numerous future billfish catches became stepping stones to what would become a well-rehearsed skit that would be reenacted many times to success. Once the word got out—which Doc and Helen willingly helped to spread—others quickly jumped on the procedure. Stu Apte, Lee Cuddy, Billy Pate, Bob Stearns and many others began catching big fish and breaking records. According to Lefty Reagan, Doc Robinson—being the detailed person that he was—enumerated eight basic steps necessary to successfully employ the teasing method to catch sailfish and marlin:

1. Fish where billfish are already known to proliferate.
2. Utilize heavy-duty fly gear with leaders expertly tied.
3. Learn how to construct and troll hookless baits.
4. Change teasing tactics based on differences between target species.
5. Practice the precise timing necessary between the fly caster, teaser/mate and captain.
6. Go mainly with blue foam-head poppers because they seem to draw more strikes.
7. Coordinate maneuvering the boat in concert with the angler's line.
8. Devise an end game for landing fish.

Doc and Helen Robinson went with 12-pound-test tippet until rules were later established to allow 15-pound ahead of the 12-inch trace. The Robinsons experimented with many patterns and finally settled on an oversize popper.

The teasing itself involves the right-handed fly angler standing on the left side of the cockpit (as one faces forward) while a second person—often a mate or another angler—referred to as the "teaser" keeps to the right side and the captain watches from the bridge.

Baits such as mullet or bonito strips are trolled in a spread behind the boat, the baits tied to the end of the leaders without any hook. It's very important here that the baits are securely tied so they can be billed and mouthed without falling off. When a fish such as a marlin comes up behind one of the baits or actually strikes it, the teaser seductively winds it in. Skill is required in letting the fish taste and see the bait so it stays fired up and follows it to the boat.

Now the crux of the whole drill: When the motivated marlin is brought within 15 to 20 or so feet of the transom, the fly angler or teaser yells "neutral" and the captain takes the boat out of gear. The teaser-mate must jerk the bait completely out of the water—often into the cockpit, which can be dangerous, or toward the right side of the bow so it's well out of sight of the fish. At precisely the moment the bait is pulled from the water, the angler casts the fly and lands it right where the bait existed a split second earlier. If the marlin transfers its sight and attention to the fly, chances are high that it will focus its frenzy on the fly. It then becomes a matter of setting the hook and successfully fighting the big fish, which of course is no gimme.

This can work with hookless lures as trolled teasers, but without the scent and taste factors, it's far less effective. Often hookless lures are trolled along with one or two hookless baits and if a lure is hit, it's "switched" by manipulating it close to one of the baits so the fish can be transferred. It's far more likely that a billfish will continue to follow a bait rather than a lure close to a boat without spooking. If a fish rises in the spread but seems tentative, the teaser bait can be dropped back, and likewise flow all the subtle nuances one learns. The Robinsons and others soon acquired a lot of helpful observations that upped their hook-up percentages.

"Marlin and sailfish act differently, so teasing has to vary accordingly," Doc said. He, Helen and Reagan altered the process based on each species they encountered, becoming experts at the technique.

Lefty Reagan's role was crucial in finding fish, in making sure the boat was in neutral before Doc or Helen cast and in assisting with the ensuing fight. Reagan had to check the boat at proper angles, put the bow to one side of the line when the fish is running so his angler can easily retrieve line, keep the line out of the props and of course help land the fish with the mate once it's bested. In other words, a lot can go wrong, magnifying even more the accomplishment of whipping a fish like a marlin on fly instead of conventional tackle.

After Doc's death, Helen didn't just fade away. She produced *Marlin to the Fly,* a TV documentary for the Public Broadcasting System. It depicted how she, Doc and Reagan devised the teasing method and other secrets they discovered about fly fishing for big offshore game fish. Before Helen died in 1989, she was honored by the British Broadcasting Company in a special they produced titled *The Old Lady and the Sea.*

You gotta believe ol' Doc was mighty proud.

6

Ernest Hemingway, 1899–1961

KEY WEST

I've always held the same kind of fascination with Hemingway as legions of others. It's the image of a macho man, someone with an urge to prove he's tough, strongly opinionated, a womanizer and a boozer. The trail of his life bespeaks a man of adventure, a person with perspective and a gift for creativity. Hemingway's stoic novel characters showed the ability to persevere, and he attracted the level of popularity reserved for superstars right up until his suicide. In fact, his legacy is still debated.

I met a number of people when I lived in the Florida Keys who said they had known Hemingway and fished with him, but I'd nod politely the same as when someone tells me they were among the throng at Woodstock or Jimmy Buffett is a "good friend." Truth is, after 1940 Hemingway seldom visited Key West or even Florida, for that matter—long before most of even the oldest name-droppers were old enough to share a whiskey with him.

As is so often the case, fishing trips with his dad nurtured Hemingway's love for the sea that would last throughout his life. From his beginnings in the streams and mountains of Idaho and Michigan, Ernest Miller Hemingway moved about the planet like few others. For one thing, he could afford it, and for another, he got bored at even the thought of staying in one place forever. That he lived in Key West for 12 years is a testament to the compatibility of the place with his character.

Hemingway arrived in Key West with his second wife, Pauline, in 1928. They'd previously been expatriates living in post–World War I

Josie Russell—owner of Sloppy Joe's, where Hemingway often swigged scotches and soda—toasts Papa's marlin catch. Photo courtesy of the International Game Fish Association and Fashion Licensing.

Paris. The chemical reaction between Hemingway's hard-drinking demeanor and the rough-around-the-edges flavor of America's Southernmost City seemed a matter of destiny. Hemingway enjoyed being able to walk into a gin joint without the local bar patrons making a big fuss over him.

Key West is more than 100 miles from Florida's mainland and connected by U.S. Highway 1. The terminus of the highway is marked with a "0" mile marker, which even today is a tourist attraction. Here Hemingway found fewer paparazzi than places like New York or Los Angeles, the solitude when he needed it to write and an ever-expanding herd of wild cats he fed and befriended within his walled property. The bar visits produced a handful of part-time charter guides who not only fished like him but also enjoyed pickling their livers. Key West was his kind of town.

He and Pauline moved into a large carriage house on Whitehead Street, dividing their time in the ensuing years between winters in Key West and summers in Wyoming. The house was a present from Pauline's uncle, containing a den on the second floor from which Hemingway conducted much of his in-home book research. Huge oaks and tropical hardwoods crowded the corner property and still do so today. Hemingway, nicknamed "Papa" by family and soon by some in the public, stuck to a daily routine to suit his writing creativity. His mind moved faster in the earlier part of the day, he found, so he'd rise early enough to watch the sun streak away the darkness.

After a leisurely walk to the second floor of their pool house where he typed away at a small desk, he was apart from distractions by visitors or Pauline's goings-on. Hemingway would write from morning to early afternoon in the small secluded office, taking frequent breaks with short walks and mingling with the ever-increasing gang of cats that themselves would become celebrities of sorts and the subjects of coffee-table books.

At around 3:30 in the afternoon, he'd saunter into Sloppy Joe's, which is currently where Capt. Tony's Saloon is located. Here he'd get soused with friends and fans, let his mind fill with scotch and soda instead of the details of whatever novel he was working on—he could unwind and unclutter his mind in his own way. It's also how he weeded out the fishing guides he favored from the unending offers to take him fishing.

The first invitation he accepted came from Charles Thompson, the unassuming owner of a hardware-supply business in town. Hemingway was intrigued by his tales of lightning-fast bonefish blitzing across the flats when hooked, of tarpon frantically leaping in Key West Harbor and of rod-bending battles with barracuda and snapper on wrecks. Grouper could be taken by the dozens atop rock piles, and sharks hooked just about everywhere.

Thompson's 18-foot boat fit two or three fishermen well enough, but it proved not at all comfortable when the wind blew and foamed the seas—a frequent malady due to the ever-present trade winds off Key West.

Back at the dock with another marlin; Hemingway averaged about one marlin catch a day in the Gulf Stream. Photo courtesy of the International Game Fish Association and Fashion Licensing.

Enter Capt. Eddie "Bra" Saunders, an old salt by the late 1920s who knew surrounding offshore waters better than anyone. He'd started his charter business before the turn of the century, and Hemingway was riveted by the prospect of fighting fish that weighed hundreds of pounds. He'd already yearned to test his muscle and determination against really giant fish, and the same went for his pal Charles Thompson. Together they joined Saunders to prowl the Marquesas Keys, the Dry Tortugas and the Gulf Stream. Hemingway caught wahoo, big dolphin and added sailfish to his burgeoning list of conquered fish species. But the huge marlin that he heard were being caught off Cuba really lit his fire.

When Joe "Josie" Russell, owner of Sloppy Joe's, found out Hemingway was not only a bar patron but a big fan of offshore fishing, the men agreed that a trip for trophy-size blue marlin was a done deal. They became fast friends, and the fact that Russell owned a large boat named *Anita* meant they could comfortably make it to Cuba and back, barring a serious storm. To say Hemingway became totally hooked on fishing—particularly big-game offshore style—during his initial Key West years is an understatement. Hemingway and Russell visited Cuba many times, and on one of these trips they ran into a fellow named Carlos Gutierrez, who'd established a reputation for mastering blue marlin.

They hired him as a mate and took to the deep Gulf Stream off Havana, the result being Hemingway finally going mano a mano with blue marlin. From those excursions in the early 1930s, he branched out his fishing experiences to the Bahamas—particularly Bimini for bluefin tuna. Many pictures of Hemingway next to huge bluefin on the dock in Bimini appeared around the world in the 1930s.

In 1934 Hemingway decided that he'd had enough of paying for charters or grubbing trips on the boats of friends. Now familiar with the best attributes of and needs for offshore fishing, Hemingway built a customized 38-foot power yacht he christened the *Pilar*. It became one of the first to sport a flying bridge and a cockpit with the best fighting chair and big-game gear money could buy. In his Havana jaunts he'd met Gregorio Fuentes, another master of marlin and offshore fishing, and Fuentes agreed to serve as full-time skipper of the *Pilar*.

One species drew Hemingway's ire, no doubt due to a hungry tiger or bull shark ruining more than a few potential world-record tuna and marlin. On a trip to Bimini aboard the *Pilar* in 1935, a shark struck a trolled bait and Hemingway gaffed the animal as it flopped and popped its jaws. He grabbed a pistol and in a frenzy fired away at the gasping shark. His state of mind questionable due to the searing heat and more than a few scotches and water, Hemingway shot himself through both legs during the melee. He was rushed to a Key West hospital, where he spent a week recovering enough to hobble around with crutches for a while.

Not one to be forgiving, Hemingway would at various times stash aboard the *Pilar* a Thompson machine gun or a U.S. Army tripod "nest" machine gun, both of which he delighted in hoisting to riddle with lead any hooked or unhooked shark that appeared even remotely near his boat. It's even been reported, though unsubstantiated, that Hemingway also used the weapons to fire at trolled fishing lines that periodically would trespass behind the spread of the *Pilar*. True or not, suffice it to say that other anglers kept their boats a goodly distance from Hemingway's.

Speaking of sharks, while living near Havana during World War II, Hemingway volunteered to partake in "combat patrols" in Gulf Stream waters for the U.S. Navy to spot and destroy German U-boats. His plan involved sneaking up on a sub when it was at the surface, then quickly jumping aboard and dropping a grenade down the hatch. Of course, he'd finish off anyone jumping overboard with the machine guns. His son Jack accompanied him on some of the patrols, but the only known victim was a shark just outside Havana's harbor that they repeatedly shot until little flesh was still intact.

Hemingway loved big-game fishing as much for the enjoyment he derived from the action as being admired for something other than his novels and raucous lifestyle. Even so, it's been reported that at one point, author Zane Grey invited Hemingway to go on a worldwide fishing competition with him, but Hemingway declined the offer on the basis that he didn't want to participate in what he felt would be nothing more than a publicity stunt. Whatever his reasons, Hemingway seemed more intent on achieving personal accomplishments in angling—all

Hemingway could often be seen at the International Fishing Club in Havana Harbor, as in this 1954 scene with Gregorio Fuentes and their catches. Photo courtesy of the International Game Fish Association and Fashion Licensing.

In a typically cluttered scene in the cockpit of the *Pilar*, Hemingway accepts a celebratory handshake from Elicio Arguelles. Photo courtesy of the International Game Fish Association and Fashion Licensing.

the while not at all shy about being photographed next to conquered giants—than hobnobbing on the water with other celebrities who were accomplished anglers. Perhaps he simply didn't like sharing the limelight.

The legendary Lefty Kreh spent two and a half days on Hemingway's boat in Havana in 1959. "It was during the 14th White Marlin Tournament," said Kreh.

"As a budding outdoor writer I asked Hemingway, 'How do you tell good writing?' He thought for a moment and answered, 'It can't be edited.' I don't think that answer can be improved upon."

Erl Roman, the *Miami Herald* outdoor editor who, beginning in the 1930s wrote hundreds of articles about Florida guides and anglers, documented that on May 21, 1935, while Hemingway was a resident of Key West, he boated a 381-pound bluefin tuna. Carlos Gutierrez served as skipper aboard the *Pilar* when this catch was made off Bimini. The ensuing publicity circled the globe until everyone involved in the big-game fishing circles knew about it.

Two days later, Hemingway notched another bluefin that reached the boat without shark mutilation, tipping the scale at 319 pounds. For gear enthusiasts, he used a Hardy reel and rod with 54-thread Edward vom Hofe fishing line. Roman had convinced Papa to fish off Bimini that season rather than Cuba, and after thanking him profusely, Hemingway seldom missed reading his *Miami Herald* columns.

Hemingway continued conquering giant fish even as his literary career culminated in 1952 with a Pulitzer Prize for *The Old Man and the Sea* and in 1954 with the Nobel Prize in Literature for the same. The timeless story embodied his own ambivalence about killing big fish while respecting their majestic power and will to live.

Hemingway was rightly proud of the prizes, but he also cherished his rise as a respected angler who had come full circle from what the young man witnessed in 1921 in the harbor of Vigo, Spain—a huge tuna somersaulting out of the water. Hemingway later said the fish crashed back into the water "with a noise like horses jumping off a dock" and that anyone besting such an animal on rod and reel should "enter into the presence of the very elder gods."

In the late 1950s, Hemingway's hard life began catching up to him. Often bedridden due to failing eyesight and a body battered from two plane crashes in Africa, Hemingway was also suffering from liver damage and bouts with depression. The final blow came when his doctor announced he was beset with an incurable hereditary disease that would slowly deteriorate his mind. That news, combined with losing his house and most of his possessions after Castro's revolution in 1959, shifted Hemingway's depression into high gear. He moved back to Idaho, contemplating the inevitable.

Unable to come to grips with a sedentary life precluding his ability to fish the oceans and with the prospect of no longer being capable of writing, Hemingway finally ended it all with a self-inflicted rifle shot to the head. He departed this world with suitable drama, reflecting a rollercoaster life filled with travel, action, fame, fortune and in the end, control over the direction of his own mortality.

Those who actually did fish with Hemingway came away with an admiration for the man's audacity, his lust for life, his irreverence for authority and a strong appreciation for what he could do behind a big-game rod. Hemingway spent much of his life in solitude, writing drafts, editing, typing manuscripts and conjuring plots. That made his time on the water that much more special to him. But by any means of measure, his contributions to public awareness of fishing as a sport will always be invaluable.

7

Philip Wylie, 1902–1971

MIAMI

It might seem incongruous that someone who successfully inflamed so many opinions found inner peace on the decks of charter boats in the Gulf Stream.

Then again, such anomalies never fazed Philip Wylie. He sharpened his pen on topics that made readers uncomfortable yet reflective, the most celebrated and controversial example of this being *A Generation of Vipers*. The book—published during a huge wave of patriotic fervor due to World War II—questioned many of the ingrained values Americans had come to embrace. Wylie took to task both the liberal and conservative establishments, but we'll get into that down the road.

Wylie's edgy side evidently sought a softer outlet, however. His series of stories on the offshore exploits of the charter boat *Poison* became a huge factor in public recognition of sport fishing. "Crunch and Des"—the story of Capt. Crunch Adams and his mate Desmond "Desperate" Smith—extolled the adventures of a charter boat operation and ignited great national interest in a profession few knew anything about.

Most of the 69 "Crunch and Des" articles appeared in the *Saturday Evening Post*. The chartering duo's experiences spun off an even more popular series in the mid-1950s on a new media sensation called television. Thirty-seven black and white episodes of *Crunch and Des* were filmed by NBC on location in Bermuda, although the fictional boat fished from New York to Key West.

As with most of Wylie's writings, "Crunch and Des" reflected his own life experiences. That included his love of saltwater fishing off Miami and the colorful charter boat community in the late 1930s and '40s he

Wylie surrounded himself with fish when penning the famous "Crunch and Des" stories. Photo courtesy of the International Game Fish Association.

grew to know and admire. Wylie readily admitted that Crunch and Des were inspired by Harold Schmidt and John Smedburg, with whom he enjoyed many sport-fishing excursions out of Miami's famed Pier 5 dock.

The moral of each episode of *Crunch and Des* may have been pre-dictable—good people and good intentions triumph over bad—but the allure that captured everyone's interest involved the reality of what charter fishing is like. This was accomplished with accurate portrayals of the essence of a day on the water in a charter boat, including the layout of the decks, gear, baits, tackle, techniques, fishing jargon and even the behaviors of different species of fish when hooked. The scenes and action changed a bit depending on whether a marlin, tuna, wahoo, dolphin, grouper, shark or other species was the combatant.

Philip Wylie meant much more to the establishment of sport fishing than his writings, however. He recognized the need for establishing rules and order in the world of fishing. In 1941 he became vice president of the International Game Fish Association (IGFA), helping to devise standardized rules on tackle and conduct. Wylie also reviewed world-record applications and contributed his suggestions on what constitutes good sportsmanship.

Wylie's support of the IGFA resulted in public exposure for the organization in such pieces as Wylie's *"Big Fish and High Seas,"* which appeared in *Esquire* magazine in 1952. In the article he said: "That's the story of IGFA. Its worth to human relations the world over cannot be exaggerated. Its value as an umpire in a great sport is deeply appreciated by many and should be understood by all."

Michael Lerner, the retail magnate of the chain of clothing stores bearing his name, also was an early advocate of IGFA. Wylie worked as a director for the Lerner Marine Laboratory in Bimini, which further developed his knowledge of fish and angling talent.

Wylie never shied from taking on the emerging fisheries issues of the day. As far back as the 1940s, Wylie raised flags about the degradation of Biscayne Bay and the Everglades. He wrote about a Miami slum and took the city to task for indifference—someone in the mayor's office got the message and instituted a program to at least try to do something about it.

In 1955, Wylie penned an article that appeared in *Sports Illustrated* titled "Freedom Underseas." He railed against the discourtesies of skin divers crowding out traditional fishing locations.

"The presence of people, male or female, amidst the intended quarry is distressful," wrote Wylie. "Fish sought in their own element are not in a mood to take baits lowered through a layer of pursuing swimmers."

Wylie went on to state, "It is this writer's opinion—after long and fairly considerable experience in both fields—that some areas of the sea are too dangerous for skin divers and should be taboo."

He thought that the differences between divers and anglers indicated a brewing war, and how prophetic that turned out to be. Since the 1990s, federal fisheries managers mainly under the auspices of the National Oceanic and Atmospheric Administration (NOAA) have been pushing no-fishing zones at a frenetic pace.

Divers have aligned with NOAA on voting councils and "advisory" committees, obtaining as an obvious benefit unfettered access to wrecks, reefs and other areas banning anglers.

Undoubtedly Wylie wondered how the prospect of unlimited numbers of divers interacting directly with the resources made sense in areas supposedly set aside for "protection." Wylie, based on his fierce activism and opinion of divers, would likely be one of the most vocal opponents of no-fishing zones and, per his *A Generation of Vipers* reflections, claim that the zones are a thinly disguised federal takeover of our shorelines.

That Wylie disdained divers ruining prominent fishing sites—their very presence biasing the behavior of fish—is evident in his article. In it he also cites economic reasons for why divers, no matter how numerous, would never make up the difference in lost revenue from displaced fishermen. That unfortunate situation indeed may become more and more common to resort areas and countries dotted with the ubiquitous no-fishing zones.

During the mid-1950s, Wylie slowly switched from becoming a fish catcher to more of a fish watcher. It was not that he grew a dislike for fishing or suddenly favored diving—far from it. Instead, Wylie wished to spend less time improving his casting and techniques in order to concentrate on fish behaviors, habitats and life cycles. Drawing on what he'd previously learned at the Lerner Marine Lab, Wylie contributed a great deal to further understanding how to best sustain and enhance the resources of many saltwater species.

Let's hit the reverse button for a moment and return to *A Generation of Vipers*. Wylie's state of mind when writing the book is angry, representing quite a contrast at the time to his relaxation zone while fishing. According to those who regularly shared a boat with the author, he was generally mellow and laid-back. Only when someone directed the conversation away from fishing or toward things inconsequential did Wylie become animated and hot tempered.

Wylie supposedly wrote *Vipers* in less than two months in 1942, and neither he nor the publisher thought it would be a big seller. Considering how he used everyone as a punching bag, its popularity is remarkable. Wylie penned a critique of American society that one might figure would have netted him a lynching during a time of brotherly support in

An active day offshore with bonito and a sailfish draws a smile from Wylie (left).
Photo courtesy of the International Game Fish Association.

World War II. The book amazes for its audacity because it takes to task just about everyone—professionals, businessmen, clergymen, politicians and regular citizens for not recognizing the deficiencies of others and their own apathy. Interestingly, at one point Wylie served as a special advisor to the chairman of the Joint Committee for Atomic Energy, and it's possible his dismay with bureaucratic incompetence spurred his later criticisms of "the system."

Backing up to 1937, Wylie was invited to join the Miami Beach Rod & Reel Club. He moved to Miami Beach and greatly looked forward to visiting the club, chatting with other anglers, sharing ideas and tips, entering catches in the competitions and just being a part of south Florida's incomparable fishing community.

While not considered by most to be in the expert class, Wylie exhibited good fishing skills. Although a slight man, he showed tenacity in sticking with a fight to the point of exhaustion. He displayed that determination as far back as 1937 when he tangled with, and whipped,

Wylie was famous for penning numerous titles, including the controversial *A Generation of Vipers*. Photo courtesy of the International Game Fish Association.

a blue marlin while fishing out of the Key Largo Anglers Club—a feat that few others had managed up until then. He also met his future wife that year. Life got even better as he gained prominence in the 1940s and the '50s with his Crunch and Des media blitzes, including press about the releases of the book, articles and especially the TV series. Wylie was on top of the world.

Born in Massachusetts, he became used to a wanderer's life with a father who was a traveling Presbyterian minister. They moved from state to state, and the young Wylie sampled the fishing waters whenever he could. He got his start in 1925 as an editorial staffer with *New Yorker* magazine and found his calling—writing.

Wylie tried his hand at writing a novel in 1927. That didn't produce significant revenue or acclaim for him, but it did fetch interest from MGM Studios and Paramount Pictures and he became a script writer.

In 1930, Wylie made a trip to Coral Gables during the winter and found the warm climate very agreeable. Quite accidentally, he was

The youthful writer clutches his camera while posing next to a marlin, circa 1930. Photo courtesy of the International Game Fish Association.

invited to come along on a fishing charter, and though ambivalent at first about going offshore among large waves and fabled sea monsters, his fears unfurled as he tangled with several smoker kingfish and really enjoyed it.

The effect on Wylie was immense—he loved south Florida, and the encounter with big saltwater game fish made him wonder why he was ever enamored with smaller freshwater quarry. From then on, Wylie relocated to Miami every winter, spending summers in New York and Connecticut.

Always witty and pithy, here are some of the more popular Wylie quotations:

- "Without criticism, progress is impossible."
- "God must hate common people, because He made them so common."
- "One good teacher in a lifetime may sometimes change a delinquent into a solid citizen."
- "Ignorance is not bliss—it is oblivion."
- "If liberty has any meaning it means freedom to improve."

For those who knew Wylie as a journalist, an advocate for conservation, an angler or just a friend, he made a lasting impression. For those of us still wetting a line, his contributions to our sport through his writings cannot be overstated.

8

Bill Fagen, 1904–1975

MIAMI

Home life in Ormond Beach, Florida, just wasn't agreeable while growing up, so Bill Fagen decided to hit the road. The young man headed west on a train from Jacksonville, and one of its stops was New Orleans. Fagen jumped from a boxcar with a burlap bag over his shoulder that contained all his worldly possessions. He melted into the crowd, making his way to the waterfront as the train continued westward.

His curiosity boiled over. He'd heard plenty about "The Big Easy" back in Florida and its reputation as a place open to anything and everything, a bawdy town where a go-getter and hustler could make some easy cash. Fagen figured that maybe here he could learn the ropes and become a success at something instead of being shooed away like at home.

With a harbor cluttered with private yachts and merchant vessels, Fagen immediately ran into crew members drunkenly stumbling along narrow streets in the French Quarter. Many of the boats needed low-paying gofers, it seemed, and Fagen didn't mind starting at the bottom. Likeable and never one to shrink from hard work, he hired on as a deckhand for a private yacht. When that voyage ended, he hopped aboard another yacht sailing out of Biloxi.

Fagen enjoyed his time at sea, learned the rudiments of navigating a boat, saw what it took to please wealthy clients, and learned how to lay low when people got carried away by the whiskey man. Fagen made a few bucks here and there, but another calling paid better: rum running. The salt air and liquor had proved magnetic companions for centuries, and the hearty fellows with whom Fagen ran liked the idea of taking on

Letting down the outriggers as they head to the Gulf Stream. Though unimpressive compared to today's charter boats, in the 1920s and '30s, *Florida Cracker II* was the head of its class. Photo courtesy of the International Game Fish Association.

a few kegs of rum aboard their vessels before hitting the Gulf of Mexico and sailing far and wide.

Many of them already knew how to make money delivering rum, too, and soon Fagen became a willing student. Still too young to serve in World War I, he was plenty old enough to understand supply and demand. Although Fagen did business with shady characters, so did everybody in the shadows of ship piers and docks. He rationalized that any ill-gotten gains would simply be a means to an end, a necessary evil that would help him eventually stake a claim in some sort of business.

By this time an industrial zeal had gripped the United States, with Ford's Model T appearing everywhere roads were passable and the spectacle of overhead biplanes becoming commonplace. Some of the crew and yacht owners liked to fish, and it thrilled Fagen to witness skirmishes with cobia, tarpon, gag grouper and occasionally even blue marlin in Gulf waters. At times he ventured to Venice to fish the coastline marshes of Louisiana for redfish and trout. The anticipation that with each cast, at any moment, a fish might strike totally enraptured him.

Operating a merchant vessel or running some rich guy's yacht had appeal to Fagen, but the prospect of sailing the seas, fishing and somehow making a living doing all of that really fascinated the young man. He decided to somehow buy his own boat and make his name as a charter boat captain—a daring and chancy venture, he knew.

Fagen's cash stash grew and, now in his early 20s, he sensed it would be wise to get out of town before someone else cleaned him out. That was the sort of dog-eat-dog world of the ports and wharfs where he toiled and sometimes played. He'd also grown tired of dealing with the unsavory characters that would get tanked and roll unwitting tourists, and he wanted no part of that ilk. And so it was that Fagen journeyed to Miami at the beginning of the Roaring '20s. No one's quite sure how he ended up there—probably off the boat of a wealthy and well-traveled yachtsman. Fagen had heard plenty of intriguing tales about the spectacular fishing and burgeoning tourism interest in south Florida, and apparently he'd decided it was time to experience that for himself.

It all clicked into place. Bill Fagen liked to fish, was comfortable with Florida weather growing up as a child and thought a fresh start in a new place sounded good. In any case, once in Miami it didn't take long before he found his way to Pier 5, the already famed fishing charter dock across from the growing glow of the city's downtown on Biscayne Bay. Pier 5 would become a pivotal meeting place of innovators for the sport, where such things as outriggers, strip baits and drop-back techniques for sailfish would be employed. The nerve center of matters related to recreational fishing, Pier 5 became the stage where Fagen watched, listened, learned and grew. In years hence his peers would be watching, listening and learning from him.

In time the right opportunity presented itself, and Fagen jumped at the chance to turn his dreams into reality. More than ready to control his own destiny, in 1925 he caught wind of a boat for sale—but not just any plodding old charter boat. This was a special craft that combined speed with good construction, making it large enough to cross the Gulf Stream to the Bahamas or Cuba and suitable for rigging up as a fishing vessel. He named the 38-footer the *Florida Cracker II,* and it came equipped with two six-cylinder Hall-Scott 120-horsepower inboard engines.

The boat would almost immediately become the subject of dock talk throughout south Florida. It ran at an astonishing top speed of 26 miles per hour—unheard of in those days for a wooden boat measuring nearly 40 feet. In fact, most vessels of that size lurched along at about half that speed. It would give Fagen a huge advantage for charters and especially tournaments, as he could leave at the same time as the other boats and beat everyone to the choice fishing grounds. He could also fish a bit longer than the rest and get back to the dock at about the same time they did.

In the late 1920s, Thor decided to rearrange south Florida a bit. Miami's population had practically disappeared after the horrendous 1925 hurricane. But soon the real estate speculators would return, and in the meantime Flagler's railroad and passenger ships continued to deliver huge numbers of curious tourists to Miami's waterfront during the icy winters up north. The rich and famous extended their reach beyond Palm Beach, flocking to what was being touted in the press as the new tropical paradise—Miami Beach.

Fagen checks the scale reading for a swordfish; notice the fellow in knickers in the background. Photo courtesy of the International Game Fish Association.

Despite the oncoming hard times with the Great Depression and World War II, Bill Fagen stayed busy. He knew all about the tourism industry from his days in New Orleans. He'd watched smart businessmen lure visitors with news to the press about upcoming festivals and how alluring stories about the good fortune encountered by other travelers attracted yet more visitors. Fagen would therefore spend summers in Montauk, New York. As he fished there, he learned who the monied people were and where the well-connected crowd hung out.

Fagen spoke to them of the confluence off Miami of the Atlantic Ocean and the Gulf Stream, and how that attracted huge swarms of baitfish and the big-game fish pursuing them. It was like shooting ducks in a pond, he would say, and real-time and wannabe anglers salivated at his tales of daily battles with sailfish, wahoo and marlin. He described the live reefs teeming with snapper and grouper and the discoveries of virgin waters off the Florida Keys featuring massive schools of humongous tarpon. Fagen knew how to spin a story.

Fagen asserted on one occasion that "some of the best fishing in the world is in the Gulf Stream from Miami Beach to Fowey Rocks Lighthouse" and said, "I found some of the best fishing in my career as a guide in the Florida Keys." He spoke of kingfish running as high as 70 pounds, with "plenty of sails, tarpon and other sporty fish."

It didn't hurt Fagen's cause when his anglers returned to their hometowns verifying that the man's claims had basis in fact. Fishing really was spectacular in those days, just as Fagen claimed—at least for those with the skills to run a successful charter operation. As word of mouth spread, the steady customer base grew for all of the charter captains plying south Florida in the 1930s.

When an angler aboard the *Florida Cracker II* caught a shark estimated at 600 pounds in 1928, Fagen made sure pictures of it were sent to the media. At the time it was thought to be the largest fish ever caught on 24-thread line, and Fagen wanted the world to know about it.

He did the same when a massive bluefin tuna allegedly weighing 700 pounds was bested off Bimini, as well as a shark estimated at 785 pounds. The truth of the matter is that dock scales at that time weren't believed to be capable of even weighing fish that large, but so much

There was nothing much Bill Fagen or others could do about sharks frequently ruining catches such as this blue marlin. Photo courtesy of the International Game Fish Association.

for small details. Whatever the true weights, Fagen made hay with the captures along with the added tidbit that daily catches were being tallied on sailfish and blue marlin.

In every sense of the word, Bill Fagen was quite the promoter as well as a first-class charter boat captain. One might not think so when first laying eyes on him, the lean and bespectacled fellow looking more like an accountant than the common expectation of a burly hairy-chested skipper. Few could match his competence at the wheel, however, be it maneuvering the boat, spotting signs of fish or delivering plenty of action for charter customers. People quickly grew to respect Fagen and to recognize his skills versus the best captains of his day in any kind of sea conditions.

One well-publicized and puzzling episode appeared in a Miami newspaper article in 1925. It related how Fagen had harpooned a 30-foot shark while fishing on the edge of the Gulf Stream. Initial reports surmised the beast was a killer whale, but most anglers and biologists of the time considered that unlikely. A similar incident in 1912 with Miami skipper Charlie Thompson involved a whale shark, and unlike Fagen's monster, the Thompson shark was photographed and brought to the dock with much fanfare. In any case, Fagen did not boat the 30-footer and he later told curious skippers and onlookers at Pier 5—including, evidently, the newspaper reporter—that the damage to his boat occurred when the massive animal, chasing a sand shark, blithely caromed into the hull of the *Florida Cracker II*.

This cracked several planks below the waterline, but Fagen patched the leaks and the bilge pumps did their jobs well enough to allow time to reach Miami's Government Cut and safety. A somewhat bizarre story, to say the least, since whale sharks are plankton eaters and rarely had anyone ever seen a killer whale in local waters. It caused some to murmur that in reality Fagen ran into a coral head on Carysfort Reef off Key Largo and was covering his tail with a tale, so to speak.

That anomaly aside, other reports of Fagen's accomplishments provided all the credibility of his ability that anyone needed. According to Erl Roman, the outdoor editor for the *Miami Herald* from the 1930s to the '50s, Fagen took Pennsylvanian George Steward Jr. to Bimini aboard his boat *Florida Cracker II* in April 1928. Although targeting bluefin tuna, he led Steward to three blue marlin catches, the largest tipping the scale at 138 pounds back at Florida's Pflueger Taxidermy. In any era, three marlin captures in one short trip off the Florida–Bahamas region can be considered great. In 1935, angler Tommy Shevlin notched a world-record 636-pound blue marlin off Bimini aboard Fagen's boat. A frequent charter customer, Shevlin went on to take nearly 120 blues aboard *Florida Cracker II* over the years as well as numerous bluefins.

Roman and others began spotlighting Fagen's prowess as his accomplishments continued to pile up. His clientele included Herbert Hoover and many of the nation's top businessmen. He also fished with a fellow named Ernest Hemingway, who gave him an autographed copy from his own collection of *A Farewell to Arms*. Through Hemingway, Fagen's client base increased even more. It never hurt to be photographed with the great novelist, and to have him tout your ability to his peers would be priceless. Hemingway invited Fagen to fish with him aboard the *Pilar*, and on other occasions for purposes of added safety Fagen followed the boat along to the Bahamas in his *Florida Cracker II*.

Fagen, based out of Pier 5, was one of the first to explore waters beyond Bimini at locations such as Chub Cay and Walker's Cay. He also visited New Zealand, South America and Africa in pursuit of adventure and big fish. But no matter where Bill Fagen set his trolling spread or planted his feet, he never tired in extolling the virtues of his favorite fishing grounds in the world: Florida's Gulf Stream. His legacy continues.

9

Bill Smith, 1909–1996

KEY LARGO

We sat next to each other at a Friday-night kickoff party for a fishing competition in Key Largo in 1989. Both of us were on the tournament rules committee. I didn't know Bill Smith from Shine-Ola other than as one of the old-guard guides. Little did I realize at the time that his life was intertwined with the formative fishing history of the area—as was his wife's—and that I'd one day write a book with him as the subject of one of the chapters.

At first blush, my impression of Smith was of a dour man who looked eternally grumpy. I later found out that that could be attributed not to his personality but instead to the warfare of time; the sides of his lips turned downward at the edges and his skin looked ravaged as often occurs from years of sun exposure. Our eyes locked and he didn't smile.

"You okay?" I asked, a bit intimidated. At that time I'd been writing a fishing column in the Keys for a weekly newspaper plus doing a radio show with Rick Berry, who was then a *Miami Herald* Keys writer. Smith's name seemed familiar, and as a local in the angling community, I assumed he'd also heard of me.

"Yeah, *I'm* fine," he said, the words coming slowly yet forcefully. "It's just that I don't care for most newsmen because they can't even spell names right, much less get their facts straight."

After a pregnant silence, I replied, "First of all, I'm not a newsman, I'm a columnist. And considering your name, I find it amazing anyone's had trouble spelling it."

A smile, finally. "Not trouble with mine, but people I know like Jimmie Albright," said Smith. "We'll see how you do. And another thing: I have trouble getting through your articles without falling asleep."

This is the picture (and the fly) with Smith's handwriting about his 1939 bone-fish-on-fly benchmark. Photo courtesy of the International Game Fish Association.

Noting he'd gotten my dander up, he winked, smiled again and totally disarmed me. The man possessed a very wry sense of humor and I'd just been introduced to it. In future conversations with Smith, I was suitably braced as I grew to appreciate his wit.

Also by then I'd found out more than a few interesting details about Bill Smith. It didn't take much to get him talking, and once started, you might as well pour a glass of your favorite adult beverage and sit a spell. Between those infrequent talkative sessions, we came and went as locals do in a small town. I lived in Tavernier—a flyspeck of a community between Key Largo and Islamorada—in the late 1980s to the early 1990s. Although the throng of fishing aficionados in the Keys has always been proportionately large, you'd run into pretty much everyone sooner or later, whether they wetted a line occasionally or not.

During one of our gab sessions, Smith offered the scenario about a particular date in Florida fishing lore that directly involves him: the day the first angler took a bonefish on fly. Suffice it to say that I quickly came to recognize that that achievement—though significant—was hardly the beginning and the end of the story of his illustrious guiding career.

Smith arrived in the upper Keys in 1928 from Melbourne, Florida, at the spunky age of 19. He decided to try his hand at guiding, and that didn't sit well with the handful of local skippers already trying to eke out a living. On one occasion, Leonard and Gene Lowe blocked Smith's access to the dock on his return, so the lad tossed anchor, jumped into the water and swam in anyway. The Lowe brothers figured that if the kid was that tough, he would indeed become a fitting guide.

One evening Smith went to an Elk's Club dance in Tavernier and arrived barefoot, which became an issue with the doorman. Upon being told that shoes were required in order to enter, Smith pointed at a roach on the adjoining wall and said, "I don't see *it* wearing any shoes." That kind of silver tongue and wry humor not only got Smith into the dance, it served him well in many precarious predicaments throughout his lifetime.

Even so, as hard as Smith worked to get clients and find them fish, it seemed like an eternal struggle. For a while in 1932, he guided for Fern and Bill Butters of the Hotel Matecumbe while freelancing for

For fishing in deeper waters, Smith utilized this boat typical of the '40s. Note that he named it using parts of his and wife Bonnie's first names. Photo courtesy of the International Game Fish Association.

other charters. In that era and for a long time to come, the only people visiting the Keys were the wealthy, most of whom didn't fish. After the massive hurricane of 1935 that killed numerous Keys residents and washed into the bay most of the buildings and structures—and all of the boats—one needed to juggle several balls to make ends meet.

Fortunately for residents like Smith, catching fish to eat and filling a boiling pot with lobster were child's play on any foray into the Atlantic or Florida Bay. The waters teemed with snook, snapper, grouper, mackerel and numerous other fine edibles such as blue crab and conch. A steady diet of seafood platters didn't make anybody mad, least of all Bill Smith.

Good eating aside, the other elements did not come together like a perfect storm for young men who wanted to make a living taking people fishing in the Florida Keys. Tourism peaked with the Long Key Club beginning in 1906 and lasted until the famous camp was demolished in the 1935 hurricane; interest again died down during the Great Depression and World War II. While most tourists hadn't as yet discovered the magic of Florida Keys fishing, more and more anglers from Miami were doing so. Bill Smith saw the ebb and flow as a part-time guide in the 1930s and was well positioned to be one of the top guides when things did click. Along the way he certainly paid his dues.

"Everyone talks about the 'good ol' days' in the Keys, but I don't know any other way to describe them," said Smith. "It wasn't easy living because of the isolation when it came to comforts we all now enjoy, so it was a bit primitive. Running water and electricity didn't go into effect until the '40s, so you had to be self-sufficient. We understood the pluses and minuses and came here to get away from pollution and crowded highways and waterways. It was worth the inconveniences.

"You didn't have to run 20 or 30 miles like you do now to maybe— and I stress *maybe*—see roseate spoonbills, flamingos, herons, egrets, royal terns and other birds. We walked to the water's edge just about anywhere and there they were," he said.

"I think some fish like tarpon and bonefish ran a bit smaller in those days, but the numbers more than made up for it. Once we broke the codes on what each fish liked to eat and where they were likely to be on different tides, we seldom came back to the dock empty-handed. You also must realize that fish spook easier now because of all the boat traffic and fishing pressure."

Smith believes that the first negative impact to fish stocks occurred when the commercial docks opened in the 1940s.

"Those big boats came back to the dock overflowing with fish of all types," said Smith. "They would brag about who caught the most, and it sickened me. I didn't want my anglers doing that, so they released anything they weren't going to eat or mount. That sometimes cost me business, but so be it."

He learned how to fly fish in the early '30s for his own interest and because he believed one day it would be a specialized part of sport fishing. "Everyone used plug-casting tackle with braided lines, and of the few tackle shops in the area that existed back then, none carried all that you needed for light-tackle fishing," Smith said.

"So, I made jigs out of lead and plugs out of wood for clients and my own fishing." He also started tying flies. Smith continued to make flies and wooden plugs even through his retirement years.

"I remember Bill's tarpon lures were made out of balsa," said Miamian Al Pflueger Jr. "It had an orange head and body, and I know Bill caught many, many poons on them."

No reflections on Bill Smith would be complete, however, without his feat in 1939 of being the first ever to catch a bonefish on fly. We need to go back to 1934 to put it all in perspective. Smith worked for Ed Butters at the Matecumbe Hotel and met Islamorada resident and fly-fishing authority George LaBranche. LaBranche wrote books about dry–fly fishing and other topics. He also loudly proclaimed that since bonefish dine on crustaceans and shrimp, they would never eat a fly. Considering LaBranche's status, pretty much everyone went along with what he believed as gospel—hey, the man had *written books* about fishing. Accordingly, no one really tried pitching flies at the species in a concerted way.

As a result, bonefish were seldom a target species at all prior to 1930. Incidental catches of bonefish had probably occurred as far back as when the Indians inhabited the area. Joe Brooks, in his *Outdoor Life* magazine columns, included reports of bonefish catches in the Keys in the late 1920s by those busy pursuing tarpon.

After guiding through most of the 1930s, Smith took a man fishing in 1938 who would put him into direct confrontation with George LaBranche's theory about bonefish not taking flies. An Alaskan fly angler named George Crawford wanted to fish for tarpon with Smith for a few days. According to Smith, Crawford had written the song for the U.S. Air Force (then the Army Air Corps) that starts, "Off we go into the wild blue yonder." He'd brought along flies he used for taking salmon, and he wasn't having much luck with them in the salt.

"I asked Leo Johnson, a friend in Islamorada who also guided, what he was using to catch tarpon on flies," said Smith. "Leo explained that he simply wrapped pork rind around a hook. I decided to modify the idea, so I added hackle feathers to the hook and rind when I got home."

The next day, Crawford again struck out on silver kings, but this time he tossed the pork rind flies at several schools of bonefish. Crawford caught two, and after pulling into the dock, Smith put the fish into a sack and drove to the local grocery store—the only place in the region with accurate scales—to weigh them. As chance would have it, as Smith and Crawford walked out of the store, in walked George LaBranche. After asking Smith what they'd caught and being told bonefish on fly, LaBranche huffed and demanded to see the evidence. Upon so doing, LeBranche went into a tirade.

"He totally scoffed and put me down," Smith recalled. "It embarrassed the hell out of me. He ranted that the addition of pork rind or anything else that could be considered bait rendered the fly nothing more than bait. I knew he was technically right, and right then and there swore I'd somehow catch a bonefish on purely a fly.

"It took me months, but I finally came up with a small portion of ostrich feather over brown squirrel hair and a red-and-yellow hackle tied with red and orange thread on a 1/0 hook. I tied a lot of flies until I came up with that version.

"One afternoon in 1939 I hit the Islamorada flats armed with those flies. I saw many bonefish and cast at them, and it didn't take long at all for one of them to chomp it—about an eight-pounder," Smith recalled.

Fortunately, he had witnesses in nearby boats: a Mr. Norfleet and his guide, Bert Pinder. Since Norfleet knew George LaBranche, Smith asked if he'd inform him about the catch. Even though LaBranche remained skeptical, the believers now outnumbered the non-believers. In fact, LaBranche was to catch his own gray ghosts on fly years later with Frankee Albright, evidently after succumbing to the reality of the new game of catching bonefish on fly.

Smith figured he needed to give an identity to the soon-to-be-famous fly that started it all, and he chose the Salt-Us after a regular guiding client named Mr. Saltus. Smith also figured that if bonefish would eat a fly, a permit probably would too. He put in more hours at the tying table to design such a pattern, and it too ultimately proved a success. Many who attribute Smith with catching the first bonefish on fly don't realize he did the same with a permit. Smith named that pattern the Timrep—permit spelled backwards.

The year 1939 is credited by Smith and others of that era as the date he caught the first bonefish on fly, and there's little need to doubt it. Well, maybe one source disputed it. Erl Roman, then the outdoor editor of the *Miami Herald*, reported that it occurred on June 30, 1942,

Smith continued tying his famous flies even after he retired from guiding. Photo courtesy of the International Game Fish Association.

because he wrote that Smith called him that day to report it. According to Smith, however, he merely told Roman details about the catch in '42, while the actual catch had taken place three years earlier.

In any event, Roman also ran a picture of Smith hoisting the eight-pounder in the newspaper, and it set off an immediate reaction among Miami Beach Rod & Reel Club members—the most prestigious fishing group in Florida at that time. These members included Frank Baxter, Homer Rhode, Lee Cuddy and H.J. "Red" Greb. Fishing guides took note too, and by the late 1940s and '50s, just about all light-tackle guides in south Florida had become adept at scouring the flats of the Keys and Biscayne Bay for bonefish on fly. How much longer that would have occurred had it not been for Bill Smith is anyone's guess.

While guides in particular were becoming proficient with fly-fishing gear even in those days, then as now, novices (i.e., paying customers) found the specialized techniques beyond their capability. Consequently, spin-fishing immediately became the gear of choice for bonefish beginners. That began with a nudge from Bill Smith too.

Bob McChristian operated Mac's Tackle Shack in Miami. A fellow named Bache Brown had introduced spinning rods and reels to the U.S.

market, and McChristian sold them out of his shop. While in town, Brown also asked Erl Roman to help bring the new gear to the attention of south Florida's angling community. Roman had disdained fly gear ever since a jack crevalle gave him more of a fight than he could handle way back in 1927 at the mouth of the Coral Gables Waterway. Roman, somewhat steadfast in extolling the superiority of plug casting, nevertheless referred Brown to Bill Smith "down in the Keys." Smith instantly grasped the greater ease of use with spinning gear and what that could mean to the guiding business; clients constantly had difficulty with the timing requisite of plug-casting reels, causing unending tangles.

Smith even invited Brown to spend a week with him in Islamorada. After just the first day on the water, both men came away amazed at the ease in getting baits and lures on the table in front of tailing or mudding gray ghosts. Not only did they prove that spin tackle indeed could successfully be used in targeting bonefish, the fact that inexperienced anglers could cast reasonably enough to at least soak their own baits in the right spots instantly made it more feasible to use for the average customer.

Bill Smith's better half became well known too. He married Bonnie in the late 1930s, and she was one of the three Cass sisters who guided in the Florida Keys during World War II and beyond. The other two were Frankee Albright and Beulah Cass. Bonnie introduced Frankee to Jimmie Albright when he was on leave from the U.S. Navy while his ship was docked in Ft. Lauderdale; they married, and Jimmie went on to become one of the most celebrated guides in the Keys, thanks in large part to the tutelage of Bill Smith.

"Living in the Keys before the 1960s was grand," Smith reflected, his face tightening and eyes becoming brighter. "An advantage of a small community is helping one another. If someone needed a roof patched or a boat fixed, you knew who to see and they'd never refuse help—everyone pitched in for fellow locals. The Keys are still a great place, but it will never be the same peaceful place that I once enjoyed."

I still find the Florida Keys to be entrancing and one of the great fishing destinations of the world. But Bill Smith certainly made it even more special.

10

~~~~~~

John Rybovich, 1913–1993

WEST PALM BEACH

About 10 years ago I turned off Old Cutler Road into Gables By The Sea south of Miami. I was on my way to Key West and wanted to stop and say hello to a friend. His ornate house consisted of a magnificent structure on a wide canal leading to Biscayne Bay, and a Rybovich sportfishing boat sat majestically behind the property. My buddy took me aboard the boat, and I couldn't stop shaking my head in awe at the Rembrandt-like craftsmanship.

I also strode through his massive garage to gawk at a collection of vintage sports cars. Noting my fascination with a new Lamborghini (parked next to a just-delivered Ferrari), he asked if I'd like to drive the gorgeous blue machine to Key West and back. I protested rather weakly and since he insisted, I finally accepted the invitation. Cruising down U.S. 1 in that sexy 'Ghini, you couldn't have wiped the smile off my face with an industrial sander. I felt mighty special for those three days. Call me shameful and shallow, but the adulation and approbation were unforgettable.

Owning a Rybovich sport-fishing yacht puts you in that same first-class mindset. You're moving about in the best there is, the lines and beauty of the boat something even the most jaded owner never tires of admiring. When others view its sleek contour, the hull gracefully sliding through the swells or just reposing at the dock, someone is going to gasp, "Look, that's a *Rybovich*." Some might say it's snobbery, but I prefer to think of it as rightful pride.

Johnny Rybovich became the face of Rybovich & Sons Boat Works from the late 1940s through 1975 and still is even to this day, long past his death. His story begins with the vision and tenacity of his father, a huge dose of teamwork and his two brothers.

John "Pop" Rybovich indeed laid the groundwork for all that would unfold, namely a product that became significant in the world of big-game fishing. The curtain opens well over 100 years ago in 1902 when Pop arrived in America on a ship. He made money the old-fashioned way: with his hands. Pop, an expert cabinetmaker like his own father, met his bride-to-be and they moved to Palm Beach in 1911. He fixed up a boat, then another, and soon opened a boat-repair business on oceanfront property he purchased in 1919.

The repair biz often involved converting cruising and commercial boats into sport fishers. The plant hummed along busily until a massive hurricane laid bare the region in 1928; the Depression kicked in soon thereafter. His head bloody but unbowed, Pop hung tough and he was able to draw sons Emil, Tommy and Johnny into the trade.

The hell of World War II proved to be a vital classroom for the boys. They not only returned unscathed but with talents they immediately put to work for the family business. Johnny acquired leadership skills as a U.S. Army captain, Tommy flew bombers over Europe and Emil served as a marine-engine mechanic. It was time to make their mark in the narrow field of offshore production of big-game fishing boats. Tommy displayed his carved models in the design room, Emil focused on more efficient engines and Johnny's take-charge personality thrust him into the limelight as the figurehead for the very robust company.

"Johnny, as the oldest of the three Rybovich brothers, was the head man in charge of running the office," writes Pat Rybovich, daughter of Tommy, in her coffee-table book *Rybovich*.

Pat states that Johnny was the only one of the three brothers who enjoyed billfishing. Due to Johnny's passion for fishing, the cockpit was carefully planned with the anglers and mates in mind before the rest of the interior was considered.

Pat also confirmed that her father, Tommy, was the design genius responsible for the remarkable Rybovich profile and the extraordinary craftsmanship. Pat related that Tommy loved to carve model airplanes as a kid and that lulls in his World War II service were spent coming up with design ideas for a sport-fishing boat. Tommy's design process

Johnny (right) and friend Thomas Shevlin—himself a top-notch Palm Beach angler in those days—pass judgment on the suitability of a rig before heading offshore. Photo courtesy of the West Palm Beach Fishing Club.

involved carving a wooden model hull for review, which proved to be far more practical than one-dimensional blueprint drafts.

As for Emil, his background in keeping air-sea rescue boats in top mechanical condition paved the way for his role as the Rybovich master mechanic and engine innovator.

Johnny recognized what offshore anglers needed, Emil made the boats perform and Tommy transformed them into works of art.

That complementary teamwork clicked. Their first post-war project hit the brine in 1947 when a customer ordered a 34-footer and subsequently three more. That initial boat featured two eight-cylinder Chrysler engines, innovator aluminum outriggers rather than bamboo, a large cockpit with a custom Rybovich fighting chair, and the distinctively handsome wood finishes that elevated a Rybovich above anything else at the dock.

Rybovich tends to a West Palm Beach Fishing Club display board; he served as the club's president a total of 15 years. Photo courtesy of the West Palm Beach Fishing Club.

The boatyard hit its stride in the 1950s with the addition of a V-hull, multiple steering stations and the design that continues to make a Rybovich boat an object of beauty and utility. Instead of just making converted commercial vessels, they were now taking orders for up to five custom-made sport-fishing boats per year.

In the 1930s, Johnny and Pop did stints as charter boat captains and determined what features would be improvements and innovations, such as a transom door and hull flares to deflect sprays and sneezes. The interiors offered a comfy salon and full galley, roomy showers, aluminum outriggers and towers, below-gunnel cleats, bait wells and plenty of other amenities. Salons soon were air-conditioned, and ice-making machines and microwaves became standard along with top-of-the-line navigational doodads.

"We never built two boats alike," said Emil. That was true. But Johnny's slogan "We are fishermen first and boat-builders second" wasn't quite kosher since brother Tommy didn't care for fishing or boating.

Nonetheless, nobody could deny the superiority of what the three men were collectively producing.

Serious marlin and tuna pursuers at last could possess a custom offshore-fishing dreamboat that combined utility and luxury. Sure, a Rybovich cost four or five times more per foot than its competitors, but the company's backlog of orders shouted that plenty of customers would cover any premium. History has shown that there will always be buyers who will settle for nothing but the best.

Johnny knew the dynamics of supply and demand. He purposely kept production low enough to maintain a standing-room-only ardor among the deep-pocketed suitors while earning the family a sizable ROI. "If you don't flood the market with a good product, the market stays high," he said.

The only caveat is that playing hard to get with the highest price tag comes with expectations that must be exceeded, not merely met. Rybovich accomplished that in spades. While most boat brands prominently flashed their name on the hull in the manner of a car manufacturer, Rybovich vessels eschewed the promotional vulgarity of a factory nameplate; the understatement itself exuded class, and the classy took notice. Besides owning a quality product, a Rybo buyer didn't suffer from post-purchase blues: If someone broke down, Emil would immediately hop aboard his Beechwood aircraft and be there to remedy any issues.

Johnny, while keenly sales-minded, didn't have any inhibitions when offering advice to present or potential customers, whether it directly benefitted him or not. He at times expressed a preference for smaller boats that Rybovich didn't even manufacture, enumerating the advantages of lower costs, less crew hassles and greater maneuverability than big boats.

He also at times dissuaded buyers from adding options he didn't think they needed. That type of brutal honesty didn't go unnoticed. In fact, it further cemented not only his credibility but that of the Rybovich name; repeat owners were the norm because the only thing that could top a Rybovich was another Rybovich.

Al Pflueger Jr., a Miamian who's been a regular visitor to the winner's circle in numerous tournaments, fished with Johnny in several sailfish events. "The craftsmanship of his boats was second to none," Pflueger said in his typically succinct manner.

While their boats notching tournament victories swelled the chests of the Rybovich brothers, Johnny immodestly postulated that most competitions depend more on the quality of the angler and crew than anything else. It's true that an untalented driver probably won't win the Daytona 500 even if he's behind the wheel of the best race car. Nonetheless, put a topnotch rod pumper, skipper and mate in the cockpit of a Rybovich, and it wouldn't be advisable to bet against them. The crews on their Rybos took plenty of titles in competitions such as the Cat Cay Tuna Tournament, Masters Invitational Tournament of Champions, Silver Sailfish Derby, Sailfish Club Gold Cup and numerous others.

Just ask tournament veteran Marsha Bierman, who with hubby Lenny and Ft. Lauderdale skipper Tommy Zsak developed the short-rod standup technique they made famous starting in the late 1980s.

"From what I heard, competitors did a lot of fence-hopping at the Rybovich boatyard in the middle of the night with tape measure and writing pad," said Bierman. "They were so eager to mirror the Rybovich success that they felt it was worth the risk of being caught in their attempts to copy perfection.

"Lenny and I were fortunate to have owned two Rybovich sport-fishing boats, a 42- and a 43-footer," she said. "Both were extremely sexy vessels and made us oh so proud.

"Upon acquiring our first Rybovich, we suddenly found ourselves in West Palm Beach on Friday afternoons to Sunday evenings at the Rybovich yard," said Bierman. "We'd spend the weekend sanding, polishing and varnishing with stints in between fishing offshore. One day we're sanding away on the hull and I turned around and there was John Rybovich, sandpaper in hand and working right along with us on our boat.

"An unusual characteristic of John is that he always spoke at one level, never raising his voice," Bierman recalled. "He could be in a library or the middle of a hurricane and never change volume. With Lenny's hearing difficulties, I'd later have to tell him all that John had said."

Johnny Rybovich had a passion for conservation and he fervently spoke out about it. Miamian Bob Stearns, a highly regarded journalist

Rybovich with Ernest Hemingway at his Cuban farm in 1954 behind the first "Old Man and the Sea" trophy. Photo courtesy of the West Palm Beach Fishing Club.

both nationally and throughout Florida, served as witness to Rybovich's footprints in trying to improve the state's fishery resources.

"He and I worked on a committee that led to the establishment of the Fish and Wildlife Commission," said Stearns. "When he spoke, he commanded everyone's complete attention. One and all respected him."

Rybovich served three separate terms as president of the West Palm Beach Fishing Club (WPBFC). He furthered catch-and-release angling and worked tirelessly on behalf of the good works of the WPBFC. Rybovich was one of the founders of the Sailfish Conservation Club and pushed its fund-raising efforts to encourage the release of sailfish. He also sat on the Florida Department of Natural Resources' advisory board and was responsible for the establishment of the DNR's Sailfish Research Program. He volunteered as a founding director of the National Coalition for Marine Conservation and was a member of the

Billfish Advisory Panel for the South Atlantic Fishery Management Council.

Given Rybovich's major influence in the development of artificial reefs starting in the 1960s, it's only fitting that in 2007 the 1,768-ton cargo ship *Korimu* was scuttled in 220 feet of water and named the John Rybovich Endowment Reef. The wreck serves primarily as a fishing reef and was made possible by the WPBFC and Palm Beach County's Environmental Resources Management Department.

In his role with the company, Rybovich encountered the big names of those times. It's believed he first met Ernest Hemingway in 1935 when the author brought his boat *Pilar* to the Rybovich boatyard for maintenance. The men quickly bonded, and the friendship lasted until Hemingway's death. In the 1950s, during one of Rybovich's terms as President of the WPBFC, Hemingway sponsored the "Old Man and the Sea" trophy for their annual Silver Sailfish Derby. Rybovich also fished with DuPont, Firestone, Gillette, Maytag, Ballantine and others—all of whom he'd press into action for conservation causes dear to him.

Any story about Johnny Rybovich wouldn't be complete without discussing the person who completed him: his wife, Kay. He married Kathryn Jordan in 1941. Johnny and Kay spent 1943 to 1946 separated due to the war years. All that long-distance longing ended when the couple reunited in order to pitch in with Johnny's father and brothers in the Rybovich boat-building business in West Palm Beach.

Kay, like Johnny, showed a preference for light-tackle fishing and she became a tournament winner and fierce competitor. She helped found the International Women's Fishing Association in 1955 and took a big part in the activities of the WPBFC.

In 1972 the boat's creator, Tommy, died of lung cancer at the age of 52. As neither Johnny nor Emil were boat builders, a decision was made to sell the yard. In 1975, Johnny and Emil—the only two surviving family members of Rybovich & Sons Boat Works—finalized a deal whereby they'd stay on with a management contract for five more years. Johnny's presence and impact did not diminish, however, and he remained active as an angler and conservationist. He became a regular contributor to *Boating* magazine, writing a column that called anglers to action for conservation projects and causes.

Although Rybovich's first love was sailfishing off Palm Beach, he began spending less time there and headed elsewhere for that purpose. He said it just wasn't the same as the good ol' days of the 1940s, when boats raised up to 10 sails a day. While acknowledging partial responsibility for the sophistication of fishing boats, Rybovich spoke fondly of more primitive times without outriggers or flying bridges and of the boats that moved at a snail's pace.

Tackle performed well enough, he felt, and you didn't have to go that far anyway in those days off Palm Beach. Rybovich laughingly spoke of a 35-foot boat named *Driftwood* that he owned way back when. It sported only a 50-horsepower engine and he said, "We used to joke that if we ever got as far north as Ft. Pierce, we'd have to sell the boat, because it was too slow to ever get back."

Fishing laments and all his good works aside, no one ever doubted that Johnny Rybovich's memory would live on separately from his high-profile position with arguably the greatest boat-building company of all time—and that's a pretty high watermark in anyone's measure of Florida's historic fishing and boating innovators.

11

Jimmie Albright, 1915–1998

ISLAMORADA

I moved to the Florida Keys in 1987 and soon started writing fishing columns for a local newspaper. Although he no longer guided, I still wanted to meet the legendary Jimmie Albright for an article.

"Heck," he replied when I called him. "If you've got a boat and know how to run it, let's go fishing for a few hours."

Thrilled beyond measure, I assured him I could run my 20-foot MAKO just fine but admitted to being green when it came to the intricacies of navigating the labyrinth of Florida Bay flats. Albright said not to worry and to leave that to him.

Several days later, off we went in my boat from Tavernier Creek Marina, Albright directing me as I raced through channels and small passes. We soon reached a tranquil cove protected from the wind and I staked out. He pointed at the mouth of a creek.

"Wade over there as quietly as you can and when in casting range, send that big shrimp right into the mouth," he whispered.

As I carefully slid over the side, the entire half of my lower torso sank deeply into the silty mud. With my shoes locked and immoveable, the current cleared the murky water just above my waist. The form of an angry blue crab came into view—its claws in full battle array—and it made a threatening dash directly toward my favorite organ. I grabbed the side of the boat with both hands and catapulted onto the deck without my chest touching a thing.

With my shoes now a permanent fixture in the mud and my body reminiscent of a Dove bar, Albright laughed until his face turned from red to blue to purple.

Jimmie Albright (kneeling left) with veteran guide Cecil Keith (kneeling right) and two anglers posing with their tarpon catches in the 1950s. Photo courtesy of the International Game Fish Association.

"Welcome to Florida Bay," he finally squeezed out, his body convulsing in ever-increasing crescendos. I thought it was funny too until I feared the old fellow might suffer a heart attack from all the sputtering mirth.

We never went fishing again.

"Jimmie had integrity," said Richard Stanczyk, owner of Bud N' Mary's Marina in Islamorada. "Some say that his attitude bordered on arrogance at times, but he told it like he saw it.

"I caught my first bonefish on fly with him," Stanczyk continued. "Jimmie Albright is one of the reasons I moved to the Keys in 1969. I saw how successful his career was and realized a marina operation would work down here too."

Al Pflueger Jr., who with his father built a pioneering worldwide taxidermy business based in south Florida, considers Albright one of the best ever.

"In the 1940s and '50s, you didn't have a lot of guides in the upper Keys because of the limited tourism back then," said Pflueger. "But Jimmie Albright, Cecil Keith and Jack Brothers were the cream of the crop of backcountry guides."

Few people during that era lived full time in the islands between Key West and Florida's mainland southwest of Miami. In fact, Albright's post office box in Islamorada was simply the number 4. Comforts were scarce, with no electricity or running water. Nonetheless—and despite frequent forays to the Bahamas, Newfoundland and other far-flung places to chase bluefin tuna—he and his wife, Frankee, built a comfortable nest in Islamorada.

How Albright ended up in the Keys to begin with involves a smattering of fate. In 1933 he arrived in Miami at age 18. After a stint as a lifeguard, Albright mated on charter boats. When only 21, he secured his own charter boat, a 33-footer already named *Jambar*. He fished off Miami and throughout the Bahamas for big-game species until the war broke out. He joined the U.S. Navy in 1941, remaining in the service until '46.

It was during the war that Albright arrived in Ft. Lauderdale on a navy vessel for a brief respite. He'd previously been assigned to teaching other sailors how to tie knots—a skill that would later prove invaluable. Albright decided to go fishing on his leave time but wanted to try something other than an offshore trip, having seen enough bouncy seas aboard ship. He booked a light-tackle outing in the Keys with Capt. Bonnie Smith. Not only did she put Albright on his first bonefish, Smith later introduced him to her sister Frankee.

Frankee and Jimmie hit it off immediately and were married after the war. Bonnie's husband, veteran fishing guide Bill Smith, took the fishing-savvy brother-in-law under his wing. He taught Albright the basics of flats fishing and about the more prominent locations to intercept bonefish, permit, snook, tarpon, redfish, trout and other species. Smith loaned him rods, reels and even his boat on occasion. The whole process hit Albright like a wonderful dream, a means to an end that sparked an enormous passion for hunting tarpon, bonefish and the like on light tackle. He figured that it just worked better all the way around than offshore charter fishing, and though he bore a tough constitution,

Albright also knew how to catch the big ones offshore. Here he holds a billfish on his lap that Joe Brooks boated. Photo courtesy of the International Game Fish Association.

the thought of slamming around in four- to six-footers all day in the 33-foot *Jambar* didn't seem nearly as inviting as flats fishing. He sold the boat and invested in a small skiff, thus becoming a "mud guide."

Albright points to June 11, 1947, as a landmark day on which he guided Joe Brooks, at the time America's top angling authority, to catches of three targeted bonefish on artificial lures. The fact that Brooks, editor of *Outdoor Life* magazine and a world traveler with innumerable contacts, would faithfully publicize and consequently immortalize those catches in print didn't hurt Albright's reputation and acclaim one bit.

Brooks' catch wasn't the first time a bonefish succumbed to being caught, of course. Many years prior to 1947, Bill Smith and others had successfully caught bonefish on bait, and Smith nailed a bonefish on fly in 1939. Reports of another incidental bonefish catch on fly have floated about since as early as 1924. But prior to 1947, it wasn't believed to be

1972

AL PFLUEGER
GUIDE — JIMMY ALBRIGHT

A press photo of Albright with Al Pflueger Jr. after a day spent fly fishing for poons in 1972; as was often the case his entire life, "Jimmie" is misspelled. Photo courtesy of the International Game Fish Association.

feasible to go after bonefish as a guiding specialty on lures or flies. In fact most anglers of the day and the few light-tackle guides around back then were pooh-poohed for any notion of that being practical. Spin gear was catching on, and the easier technique made for happier clients.

Up until the 1940s, it was thought that bonefish were too wary if not too wise to eat a fly pattern and that even if one did so, it'd probably run so fast the result would be a broken tippet or spooled reel. That no one had carefully planned the proper techniques other than Bill Smith before Albright and Brooks did so indicated impending doom, but this proved to be incorrect.

Negative attitudes aside, it must be appreciated that the fly gear of the time was nothing like it is today, just as equipment of tomorrow will be superior to what we have now. It's the same in golf, as one can only imagine what the record books would look like if former stars such as Snead, Hogan and Nicklaus had in their hands what the players of the twenty-first century use. In Albright's heyday, it was common for even his heavy bamboo Orvis Battenkill rods to shatter or for their snake guides to twist off when a sizeable fish took up the challenge.

"We sometimes placed rivets in the Medalists [reels] so they stayed together," said Albright. "The alternative was to over-tackle the smaller fish, but that really defeated the whole intent of fly fishing." Joe Brooks in particular, Albright noted, was a "traditionalist" like himself, and the notion of heavy tippets for light fish was simply not in the cards. About 14 years later, Brooks would write another world-record account of a tarpon he bested in Little Torch Key with Stu Apte—the latter being another traditionalists who eschewed heavy tippets.

Albright's growing reputation soon drew the attention of tackle manufacturers. They wanted him to test equipment to see how marketable their products might be. Albright was therefore one of the first to try out the reels being made by hand in the mid-1950s by engineer Gar Wood, who not coincidentally happened to be a passionate fly fisher. Wood's reels became the prototypes for the Fin-Nor production models in 1958 known as "wedding cakes."

Wood's solid bar-stock aluminum reels offered durability and dependable drags, and they just plain looked good. The reels became an instant hit in the fly-fishing world, and guides such as Albright would use nothing else. The same thing occurred when fiberglass came along in the early 1960s, right about the time that world records on almost all species began to tumble. Better yet, in the still-burgeoning world of saltwater flats guiding, the gear could stand up to constant use and therefore needed replacing less often.

Another aspect of Albright's growing fame involved the glowing company he at times joined on the water. He fished with Ernest Hemingway ("He liked me to call him Ernesto," said Albright), Jimmy Stewart ("He kidded me about the weird spelling of my first name"), President Herbert Hoover ("He didn't talk much") and just about any other luminary who fancied light tackle and skinny water. In 1964, Albright fished Dan Topping, then owner of the New York Yankees, on his yacht *Yankee Clipper* off Bimini. But long before Topping came on the scene, a fellow wearing a uniform that Topping's pinstripers knew all too well—that of the Boston Red Sox—became a close pal of Albright's: the lanky Splendid Splinter himself, Ted Williams.

They formed quite a duo on the flats of the Florida Keys. Albright, the king of upper Keys flats fishing, and Williams, who could out-fish just about anyone around including the guides, began racking up the achievements. Rumors of their great angling success at first were met with scoffs and even derision by a good number of their contemporaries. However, it soon became apparent to even the biggest naysayers that the tales were true—pictures didn't lie (at least back then)—and eventually the techniques they employed for taking bonefish and even big tarpon on fly were being emulated near and far.

"Ted Williams was the best all-around fisherman I ever saw," Albright said on many occasions. "His vision can only be described as incredible—he could spot fish faster than an osprey—and I've never seen anyone remotely in his class with any type of rod."

The admiration was mutual. Ted Williams made no bones (pun intended) about his respect for Albright. "I treasured my long friendship with Jimmie," he once told me during a phone interview. "He's one of the few who gave me straight answers all the time.

"We both were experienced with light-tackle fishing, but together it seemed like our success rate together more than doubled the results," Williams said. "We just meshed when it came to collaborating on where

Even in his later years, Albright seldom came home empty-handed. Photo courtesy of the International Game Fish Association.

fish would likely be and the best flies and angles to catch 'em. I liked being on the water with plenty of other guides, but none as much as Jimmie."

Albright perfected the nail knot, which is used to tie the leader to the fly line. He is widely credited for devising the knot named after him (Albright Special), though Capt. Ralph Delph of Key West remembers differently—even if others disagree.

"Not many people know this today, but Jimmie didn't actually invent the Albright Knot," said Delph. "He instead adapted and perfected it from someone else who showed it to Jimmie when he was teaching others to tie knots in the navy. He used it for fishing, however, before anyone else did, so in that respect it was indeed an innovation. But I admired his honesty for confiding that to me.

"Jimmie also was incredibly tenacious," Delph added. "He fought big fish like tarpon hard—he never backed down an inch."

Another colleague thought highly of Albright for covering his back. "I used to go down to the Keys when they first started regular bonefish and tarpon tournaments in the 1960s," said Miamian Bill Curtis. "I got to know Jimmie, George Hommell, Jack Brothers and other guides really well. But back in those days, for some reason guides in Marathon didn't get along with guides from Islamorada or Key West, I suppose due to territorial concerns.

"Anyway, I'd heard about that but didn't know if that applied to a Miami guide, so I went ahead and entered a major bonefish event called the International Bonefish Tournament in Marathon," Curtis said. "I think it was 1967 or thereabouts. The client I guided won the tournament two years in a row, and suddenly I got word that the Marathon folks decided they were tired of an outsider coming down there and winning.

"Well, Jimmie heard about it and let me know in no uncertain terms that he stood with me," said Curtis. "So after that, for a while I only fished Keys tournaments in Islamorada because I was welcome there. Jimmie even asked me to bring as many customers to Islamorada as I could whether tournaments or not, and I asked him why. 'I figure that once they see how much better the fishing is around here, they'll start coming to the Keys and hiring me instead of you.' We both laughed.

"Truth be told, anytime I had a charter scheduled in the upper Keys I'd first get hold of Jimmie," Curtis added. "He'd tell me where to find the most bonefish or tarpon and the best areas to start with based on the tides and other factors. Not many guides will share location information like that, but Jimmie did it all the time."

Nobody would deny Jimmie Albright's independent nature, obvious even in the unusual spelling of his first name. He also didn't take any lip from even the likes of the often flamboyant Ted Williams. The saying "He tells it like it is" befits no one better than Albright, which goes a long way in explaining why he named all of his skiffs the *Rebel*.

12

Harold LeMaster, 1915–1986

LARGO

Everyone who's ever bought a saltwater plug knows the name MirrO-lure. The brand's 52M and many other models can be found in the tackle boxes of most serious anglers, and they can thank Harold LeMaster for that.

The L&S Bait Company in Largo (across the bay from Tampa) produces the lures, but the company's roots trace back to the 1930s childhood home of LeMaster in Illinois. He carved a lure from a fallen oak tree, tried it out and discovered fish liked it; that original Bass-Master model is still produced by the company.

In the basement of his mother's house, LeMaster made one lure at a time. In addition to using oak, he carved lures from walnut, each requiring about a full day to take the shape he envisioned. Nickel was used for the metal parts because he found it could be pounded and formed with a ball-peen hammer and a file. LeMaster used the glass eyes of dolls he bought at the hardware store.

After painstakingly making lures one at a time for a couple of years while in his early 20s, LeMaster teamed up with his pal Phil Schriner. They couldn't keep up with the orders pouring in, so the two went to Chicago and had their first injection mold built. Once they had a mold to make more lures out of plastic, the process continued to evolve. Once they had more lure sales, the men decided, they'd invest in another injection mold. They finally hunted around and found a small plant that would be suitable in nearby Bradley, Illinois.

Years went by and then World War II erupted, and the government ordered the operation shut down, saying that LeMaster should instead put his resources into making things for the war effort. To get by, Le-Master followed his father's trade as a carpenter, but it wasn't long before the government relaxed its protocol and LeMaster and Schriner went back to making lures.

Due to health issues and per his doctor's suggestion, LeMaster moved the operation to Clearwater, Florida, in 1948. It wasn't long thereafter that LeMaster saw a fisherman casting a spinnerbait that flashed in the water. The fellow pulled in one fish after the other. It immediately struck LeMaster that perhaps bits of mirror built into a lure would continually reflect even more light. And that's how the idea germinated into the concept of the famed MirrOlure.

Bill LeMaster, Harold's son and now president of L&S Bait Company, remembers the call to action following the reflective discovery. "My mother said that Dad gathered some broken glass and somehow attached it to the side of a lure," he said.

"It probably looked very primitive, but evidently fish had seen nothing quite like it. The lures became an immediate success and of course one of our trademarks."

Bill fished often with his dad, mostly for tarpon. "From the time I was about six years old, about 70 percent of the time we'd go for tarpon. We'd arrive on the water before the crack of dawn and fish all day.

"Dad also had a unique ritual: He tried to catch a tarpon on each of his birthdays, no matter how long it took. Once he caught one of any size, he'd come back home."

Eric Bachnik, Harold's grandson and longtime general manager at L&S Bait Company, also remembers tarpon trips with him. "We'd wake up early and launch his Hewes Bonefisher to search for schools of silver kings," he said.

"Grandpa packed many different types of fruit for our outings and he claimed that was good luck. I'd joke with him about that, saying, 'The fruit isn't lucky, you are.' He had a very aggressive style of fishing, meaning very little trolling motor and more use of the outboard engine to drift or pole to get into position for a cast."

Harold LeMaster loved tarpon fishing so much that when word came down from Homosassa in the early 1980s about huge pods of big tarpon running along the shorelines, he wasted no time in finding out for

LeMaster mastered this hefty tarpon. In his later years he released them all.
Photo courtesy of the LeMaster family.

Big bass taken back to the Clearwater plant in the early 1950s. Photo courtesy of the LeMaster family.

himself whether it was true. Once confirmed, LeMaster helped spread the word about the newly discovered silver king Mecca.

"I recall Harold as one of the first guys to tell the world about the incredible tarpon fishery off Homosassa—he didn't try to horde anything just for himself," said Al Pflueger Jr., a veteran himself of many Homosassa trips in those halcyon years.

Pflueger isn't the only person who remembers LeMaster heralding the poon action around Homosassa. Miami super guide Bill Curtis would spend the entire month of April or May in Homosassa in pursuit of tarpon, but not because he heard directly from LeMaster about it.

"Lefty Kreh had been writing for a period of time for the *Tampa Tribune* back then after he left Miami," said Curtis, "and he told me what LeMaster had discovered.

"Eddie Wightman, Carl Navarre—he owned Cheeca Lodge and was the Coca-Cola Bottling Company representative for the Miami area—wasted no time getting to Homosassa," Curtis continued. "Harold was dead-on right; we found wall-to-wall tarpon all around Homosassa. They ran bigger than the Keys fish on average, with shots at world records practically every day."

Long before Homosassa was discovered, however, LeMaster hooked into one of the largest tarpon he'd ever seen—an estimated 170 pounds. It all began at 7 a.m. on June 6, 1952, and turned into a D-Day anniversary of considerable magnitude.

LeMaster's 16-foot wooden boat drifted peacefully at the mouth of Hurricane Pass about two miles west of Dunedin on Florida's west coast when the epic began. By 10 p.m. the tarpon had dragged him southward on a 25-mile trip. Thousands of spectators heard about it through the grapevine and gathered to stand along the beaches and passes as LeMaster held on tight.

The fish had taken a 60M-27 MirrOlure, and all the resulting national publicity wasn't going to do the company a bit of harm. LeMaster, 37 at the time and in top shape, figured he knew from many previous tarpon encounters how to conserve his strength. Rather than pressuring the fish and risking a break-off or the hook pulling, he let it tow the boat. At one point the tarpon swam into Clearwater Marina and near the scale used for weigh-ins.

At midnight a boat dropped off someone to try to gaff the fish. But half an hour later, the tarpon made a mighty last-gasp leap and the lure flung out of its mouth and onto LeMaster's shirt.

The battle was over, much to everyone's disappointment. But LeMaster later said he was glad the great fish got away. Early in the morning of June 7, LeMaster showered and went to bed. He slept for 24 hours straight.

Indeed, Peggy LeMaster said that her dad was always philosophical about everything. "When he hooked that tarpon in 1952, he was armed with patience and a smooth, even touch with things.

"It rubbed off, and even when it didn't, he'd let you know about it. Once when I was 10, I fished with him and I got impatient and real edgy. He calmed me down by saying, 'Peggy, take it easy, you'll last longer.' It's advice I've always tried to live by."

LeMaster moved the main plant to Largo from Clearwater in 1969 to consolidate operations. Bill LeMaster recalls the impetus for his dad also starting another operation in Costa Rica.

"A government crew from OSHA came into our plant one day unannounced," said Bill. "They wrote us up on all kinds of things that totaled $60,000 in fines. We did everything they wanted us to do even though we knew the rules and regulations weren't at all practical for our business. But right after that, Dad went to Costa Rica and built a plant without all the red tape and bureaucracy—we still operate it today."

Fishing wasn't Harold LeMaster's only passion—he also loved to play golf. As a result, LeMaster acquired East Bay Country Club in Largo. He put together a plan to get the course out of bankruptcy and into shape. He told his son Bill to quickly learn the restaurant and bar aspects of the business, and that he did. The private club almost turned a profit in a number of years, but the burden of work and distraction from the lure business forced LeMaster to sell it.

"Not many people know this, but Dad built golf clubs too," said daughter Patty LeMaster Brown. "He enjoyed engineering golf clubs for several PGA and LPGA touring pros in the 1960s, such as Butch Baird.

"It became a hobby for him, and he had an area in the shop set aside for golf club work, with parts strewn everywhere. He engineered the clubs to each person's style and swing.

Three tasty trout for dinner. Photo courtesy of the LeMaster family.

"Dad was a natural at engineering," Brown added. "Without any formal schooling he seemed to understand how things worked and how to make them work better, whether a golf club or a lure.

"Back in the old days when the shop was in Clearwater, I remember the smell of the lead pot, where they actually melted the lead and then carefully poured it red-hot into the small molds to make the little weights for the lures," Brown recalled.

Bill LeMaster said that his dad did not often joke or laugh but that some people liked his serious side. One such person was Boston Red Sox slugger Ted Williams.

"He'd drop by the lure plant in Clearwater two or three times a year in the 1950s, probably when the Red Sox were having spring practice," he said. "They'd talk and have lunch. Ted liked my dad's no-nonsense attitude without any of the pandering or idolization that Williams often grew tired of. Dad wasn't about flash, just action."

Herb Allen, former outdoor editor of the *Tampa Tribune,* did become the victim of LeMaster's dry sense of humor on one occasion.

"Harold asked me to try out a new lure in the lake behind their factory," said Allen. "I no sooner made a cast than a tarpon jumped all over it. I looked back, and there's Harold laughing hysterically at the back door of the plant—he knew that tarpon would hit anything thrown its way."

Beginning in the 1970s or so, people came to realize that Harold LeMaster was quite the successful entrepreneur. "People of all stripes came to him requesting financial backing," Bill LeMaster said.

"Usually he said no, but often he'd get involved with this scheme or that. One such venture was a small plant that sectioned grapefruit with a high-pressure water spray. It took a long time to get it right so it could be done economically, but eventually Dad sold it off," Bill said.

Despite all the side interests and distractions, from age 17 until his death, Harold LeMaster's primary interest in life involved making lures. Whether the lures were the result of hand-carving or high-production manufacturing with molds, LeMaster enjoyed catching fish on his own lures and hearing success stories from anglers using them.

LeMaster was a creative person, and being appreciated by so many for so many years gave him the motivation to do what he does best. To anglers everywhere, that turned out to be a very good thing.

13

Tony Tarracino, 1916–2008

KEY WEST

Walking down Greene Street off the famed "Duval Crawl" corridor in Key West, my eyes flitted inside yet another dusky bar. There, perched on a stool front and center, sat none other than Capt. Tony, a Lucky Strike clinging to his lips. Even in the dingy light, one could tell he appeared grizzled and unshaven, and for that matter, so did I. Gillette probably sells fewer razors per capita here than anywhere else.

I ducked into the bar and said hello, not expecting him to recognize me 10 years after the last time I'd spotted him in the same exact circumstance.

I was right, he didn't recognize me. Tarracino turned on the stool, squinted at me a moment while still shaking my hand and said, "If I'm the one who stepped on your face last night, I'm truly sorry."

Instant ice breaker, and we both guffawed. I refreshed him about our brief fishing encounters way back when. A moment of silence ensued, and I felt like the guy asking Nicklaus if he remembered our Pro-Am foursome in 1973. Tarracino finally nodded and politely blurted out that "of course" he did. It didn't really matter one way or the other, however, because just being in the presence of Tarracino always turned into a happening. There's never a dull moment. He holds court like the celebrity he is, this person and that calling across the bar counter or wrapping a sweaty arm around his shoulder, all basking in his reflected glory.

About 20 years earlier, in 1964, my dad—a lieutenant colonel stationed at Homestead Air Force Base—was in charge of security and law enforcement. A retired sergeant named John "Woody" Wood, an

Tarracino at the wheel. Photo courtesy of Rob O'Neal.

outdoor writer for a south Florida newspaper, somehow knew Tarracino and my dad. Whatever the connection, I found myself one afternoon with Tarracino, Woody and Dad crossing the flight-line at the base in a golf cart escorted by a blue Air Police truck. We arrived at a series of canals that were off limits to virtually everyone else except the base commander if he so chose, which he never did.

Virgin bass waters. With gators plunging off the canal banks as we approached, water snakes galore wriggling about and lily pads just begging for a weedless plastic worm or frog, it's no exaggeration to say we all drew strikes on practically every cast. Bass averaging three pounds, with a few in the six- to eight-pound class, were released along with slobber bluegill and even the occasional snook.

"Woody told me it's unbelievable back here, and I have to agree," said Tarracino. "Usually you couldn't get me north of Key West unless I've been ground up and spit out, but for this it's worth it. Too bad bass fight like they can't even drag a pilchard backwards, but it's still been fun."

About a month later we did it again at dusk with the same stupendous action, but this time before splitting up, we visited one of the saltwater locks at Military Canal. The canal ran from the base to Biscayne Bay, and snook could be heard popping the bejabbers out of huge schools of mullet trapped in the moonlit locks. I caught a few, but Tarracino released one after the other on a white half-ounce jig. The man knew how to catch fish.

During these interludes, Tarracino spoke of his series of *Greyhound* party boats and the heavy catches over the decades on wrecks around Key West. He offered to take us fishing anytime we wanted to visit. We took him up on this within weeks, and he wasn't woofing—we left Garrison Bight and headed into the Northwest Channel, returning to the dock with a heavy cooler jammed with mackerel, cobia and I forget what else.

I later learned from many of his friends that Tarracino felt a responsibility to be forthcoming about his fishing knowledge. He gave guest lectures about fishing and its value to Key West history to students at the Florida Keys Community College, and he made numerous guest appearances on local radio and television shows. He was the first in the area to take school kids out on his boat for free. Journalists seeking quotes could depend on colorful opinions from Tarracino, some of them printable.

After all, he was a charter skipper for 35 years. For a large chunk of that time until the mid-1960s, the only tackle allowed aboard his *Greyhound* party boats for the elbow-to-elbow anglers were hand lines—no rods and reels ("buggy whips," he called them then). Tarracino often took the wheel, the mates helping those entangled or too befuddled to drag aboard yet another flopping fish. Gradually the disdain for regular gear gave way as more anglers walked aboard holding them. Even so, until modernization could not be stemmed, the buggy whippers were relegated to atop the hard roof and away from the crowded rails below.

Whatever the tackle, few complained about the results. Any trip might feature battles with snapper (especially yellowtail), grouper (especially red), mackerel (Spanish, cero and king), cobia, bonito, barracuda, sailfish, and scads of other species. A lot of rock piles and wrecks held masses of fish off Key West then and still do. Those depleted or buried in sand by the shifting currents become replaced with new discoveries.

With the advent of more sophisticated bottom sounders showing fish on the displays and LORAN-C transitioning to GPS, it's unlikely the fishing will ever turn "bad" off Key West. Capt. Tony Tarracino and crew on the *Greyhound II* we boarded and other successions of *Greyhounds* he owned entertained thousands of visitors mixed with loyal locals. Unquestionably tens of thousands of back-at-the-dock pictures of all the great catches still fill photo albums around the world.

Born in 1916 in Elizabeth, New Jersey, to Italian immigrants Luigi and Henrietta Tarracino, Tony dropped out of ninth grade to help his father produce bootleg whiskey in the Prohibition years. During World War II, he up and moved to Seattle to take a job with Boeing, leaving behind a wife and three children. Tarracino grew streetwise in Seattle and returned to his native New Jersey after the war looking for fast money. Together with one of his four brothers, he figured out a past-posting scheme that netted them big money from horse-racing bets.

Tarracino's saloon on Greene Street in Key West, where more than a few cocktails and fish stories have been concocted. Photo courtesy the Dale McDonald Collection and Monroe County Library, Key West.

When the rough-and-tumble bookies got wise to the con, Tarracino ended up a bloody pulp in a Newark dump. Somehow he regained consciousness, fled due south and didn't stop until he reached Miami. The ponies were still in his blood, however, and in 1948 he steered a girlfriend's pink Cadillac to Tropical Park race track in Hialeah. Whatever money had resided in his wallet evaporated like a puddle of ethanol. He bid adieu to the car and the lady, and with 18 bucks to his name found a kind soul behind the wheel of a milk truck lonesome for conversation on the long drive to Key West.

The Southernmost City in the late 1940s featured a remarkable collection of wreckers, fishermen, drunks and fledgling drifters—the perfect place for an entrepreneur to rise and shine. In Tarracino's meager baggage were large dreams, however, and he perceived how the place Hemingway had ditched about a decade before his arrival would inevitably turn into a tourist magnet.

Capt. Tony (wearing the hat) and a client who experienced plenty of action on a Key West wreck in the 1950s. Photo courtesy of Wil-Art Studio, Angie Marine, and Monroe County Library, Key West.

The *Greyhound* head boats provided a steady stream of cash for 35 years—sometimes plentiful, sometimes not—but it paid the bills and gave Tarracino a local foothold. It also led to his buying Capt. Tony's Saloon in 1961, a legacy that continues to this day even though he sold it in 1989. Since the mid-1800s, the old building containing the saloon at various intervals hosted a morgue, ice house, whorehouse, telegraph station and speakeasy.

The property had been owned by Josie "Sloppy Joe" Russell since the early 1930s. Russell, also a charter-boat owner and the fishing pal of good customer Ernest Hemingway, offered locals and visitors a taste of gambling, booze, broads and rumba music.

Also in 1989, Tarracino became the official mayor of Key West, not the "sidewalk mayor" as previously conferred. He'd made a run for it half a dozen times or so before, coming close in 1985 but losing by 52 votes to a fellow named Tom Sawyer, prompting some to say the race came down to a battle between two fictional characters.

In the successful bid that resulted in his election, Tarracino humorously reacted to those who objected to his frequent use of the four-lettered favorite of all vulgarians. "I just hope everybody in Key West who uses that word votes for me—if they do, I'll win in a landslide," he said.

So, too, goes another of his favorite sayings into the ledger of history: "All you need in this life is a tremendous sex drive and a great ego. Brains don't mean shit."

Nothing could have resonated more in the big hearts, open minds and pickled livers of the proud Conch Republic loyalists in Key West. To hell with the stifling masses north of Stock Island, they felt, and electing the outrageous Tarracino sent the world that message in spades. Some exclaimed, "You say he drinks, gambles, likes sex, smells of fish and you can find his picture with the word 'eccentric' in the dictionary? He's got my vote."

Even so, Tarracino won by a mere 32 votes out of 6,000 cast—"Twenty-eight of 'em were hookers," he quipped—and he served until 1991. In that short span he saw enough of the buddy system and unyielding bureaucrats. "I enjoyed it a lot, but I had my time in the sun," he said.

There's probably not much under the sun that Tarracino didn't do or get involved in. The father of 13 children—the first born when he was 20 and the last at 70—he married three times (outliving each wife) before settling into a close-knit union with wife Marty.

It's rumored he worked undercover as a gunrunner in the 1950s and '60s and that he helped the CIA smuggle arms to pro-U.S. guerillas in Cuba and Haiti. He loved the hard life and loved the electric persona of Las Vegas—one of the few places he'd venture outside of Cayo Hueso. To have lived 92 years in such a tumultuous fashion is a testament alone to quite a remarkable life. "Only the good die young," he said in 1990, and indeed he kept on going for another 18 years.

I remember Tarracino telling me why Key West appealed to him so much. "It's an asylum, and I belong here," he said without even a hint of being disingenuous. "I could never again live somewhere like Miami or New York—it would suck the life out of my brains and body."

While many of the anglers and guides depicted in this book are included more for their uniqueness of personality than for superlative fishing achievements, Tarracino refereed as many fish fights as anyone. Numerous other outstanding captains made their marks in Key West with greater fishing skills than Tarracino, among them Lefty Reagan, Tommy Lones, Ralph Delph, Gainey Maxwell, Norman Wood, Willy De-Meritt, Bra Saunders, R.T. Trosset and others. However, no one chimed any better with the quirky charisma of Key West than Capt. Tony.

And so it is that my personal memories of Tarracino are of a capable captain, a quick-witted fellow and someone you'd best avoid in a match of one-liners. His character, humor, lack of pretense and what-you-see-is-what-you-get style is exactly what you'd expect from an icon who reflected the hearty soul of a haughty city.

14

Ted Williams, 1918–2002

ISLAMORADA

Although one of Ted Williams' best friends and a business partner in a fishing-tackle venture, the legendary golfer Sam Snead didn't always want to hear about the Splendid Splinter.

I was about 16 years old when I unexpectedly encountered Slammin' Sammy as an anxious member of the gallery at the Doral Open golf tournament in Miami. Snead strode to the tee box at the 11th hole and by coincidence stood next to me, both hands on the grip of his driver while another player teed it up.

Snead's eyes met mine for a moment and he was expressionless. Knowing his love for fishing and long friendship with Ted Williams, I nervously blurted out a question about whether they'd fished together recently.

He winced as if goosed with a two-iron. "You gotta be kidding," he growled incredulously, eyes narrowing and head shaking side to side. "I can't make a goddamn putt today and you want to talk about *him?*"

Taken aback, I said nothing. He moved away to hit his drive and I figured that was that. About an hour later, however, I stood behind the tee box at the 16th hole as his group walked up. He scanned the gallery until his eyes stopped on me. After hitting his drive, damn if he didn't saunter over.

"Listen here, kid" he rasped in his heavy Virginian accent. "Would you go to a ball park and in the middle of the game when Ted Williams just struck out three times ask him if he's fished with Sam Snead lately?"

"Um, probably not," I answered, shocked and amazed that something this trivial was still eating at him.

"Good," he snapped. "Then keep your little mouth shut about Williams or anyone else while I'm out here hacking my way around the course." With that, Snead did a 180 and walked away while muttering a comparison of me to a certain bodily opening.

I was to describe that incident to Ted Williams years later in my long phone chat with him. I'd reached him after setting up an interview through several intermediaries while editor at *Sport Fishing* magazine. I was told the conversation would last 15 minutes, but instead we talked for 45. The high pitch and forcefulness of his voice took me by surprise. I think Williams talked longer than expected because I never once mentioned his baseball career—we just talked fishing.

Back to my reference to Snead, to which Williams laughed heartily. "Oh, don't be so sensitive," he said. "Sam's bark is worse than his bite—kind of like me.

"Listen, I don't like it when people see me fishing in the middle of a flat and obviously looking for bonefish, and they bring their boat over to mine to talk. Hell, I want to fish, not discuss a game they saw me play in 1958 or be handed things to autograph. When I get upset about interruptions like that, people think I'm nasty and a mean S.O.B. instead of realizing their rudeness. Hey, if people walked in my shoes or Sam's for a day, they'd better understand."

Those who Williams considered close friends knew all too well of his famous mood swings, but that was the price to pay for remaining friends. Williams told me that first in line when it came to his fishing companions was Florida Keys guide Jimmie Albright.

"Jimmie and I were able to know what the other was thinking," said Williams. "I didn't have to tell him which casting angle I wanted, where to check the boat and all. He also realized that I already knew where to put the cast, set the hook and play the fish. My favorite outings always involved less talk and more fishing."

Albright, who said that Ted Williams was the best angler he ever knew, recalled the day he guided Williams to three tarpon catches. "Ted got three in one day, and we weighed them in order: a 76-, 77- and 78-pounder. It set new records in the MET tournament. Even so, he

The "Splendid Splinter" strikes a fly-rod pose off Flamingo. Photo courtesy of IGFA and Ted Williams Family Enterprises, Inc.

Williams relished just getting away on his own for a little fishing. Photo courtesy of IGFA and Ted Williams Family Enterprises, Inc.

wanted one over 100 pounds. It took us awhile, but we finally did the trick."

Williams fished with hundreds of guides over the years, but few impressed him. "I could tell before we left the dock if he knew his stuff just by looking at the knots tied on the leaders," he said. "Quite frankly, most of them were bush." Williams often churlishly referred to neophytes or the unskilled as bush while also reserving the term as a friendly pronoun for good friends. Such was the complexity of the man.

In Williams' opinion—one few could refute—he knew how to pole a boat better than any guide back then as well as see fish faster, cast more accurately and play them more quickly. Consequently, Williams preferred a select few when it came to regular fishing companions and repeat trips with guides.

Albright isn't the only person who claims Williams was the best angler he'd ever seen. Stu Apte feels that way, and same goes for famed Biscayne Bay flats guide Bill Curtis, who said, "The best anglers have natural grace," and that he'd never fished with anyone more graceful than Ted Williams. "He had perfect timing, combining all the best abilities of an athlete with a fisherman," he added.

The great Wade Boggs, himself a baseball-hitting legend who followed in the footsteps of Williams with the Boston Red Sox, said that while his own exceptional eyesight was 20/15, Ted Williams' was a superhuman 20/10. "He could see the stitches on a pitched ball no matter how fast it was thrown," Boggs told me. That kind of superior vision on the flats—not to mention Williams' added advantage of standing six feet, three inches tall—equates to being able to spot signs of fish faster than others.

In our phone chat, I told Williams about watching a seminar he conducted in 1965 at Homestead Air Force Base. On that afternoon I'd stood with my father at the base exchange in the sporting goods section. Williams had a plug rod, and 15 feet away in the aisle sat a trash basket about two feet in diameter. He cast a hookless jig into the basket 10 times in a row. Williams stepped back until he was 25 feet from the basket and did the same—not one miss. He then moved 40 feet from the basket and made nine perfect shots before the last one hit the rim and bounced out. Williams looked surprised and bellowed, "Not my fault, the wind caused it." Everyone laughed. He then proceeded to cast 20 times into the basket without fail, just to let us know the one miss was a fluke. The demo impressed everyone.

After I recounted that to him, Williams replied, "You know, it's always amazed me how people praise how good you are at something, whether it's baseball or fishing or tiddlywinks. It's all about practice. Practice a lot and you'll be good at it, unless you're physically incapable. I practiced my batting and fielding endlessly even during my heydays."

His advice rang a bell, because it made me remember what Sandy Moret, owner of Florida Keys Outfitters and one of the best fly casters around, once told me. As good as he already is, Moret said he practices his casting every day for at least an hour. He explained that casting is no different than any other athletic ability and must be continually honed; it's much like a pro golfer forever hitting range balls or practicing his putting.

Williams further explained the fundaments of sporting success. He said: "If you're reasonably coordinated—which I am—and you have at least average strength—which I do—and you're committed to excellence—and I flat-ass would never accept anything other than that—then anyone can rise and shine. You might not be as good as some others, but you'll be better than most."

Williams added that he took his talents and practiced, practiced, practiced even when he wanted to stop. "When I got to where I wanted to quit practicing, I'd practice another hour," he said. "It became a game with me within a game, pushing my limits and overcoming the tendency to say, 'That's enough.' Yes, sometimes that becomes self-punishment, but that's the ingredient to getting to number one."

In his acceptance speech in 1966 upon being inducted into the National Baseball Hall of Fame, Williams said this about his work ethic:

Ball players are not born great. They're not born hitters or pitchers or managers. And luck isn't the key factor. No one has come up with a substitute for hard work. I've never met a great baseball player who didn't have to work harder at learning to play baseball than anything else he ever did.

Young and old alike respected the career of the great Ted Williams, reminiscing here with Curt Gowdy. Photo courtesy of IGFA and Ted Williams Family Enterprises, Inc.

Many of those who knew or met Williams also recall his consideration on the water for fellow anglers, including Harlan Franklin, then a Key West fishing guide. While deep in the Florida Keys backcountry, Franklin sat in his 13-foot Boston Whaler on the edge of a channel.

"As I jigged, a boat flew by and I had to hold on tight when the wakes hit," Franklin said. "A few minutes later another boat did the same thing. Soon I saw a third skiff coming closer at high speed, but suddenly it slowed down to an idle and moved to the other side of the channel.

"The man behind the console asked how my luck had been. I immediately recognized Ted Williams. After exchanging a few comments about the fishing, he idled away a safe distance before pushing down the throttle and speeding off. I'd heard now and then that he was an unfriendly sort of guy, but that certainly wasn't my experience with him—he was courteous and very down to earth."

"Ted was very generous at times too," said Richard Stanczyk, owner of Bud N' Mary's Marina in Islamorada, where Jimmie Albright guided out of in his later years. "On one occasion Ted ordered an expensive repair job on the roof of Jimmie's house," Stanczyk said. "Jimmie didn't even know about it until he came back home to see it was already fixed."

Outdoor writer Bob Stearns of Miami ran into Williams unexpectedly one early morning in the 1970s. "I was backing my boat down the Lorelei boat ramp in Islamorada. He walked over, looked at my rigs and said, 'I can see you know how to tie knots. That's how I can tell if someone really knows his fishing.' From that we struck up a conversation and kept loosely in touch over the years.

"One day with a group of writers circled around me and Ted there as well, I was showing key components of my new Bonefisher skiff," said Stearns. "At one point Ted sniffed and said, 'Hey, I don't need trim tabs on my boat.' It made me feel a bit flushed and anxious, and all my colleagues looked at me for a reaction."

Stearns said he looked directly at Williams and replied, "Well, with your fat ass sitting so far forward, you don't need trim tabs; they won't do you any good."

A moment of embarrassing silence clung in the air, and all eyes flitted to see the big man's reaction. Williams cracked a smile and then laughed heartily, at which point everyone else joined in.

One of Williams' common habits was to state a difference of opinion and then place a bet on who was right. In Stu Apte's memoirs *Of Wind and Tides,* he writes of such occurrences:

> I ended up with 13 $1 bills from numerous bets that Ted lost to me. He'd write on the dollar bill what the bet was for, and then sign and date them. These are all on the now-rare silver certificates from the 1950s and early 1960s. Of course, the same thing applied to me if I lost the bet . . . difference is, I saved all of his dollar bills and he no doubt spent mine.

Bob Stearns could also claim one-upmanship of Williams on a wager placed when the slugger worked with Sears as a sports equipment consultant. "On trip to Ft. Myers at the Sears testing center, he and I got into a discussion at dinner about how much force you can put on a rod in a striking mode. He said 12 pounds maximum and I said 40 pounds or more.

"The next morning Ted brings out a 50-pound rod, handed it to me and said, 'Prove it.' I tied the line to a post and a Bimini twist knot to a spring scale. Instead of striking upward, I turned my body sideways with the rod, bent the rod with all my strength and the line snapped.

"Ted blinked in disbelief. 'Line must have been bad,' he said, so he left and came back with an 80 rig. So I did the same drill, and this time I rotated and locked it up at 44 pounds.

"Ted's mouth dropped open. 'I'll be goddamn,' he said.

"He looked at me quizzically. I said, 'Ted, you don't hit a baseball by swinging the bat vertically over your head, right? Instead you do it sideways.'

"'Yeah, you're right,' he said with a slow nod, a moment of realization washing over him."

"I told Ted that since I won the argument, I wanted a signed baseball and he agreed," Stearns said. "I still have it. He wrote on the ball: 'Fear strikes out.'"

Williams originally became familiar with the Keys and Miami waters while stationed in Florida for training missions—he was to serve five years as a U.S. Marine fighter pilot in World War II and the Korean War. He returned every spring and off-season thereafter to sharpen his saltwater skills, and Jimmie Albright would later reveal that on more than one occasion, Williams played hooky during spring training to fit in a couple of days on the flats. Williams was committed to staying on top of his baseball game, but he found time even during his playing days to fish and hunt. He tangled with a huge variety of species, including stripers, muskie, largemouth and smallmouth bass, redfish, snook and even once a grander black marlin off Cabo Blanco, Peru, after getting tipped off about the area by Doc and Helen Robinson in Key West.

Even so, Williams made no secret of the fact that his three favorite quarries were tarpon, bonefish and Atlantic salmon. He figured he'd caught more than a thousand of each of those species over the many years he pursued them, releasing almost all. He also owned a lodge on the Miramichi River in New Brunswick, Canada, giving him shots at bigger-than-average salmon during the fall run; his home in Islamorada served as headquarters for practically daily flats-fishing adventures.

Williams moved north to Hernando, Florida, about a dozen years before his death. Earl Waters, a longtime Homosassa guide, remembers meeting Williams when he first arrived in the region.

"The Citrus Hills development gave him a house and a museum, so he often fished around Homosassa and Crystal River," said Waters. "On one unforgettable day, I hooked a big tarpon off Homosassa and snapped my pushpole. Unbeknownst to me, Ted was fishing nearby with Ted Johnston and they saw what happened. They came over to my boat, Williams introduced himself and offered me his pushpole for the rest of the day. I thought that was unbelievably considerate of him."

No matter what one might think about Ted Williams, it's irrefutable that he set out from his native San Diego as a kid and rose to the annals of baseball greatness with the Boston Red Sox. The same attitude and talent that took him to the summit of Major League Baseball also served as the grit for one of the best and most talked-about anglers Florida has ever known.

15

Gene Turner, 1918–2010

ST. PETERSBURG

We met for lunch at an Italian restaurant on Tierra Verde south of St. Petersburg to discuss his life. Gene Turner, 91, came ready to talk and eat. His longtime pal, Capt. Charlie Walker, arranged the get-together and joined us. I looked across the table with amazement at Turner's clear and lucid eyes, a sign of graceful aging that's not a family heritage of mine.

"I caught my first bass at age 10," Turner blurted out before I'd asked the first question. "Eight times I've caught two bass on the same plug." I could tell he was used to chatting with journalists about his storied fishing career. "Once I caught two 15-pound grouper on the same hook—one took it and the bait and barb went through its gills, and another ate it. Can you believe that?"

Yep, I sure can. Any native angler in these parts will attest to the fact that no one has ever caught more kingfish or grouper in these waters than Turner. "Back in the early 1930s, fish weren't wary of anything," he continued. "You could throw anything at them. Even in the 1940s and '50s, if we didn't come home with at least 700 to 800 pounds of grouper on a day's trip, we'd be embarrassed."

Walker periodically smiled and nodded as Turner spoke of his past. Walker, of Pinellas Park, Florida, met Turner in 1970 while running a New England Oyster House restaurant in the area.

"Gene owned Pasadena Bayside Marina in the adjoining parking lot," said Walker. "When Gene decided he wanted to go fishing, he simply put down whatever he had in his hands, jumped aboard a boat and took

Putting a cast net to good use for live-baiting kingfish with greenbacks. Photo courtesy of Gene Turner.

off. He'd leave the big marina building wide open. He lost a few tools here and there over the years, but that never bothered him.

"One day we came back from fishing and his plywood fish smoker—about the size of a refrigerator—was completely empty. He'd just finished smoking about 75 pounds of kingfish that morning. He went absolutely bonkers. It's weird, but Gene didn't care about losing tools or expensive wood like mahogany and teak, but the stolen fish threw him into a tizzy. Next morning he arrived to work screaming and yelling at everybody. Word got around town quickly, and I don't think anyone ever messed with his smoked fish again."

After Walker finished his story, Turner said, "Don't ever mess with my [woman], my money or my fish." We all laughed as a huge bowl of antipasto arrived.

Although considered principally a kingfish and grouper master, Turner also caught a lot of tarpon throughout the years, but only incidentally. "If I knew it was a tarpon, I'd break him off," said Turner.

In 1954, Turner discovered a magical ingredient that made him forevermore the King of Kingfish throughout the region. "Back then few people even knew what a cast net was, never mind using one," he said. "I'd already been throwing a net for years to catch shiners for bass fishing. It occurred to me that Atlantic thread herring—what we call greenbacks—might be the trick, because I often found them in the bellies of kings caught trolling offshore.

"I'd anchor and start dropping live greenbacks into kingfish territory and begin tearing the hell out of big smokers," said Turner. "First I'd use poultry shears to cut greenbacks into tiny chunks and create a chum slick behind the boat. I never chummed too much so the kings wouldn't fill up—I wanted them hungry by the time they reached our rigged greenbacks."

If the tides and current weren't cooperating, Turner would slow-troll the greenbacks rather than anchor, his eyes constantly on the depth recorder and the graph paper that showed the bottom contours. He also advised his anglers to keep their rods in the holders until after a king struck and ran; that overcame the tendency to miss hook-ups. However Turner did it, the whole process of live baiting turned out to be a bombshell of a success. Turner's boat consistently returned with 30- to 50-pound kings in the fish box.

"Other guides in the area were curious as to how I caught so many big ones, and when I'd tell them about the greenbacks, they'd shake their heads as if I was lying. 'Kings won't bite them,' they all said. Well, they soon learned differently."

As happens any time a trailblazer proves that his methods work, others followed Turner's example. Soon the charter boats prospered with consistent catches of kings when greenbacks were offered as bait.

Turner learned how to catch bass and speckled perch long before becoming a U.S. Navy man or moving to St. Petersburg. Photo courtesy of Gene Turner.

Turner's credibility suddenly stood out from the crowd, calling to mind the old E. F. Hutton ad, as if to say: When Gene Turner talks, people listen. And Turner certainly wasn't afraid of talking when commercial fishing netters began wiping out stocks of everything around Tampa Bay.

"Netters in the '70s arrived here and pretty much devastated sport fishing, beginning with baitfish and on to game fish," said Turner. "I spoke out about it, organized against their practices and suddenly my boat's gas tank would be filled with water. I set up a light in the boatyard that was triggered by motion, and that stopped it."

Working to turn the tide of the Florida legislature and stubborn marine biologists, Turner finally got to their ears with the help of outdoor writers, magazines such as *Florida Sportsman* and his non-stop lobbying. It took years, but in time the evidence clearly convinced fisheries managers that, indeed, commercial fishing boats were overfishing kingfish and other stocks around Tampa Bay and Florida in general. In the early 1980s, measures were put into effect establishing quotas and bag limits, and slowly the stocks rebuilt—not quite back to what they were, as Turner quickly pointed out, but at least now most fisheries are growing instead of dying.

While Turner succeeded in spearheading conservation measures and did quite nicely as a well-known local guide, he did even better making fishing boats. In the 1940s and '50s, he made about 2,700 in all sizes, including a 45-foot houseboat model with twin diesels, a 31-foot fly bridge sport-fishing design and the rest under 26 feet. At first he built wooden freshwater boats and later saltwater as the popularity of marine fishing increased.

"I never put a name on a boat," said Turner. "In later years I also made 'em with Monel and epoxy with high nickel contact so they'd be more malleable than steel. I used the best possible materials on boats, and people kept buying them because they'd last even in saltwater under the intense rays of the sun."

Turner's freshwater fishing exploits might not be as profound as his feats in the briny, but he became as good as anyone at catching speckled perch. "I find it easy to catch more than most other people do," he said. "Perch like to gather in deep holes directly under a boat, so fish straight below and you'll bag four or five to one over lines cast way out."

In addition to his discovery of greenbacks for kingfish and how to best take perch, Turner has a tried-and-true technique for largemouth bass.

"Use two big hooks tied 90 degrees from each other," he said. "Buy fat bacon half an inch thick and cut a strip five inches long. Split the ends, put a hole in the top for the hooks, and big bass will literally smell it out—they can't resist it.

"Fish on the darkest night of the new moon and just before daybreak, start hitting the top of the water with your rod tip—a technique known as dibbling—with just one foot of line out of the tip and the rest of the line running to the grip. Use a light rod so it bends as bass run under your boat."

Nobody has weighed more smoke kings than Gene Turner (right) and his anglers. Photo courtesy of Gene Turner.

He's also designed special gaffs that are more ergonometric than models of old, allowing a more secure grip and less misses at the critical moment when the fish are boat side. Turner also came up with a fish de-hooker long before others had even seen such a gadget. He could quickly remove bait fish off a Sabiki rig without getting it all tangled or the baits severely injured.

Turner said his greatest stroke of luck was meeting his wife, Jeannie, during World War II. At the time he was dating someone else; the same with Jeannie, but suddenly their partners didn't shine in comparison. He courted Jeannie, she obliged, and their marriage lasted until his recent passing.

Jeannie, small and slight, nonetheless commands the moment with her quick laugh. Funny and down to earth, she's quite aware of Turner's reputation for being gruff at times. She knew his moods and parried them with lots of humor and little stress. "He's really a puppy dog," she once told me.

Longtime outdoor writer David Brown of Tampa might agree. He fished with Turner and quickly discovered that the man didn't just tell you what to do on his boat, he made you understand why.

"One fine spring morning, Gene hosted me and two others for a few hours of Spanish mackerel fishing at the mouth of Tampa Bay," Brown recalled.

"With Spanish or the larger king mackerel, the trick in getting a solid hook-up means holding your rod tip at about 10 o'clock while allowing the drag to moderate the tension. The one thing you don't want to do is lower the rod tip to where your line absorbs most of the pressure.

"Gene caught me making this mistake once," Brown said. "I remember clearly how the raspiness of his voice and the sudden upturn of intensity seared the admonishment into my mind like a branded calf: 'Don't point that rod at the fish, David, you're trying to catch him, not shoot him,' said Gene.

"He didn't hesitate to lower the education boom on me with such an amazing clarity that I have never, and I mean never, repeated the error."

Turner made indelible impressions on his anglers for decades during his guiding career. "I taught people to do it my way," he said. "Of course I realized that anglers can catch the same fish at times with different baits or lures or using a variety of gear, but someone is paying me to help them catch fish and I knew how to do it. If people wanted to do it their way or how some other person taught them, I figured they were wasting my time and their money—when that happened, it would be our last trip together."

While Turner used reels such as No. 309 Penns, he favored Fin-Nors spooled with 40-pound-test line. "They cost more, but I've always believed that good equipment is worth it. I didn't care for big spin rods on smoker kings because they usually kinked the line."

Entrees arrived at this point in my interview with Turner, mine being a chicken parmigiana sandwich overflowing with mushrooms and sauce. Walker and Turner ordered something else, and both dishes looked scrumptious. As we forgot the world and dived into the delicious Italian food, I somehow managed to ask Turner if anything off-beat came to mind from his vast fishing experiences.

A bit annoyed at the distraction, Turner chewed a few more moments and took a swig of water. Wiping his face with a napkin, his lips curled into a smile as his eyes brightened—I could tell he'd just recalled something.

"Way back when, I sometimes fished a lake in Tampa that had a large nudist colony on one of the shorelines," Turner said. "They dredged sand from the lake to construct a beach, and we'd anchor where that deep hole was created and catch speckled perch. Meanwhile, it was quite a nice show all day seeing the girls lounging about with 100-percent suntans.

"I like this food," he added, his eyes locking with mine. I got the message. We still had lunch to eat, and talking with your mouth full is rude.

I liked meeting Gene Turner, a man who's always let his actions speak louder than words. We'll be breaking bread again soon.

16

Curt Gowdy, 1919–2006

PALM BEACH

I walked into the small gift shop of Cheeca Lodge in Islamorada about a dozen years ago and found Curt Gowdy scanning through greeting cards on a rotating stand. I walked behind him to the clothing racks and pretended to browse while I unobtrusively observed Gowdy. He looked tired, disoriented and somehow out of place.

Gowdy yawned, glanced to the left and right, didn't change expression and continued to peruse the cards. About 15 seconds later, he yawned again, doing so with a vocal sigh. Suddenly I worried that he might be feeling the effects of either a heavy dose of medication or one libation too many.

After stretching his arms, twisting his back and yawning again, the cashier and I were starting to freak out. But before anything could be said, Gowdy seemed to remember something and out he scurried from the gift shop like a sprayed roach.

Other observations I made about Gowdy over the years weren't very flattering either. He ventured to the Keys from his home base in Palm Beach quite often, and with my being a resident for seven years starting in the late 1980s, I'd encountered Gowdy now and then at a tournament or tackle shop. It seemed like he only hung out with the same clique and never acknowledged others he didn't know.

A somewhat small and slight guy in stature, he unquestionably leveraged his popularity in a spectacular way as a TV commentator for Super Bowls and World Series games. He also produced the hugely popular *Wide World of Sports* for ABC with Roone Arledge and *The American Sportsman* TV series in the 1960s and '70s. Needless to say, Gowdy's

Having a hit show like *The American Sportsman* lured celebrity anglers such as Ernest Borgnine (far left) and Jonathan Winters (far right). Photo courtesy of the International Game Fish Association.

guests on the latter show ran the gamut from Hollywood celebs to fly-fishing pros, creating a powerfully positive image that helped further promote sport fishing in the public eye.

Even so, I took Gowdy to be aloof and earthy to a fault. He was forever haggard in appearance and often wore oversized fishing shirts that billowed like a spinnaker when he stood in a breeze. Secure in his legend and retired from all but ceremonial roles, Gowdy didn't seem to care what he did or what people might think.

Or so I thought. My opinion changed dramatically a few years before he died. He and I were listed as the anglers aboard the same skiff in an annual Redbone tournament in Islamorada. When I learned of the pairing, I dreaded the thought of spending eight hours within a few feet of someone built up in my mind as an old buffoon. Instead, it turned out to be one of the most enjoyable days on the water I've ever experienced.

From the moment we left the dock until we returned, Gowdy and I talked endlessly about various sports we both fancied, particularly pro and college football. He was surprised at my depth of knowledge for a layman, and I equally appreciated his down-to-earth manner and gregarious nature. He later said to others at the event how nice it was to "meet a new friend" by way of fishing with a different angler for a change. I beamed.

It just goes to show how impressions can be diametrically reversed once you really get to know someone. I now realize that Gowdy was simply unpretentious, not concerned with trivialities or trying to uphold a grandiose "celebrity" image. The man's heart was in the right place, and I better appreciated all of Gowdy's volunteering and the loaning of his name to endless charitable causes throughout his lifetime.

Tarpon master Stu Apte first met Curt Gowdy in 1962. ABC's *Wide World of Sports* planned to shoot a tarpon fishing segment that pitted editors Al McClane of *Field & Stream* and Joe Brooks of *Outdoor Life* against each other. By a flip of the coin, Brooks' guide turned out to be Apte and McClane's the famed Jimmie Albright.

"Curt did an intro for the show and interviewed us in front of the Bahia Honda Bridge," said Apte. "We took to our boats, and fortunately, Joe and I won the competition. What people don't know is that on the prior evening, I was sitting alone at a table with Albright and I introduced myself. He was one of my heroes when growing up in Miami— I wanted to be just like him and guide clients to big tarpon. When I started gushing to Albright about how highly I regarded him, he looked at me coldly. Evidently he thought I was being sarcastic or trying to psych him out for the competition the next day. In any case, he cussed me out really harshly. Hurt and embarrassed, I worked extra hard to win that TV event."

After getting to know Gowdy during the filming of that episode, Apte went on to field host several *American Sportsman* episodes. "One show involved Curt and I walking through the jungle in Costa Rica," Apte said. "At the time, I had no idea that Curt was deathly afraid of snakes. He kept his eyes to the ground as we walked, and I could see something really worried him. Finally Curt asked, 'Hey, are there any snakes around here?'

"I said, 'Curt, only fer-de-lances and bushmasters.' I could see him take a big gulp and he asked, 'Uh, don't bushmasters actually stalk people?' I nodded, and Gowdy grew pale and clammy while murmuring about watching out for 'two steppers,' meaning fabled snakes that strike and you only get a couple of steps before falling to the ground dead. It was all I could do to keep from laughing out loud."

Apte, in the lead on the path and ensuring no snakes were in their way, continued to enjoy the levity in Gowdy's angst.

"Gowdy pranced and danced down the path," said Apte. "He walked like Kwai Chang Caine on rice paper, his head swiveled and eyes darted about. At times I'd suddenly stop as if I spotted something, which turned Gowdy into a quivering bowl of Jell-O. Gowdy swore he'd never traverse that path on foot again, and to my knowledge he never did."

Apte said he played with the idea of tossing a plastic snake at Gowdy or placing one in his bed, but then the thought of possibly causing a heart attack dissuaded him.

Curt Gowdy was born in Green River, Wyoming, and at age six arrived with his family in the state's capital of Cheyenne. I graduated from high school in Cheyenne, and when our paths crossed for our day of fishing together, we talked a lot about the raucous Cheyenne Frontier Days celebration each year, the antelope and deer hunting available right outside the city limits, the grandeur of Yellowstone and the Grand Tetons, the special character of Jackson Hole and other such topics. We didn't know many mutual friends because of our age difference, but he spoke of Wyoming with great nostalgia.

Gowdy's journey from the Old West to stardom actually began because of a back injury. Gowdy ruptured a disk he'd damaged in a previous accident while in the Army Air Corps before World War II ended. It grounded his dream of being a career fighter pilot, and in 1943 he was discharged. Gowdy had played for the basketball team in high school, and despite being the smallest member of the squad, he led the state in scoring. He also loved football. His sporting interests prompted someone to ask Gowdy to do the announcing for an upcoming high school football game in Cheyenne.

Here's the scene: It was a cold November day of about 10 degrees below zero, and Gowdy, bundled in layers of clothing, stood on a crate

Gowdy with a bonefish on fly in the '50s. Photo courtesy of the International
Game Fish Association.

Curt Gowdy at home in Wyoming with a fly rod and a mountain stream. Photo courtesy of the International Game Fish Association.

next to the bleachers. Holding a speaker cone in one hand, he barked out the plays and commentary to about 15 die-hard parents in the stands. Although no one was in attendance from the media to witness his performance, Gowdy noticed his own racing heartbeat and excitement while doing the announcing. He instantly yearned to make it a career even while recognizing that a young man from a non-media market would have to be very lucky to get noticed.

Gowdy took a job at a Cheyenne radio station and became sports editor for the weekly *Wyoming Eagle* newspaper. He barely scraped by, but in a couple of years he went to Oklahoma City to broadcast Oklahoma University's Sooner football games as well as Oklahoma State basketball games. That experience did net listeners, and people noticed. They liked his unique voice, his enthusiasm, his talent.

In 1949, the big break occurred. At that time, radio was the only outlet for someone with "good pipes," and Gowdy headed to the top media market in the world, New York City. He traveled there specifically to audition for the job as sportscaster Mel Allen's assistant. Gowdy nailed it, and there was no stopping him after that. He began announcing play-by-play for the New York Yankees. He also hooked up with Red Barber on CBS radio to handle football broadcasts. Gowdy's career was on fire.

In a couple of years, Gowdy received an offer to become the voice of the Boston Red Sox, and he jumped at this opportunity—a job he'd coveted for 15 years. The high-profile gig solidified a friendship with the great Ted Williams, whom he'd met in St. Petersburg years before during a Yankees spring practice session. That relationship alone opened up a huge number of contacts for him in the sports world. Gowdy also got into pro basketball broadcasting, becoming the first announcer for the Boston Celtics. The unknown kid from Wyoming had made it to big-time TV and radio.

His success in broadcasting can be simply put: He had a pleasant way of putting things, with a clear and distinctive tone of voice. Over the years he'd learned to synchronize what he saw with what he said, offering not only play-by-play but also colorful insights that other announcers weren't providing. He was one of the first to effectively use stat sheets, interweaving tidbits of background info and data to make it more meaningful for the audience. His unique style and delivery had made him a hit on radio, and when TV captured the media spotlight in the 1950s, Gowdy was already a name in the industry.

Luckily, his mother pushed him to include elocution lessons in his curriculum at the University of Wyoming—something he at first resisted and years hence would recognize as fateful good fortune. Gowdy would go on to work for all three of the major networks of his day: ABC, CBS and NBC. His broadcasting credits were phenomenal, including eight Super Bowls, 16 World Series, 12 Rose Bowls and 24 college basketball finals. But Gowdy's skills weren't relegated to just baseball, football and basketball—he also covered eight Olympics games.

Early on, Gowdy wanted to go beyond the usual TV sports genres and do something unprecedented. Having met ABC's wunderkind, Roone Arledge—the man who would go on to create *Wide World of Sports, Monday Night Football,* and other colossally successful projects—Gowdy approached him with a programming idea. His pitch: How about a show depicting the beauty of the outdoors as people fished and hunted?

Gowdy recited statistics about the number of people involved in outdoor sports, but Arledge didn't think viewers would care much unless some sort of competition could occur. In Arledge's view, people wanted to see a show culminate with a winner, someone claiming victory for his or her accomplishment. Gowdy pondered the angle and soon broached the concept of a trout championship; Arledge gave Gowdy the green light. And so a competition was organized in Argentina to pit the American team of Gowdy and Joe Brooks against two Argentineans.

The *Wide World of Sports* segment was a huge success, leading to enormous positive feedback from viewers. The subsequent Apte-Albright segment in the Keys was likewise a hit. Even ABC's ad sponsors told Arledge that finally they were seeing unique programming based on the great outdoors rather than in an enclosed arena or stadium. Besides the fishing action, the show included cut-ins of the beauty of the mountains, the essence of mountain streams and the cultural flavor of Argentina. Even non-anglers loved the shows.

Arledge needed no more prodding. In 1964, *The American Sportsman,* hosted by Curt Gowdy, debuted as four one-hour specials. They became an immediate hit. ABC decided to make it a series of 13 shows the following year, and that became a 20-year ride with over 200 episodes. Gowdy, already famous from his days with the Yankees and Red Sox, enjoyed even greater celebrity status as the epitome of an American sportsman. The shows included entertainment and sports celebrities who liked to fish or hunt as well as great anglers. The broadcast sites showcased some of the most magnificent locations around the world, which in turn highlighted tourism venues and served as massive good-will messages for the fishing and hunting industries.

Gowdy became an international icon. His father had taught him to fly fish for rainbow trout and stalk antelope, and Gowdy envisioned a way to successfully combine those passions with his beloved broadcasting profession. With a career that would span 50 years, you couldn't find a room big enough to display all his trophies and awards. Even so, some of the more significant honors include the naming of a state park after him in Wyoming, the Ford Frick Award for excellence in baseball broadcasting, the National Academy of Television Arts and Sciences' Lifetime Achievement Award for Sports, the Peabody and Emmy awards, and so many sportscaster of the year recognitions that they'd take pages to list. Gowdy was a member of the International Game Fish Association's distinguished board of trustees since 1985 and a founding member of Bonefish & Tarpon Trust. He wrote two books, *Cowboy at the Mike* and *Seasons to Remember: The Way It Was in American Sports, 1945–1960*.

During my lone day on the water with Gowdy, I asked what he thought was most important about his life and career. "My family, for sure," he replied quickly. "After that, I was never happier than behind either a microphone or a fly rod, although I must confess that I achieved a lot more with the former than with the latter."

17

Duncan MacRae, 1922–2006

HOMOSASSA

Anyone journeying up Florida's west coast on U.S. Highway 19 will sooner or later drive through Homosassa. Famous for its old Florida charm and freshwater springs, the area's special appeal can really only be appreciated if one turns west off the main drag.

That's exactly what James and Mary MacRae did circa 1909. Intrigued by the promise of the area's future and a natural setting they couldn't match back home in Dunedin, they packed up everything and moved to Homosassa. Since the early 1800s, the area was mainly home to sugarcane fields and mullet fishermen. The remnants of an old sugar mill can still be seen. But the MacRaes firmly believed that others who came to visit would also recognize how special it is and want to return.

There could be no mistaking the potential for growth along the crystal-clear Homosassa River. James and Mary spent time scouting the area, talking to residents and sizing up the region's geographical pluses and minuses. Some boats cruised up the river to explore, but most didn't expend the time to do so because of a lack of ready facilities that skippers and crews desired.

With the river's access to the Gulf of Mexico, the MacRaes envisioned trading with an ever-increasing number of vessels plying Florida's west coast, and that spelled opportunity. If crews could obtain needed supplies, they'd also at times require maintenance for their boats; they'd want to take a break to eat and drink, to perhaps take home a souvenir or two. And yet no one was providing all those services in one convenient place.

MacRae cleaning a trout near the mouth of the Homosassa River in the early 1960s. Photo courtesy of Gator MacRae.

The MacRaes opened a store upriver and offered just about every-thing a traveler might desire. They packed fish and sold tools, paint, clothing, food and other basics to not only visiting trading boats but also to locals.

The MacRaes prospered—not in the sense of great riches, but their store became a known source as the word passed around. That kind of goodwill just about always leads to steady success in the retail business.

As the Roaring '20s consumed the rest of the nation, Homosassa moved along quietly, off the radar screen of industrialization. The in-habitants felt quite glad about that. Soon the MacRaes had a son they named Duncan James, and the boy grew up amid a world of proper manners, lots of fishing, respect for hard work, lots of fishing, neigh-bors helping neighbors, lots of fishing, and . . . you get the idea.

Duncan worked hard at the store, dealt with characters of savory and unsavory temperament, and watched and absorbed what it took to make money. He saw how his parents treated customers in a friendly, cordial manner, and how many of them became friends; this would serve Duncan well in his adult years.

He also watched firsthand as his father and mother dealt with unrea-sonable wheeler-dealers and others out to cheat and swindle. That sel-dom happened with locals; it was almost always out-of-towners. Then again, when you know everyone in the area and it happens to be an old southern town, most neighbors look out for each other. The MacRaes provided other merchants around Homosassa with information about good and bad customers, and they received same in return.

It's easy to appreciate this part of Florida's easy-on-the-nerves at-mosphere. Take a spin down Yulee Drive not far from Highway 19, and don't be in a hurry. Yulee Drive itself is a return to Mayberry, with a beautiful, oak-shaded yaw of a road where you amble past the sugar mill ruins, a tackle shop, a smoked fish hut, several small (and excel-lent) eateries, a school, a library and—here and there—structural evi-dence of modernization.

At the terminus of Yulee Drive one passes the venerable Riverside Resort on the right just before turning left into MacRae's of Homo-sassa. The tackle shop is next to a boat ramp, and the property features

Just about every grouper outing in the 1950s resulted in heavy catches of gags and other species. Left to right: Mike King from Auburndale, Florida, Duncan, and wife Wilma. Photo courtesy of Gator MacRae.

covered wet-boat storage, a bar and an open dining area on the water-front, a string of nicely furnished hotel rooms and what used to be an inn which now serves as a MacRae family residence.

The bar consists of a three-sided row of stools and has become a favorite gathering spot since it opened in 2001. You can also munch a nice selection of seafood and sandwiches; a take-out counter services those coming and going in boats or cars. I love hanging out here while swilling a Captain Morgan and cola—it's a cool place to people-watch and just kick back.

The old tackle shop, which was showing signs of wear and tear, is undergoing renovation. Even when change is gracefully slow in coming, sometimes improvements are just that.

Before Duncan MacRae's passing in 2006, the route to the present-day status of a resort involved many contributions by this colorful man. A talented baseball player, a young MacRae earned a scholarship to Saint Leo University before getting his commission as an officer in the U.S. Army at Marion Military Institute in Alabama.

During World War II, MacRae served in the Pacific and participated in four beachhead attacks—resulting in many wounds—with the 307th Infantry Combat Regiment. Following the war, MacRae attended the University of Florida to play baseball.

"I knew that after all the schooling I'd end up right back in Homo-sassa," said MacRae, "and that's exactly what I wanted. I spent a lot of nights on little islands in the Pacific daydreaming about the peaceful life here and how I missed it." MacRae remembered the sacrifices of those who didn't return from the war. He rolled up his sleeves and became involved in the family businesses, which by then included not only the store but also the Homosassa Inn and a number of rental residences.

He eventually met Wilma Sassard of the nearby town of Red Level at a USO dance ("He couldn't dance a lick," she would later joke). They married, entering into a union that would last 60 years. They raised three sons named Buzz, Gator and Rodney as well as a daughter, Kathy.

Noting the rising interest in recreational fishing, Duncan and his mother opened MacRae's Bait Shop in the early 1950s. Many momen-tous weigh-ins of fish big and small—including world-record tarpon

When MacRae pulled out the skillet for one of his famed river picnics, mouths began to water. Photo courtesy of Gator MacRae.

bested by legends of the fly-fishing world—would occur at the dock scale here over the ensuing decades. Stu Apte, Billy Pate, Al Pflueger, Tom Evans and many other record seekers flocked here with their fly gear every spring from the late 1970s to the 1990s.

Many sought out men who knew the waters like the back of their hands, and Duncan MacRae was at the top that list. He helped clients calculate the best tides and conditions, and of course sold them gas, bait and tackle. The skiffs arrived by the score and though this became discomforting to some, it represented a boon to the hotel, restaurant and marina businesses. Fishing boats cruised the shorelines north and south of the mouth of the river, and they indeed found and fought world-record tarpon.

Duncan knew them all or came to know them, including guides arriving from south Florida like Lee Baker, Ralph Delph, Steve Huff, Bill Curtis and dozens more. They joined the men already guiding out of

Homosassa for years such as Mike Locklear, Jimmy Long, Earl Waters and more lately, William Toney and others.

Although MacRae was known by many as "Mac," Homosassa native and fishing guide Mike Locklear preferred to call the man "Mister Duncan" out of devout respect for him.

"I've always felt fortunate to work with Mister Duncan," Locklear said. "He mentored me and became my employer, and even though in his fifties when I first met him, we became friends.

"Mister Duncan was in his element with a fishing rod or in a duck blind. He especially loved quail hunting, and you could always see a couple of his bird dogs hanging around the bait house."

Former *Tampa Tribune* outdoor editor Herb Allen enjoyed coming up to Homosassa and spending several days at a time with MacRae.

"Mac kept a cabin in the woods down the river in a hidden spot so remote that few people knew about it," said Allen.

"We'd stay in the cabin and by daybreak we'd be right where he knew the fish were. Mac also could cook with the best of them, and he'd prepare whatever we caught in a delicious lemon-butter and garlic sauce. I'll never forget how much fun we had."

As MacRae's stature and renown increased, the authorities knew the person to call whenever someone ended up in trouble around Homosassa. MacRae often helped with rescues because he understood every nook and cranny as well as the outlying waters.

Just such an occasion arose in August 1970, when a 23-year-old newlywed named Glenda Lennon went snorkeling with her new husband, Robert, during a Homosassa honeymoon. They'd anchored a 21-foot boat near a channel marker about five miles off the river's mouth, but they underestimated the strength of the freshwater flow coming out of the river. Glenda called out to Robert for help as she drifted away from the boat and farther out into the Gulf of Mexico.

Instead of taking the boat to her, he mistakenly jumped in and swam to her. As the boat began to disappear from view and with no other boaters in sight, Robert realized he couldn't tow his wife against the current to the boat while swimming himself. She also seemed to be fine once he settled her down. An experienced swimmer, Robert decided to swim back to the boat so he could pick up Glenda and return them to safety. He ultimately made it, but when he searched for Glenda, he could not locate her in the choppy waters.

That night couldn't have been worse, with a gale blowing through that held back the search teams. The weather improved a bit the next day, and MacRae immediately ran down the Homosassa River and out the mouth to the marker where the Lennons' boat had been anchored. Estimating the strength of the tides off Homosassa and wind direction, he headed into the Gulf with two others aboard his boat.

"Look for anything shiny or a flash in the water," he told them, "and don't take your eyes off it if you do." MacRae explained that oftentimes it's impossible to relocate an object in choppy waters once eye contact is lost.

After rushing to many sightings in the distance that turned out to be debris, MacRae spotted something light in color against the briny surface of the water. He ran quickly to it and found the exhausted Glenda—she had been fighting for her life for nearly 20 hours. MacRae swung her aboard and after a week in the hospital, she fully recouped. Her husband, Robert, was of course ecstatic, the public enthralled, and MacRae felt the satisfaction of having saved someone's life. The entire saga ended up in the pages of numerous newspapers as well as *Reader's Digest*.

I met Duncan MacRae several times in his later years as he sat outside the bait shop, holding court to new and old friends. I never got to know him, but I did witness some of the exciting world-record weigh-ins at MacRae's during the 1980s. In 1991 Duncan's son Gator took over the businesses, and they've grown and prospered.

"When Dad spoke, you listened," said Gator. "He wasn't big in stature, but he was big in substance. He knew what he was talking about and it made good sense to pay attention."

His son Rodney considered him a friend, not just a father. "He was a teacher of life, encouraging me to always keep my word and to act honorably."

I continue to visit Homosassa as often as possible with family and friends, giving me the additional opportunity to pen articles here and there about the endless ambiance and fishing resources. I love staying at Riverside Resort or MacRae's—one is right across the street from the other—when a stress-busting respite is needed. ˙

In 2006 the Florida Outdoor Writers Association held its annual conference in Homosassa when I served the group as executive director, with a turnout so huge the meeting rooms were overflowing. One night we held a roast of Billy Pate, who set his long-standing world record of a 188-pound tarpon on fly in these waters—it was standing room only.

Thanks to pioneers like Duncan MacRae, Homosassa will also be special to me and all the anglers who've ever visited or lived here.

18

Bernard "Lefty" Kreh, b. 1925

MIAMI

"Lefty is the best teacher of fly-casting, ever. He's dedicated his life to doing that, and he loves an audience and performing." So said fly-fishing impresario Stu Apte, and one might say that that pretty well says it all.

However, Lefty's legacy is far more than just the art of precision fly-casting—there's much more to the man than that. In fact, while most people in this book are mentioned by their last names as is the common journalistic practice, everyone knows Lefty as simply Lefty; constant references to "Kreh" just don't seem natural.

In his mid-80s and the veteran of more than a few instances of accidents, illnesses and operations, he can still outwork just about any of us. Lefty's travel schedule and regimen is simply amazing, and I've often marveled at the strength of his constitution. A lot of that is due to his wife of 64 years, Evelyn, who he lovingly says is his best friend.

Lefty met *Outdoor Life* editor Joe Brooks in 1947, and the bond between them was immediate. Brooks recognized Lefty's potential as a fly fisherman and journalist. The young man had unmistakable personality, a thirst for knowledge and an uncanny knack for casting a fly rod. Thanks to Brooks' encouragement, Lefty started a column in the *Frederick News-Post* and by 1954 he was syndicated in 11 newspapers.

In 1964, Brooks was to also convince Lefty to apply for the job as director of the Metropolitan South Florida Fishing Tournament (MET). The MET covered the southern half of the state, and the competition stretched for six months—a prestigious tournament with a million de-

Big barracuda on fly! Photo courtesy of Lefty Kreh.

tails to juggle. It was a great fit because few are better organized than Lefty.

He got the job and moved to Miami from his native Maryland. The south Florida fishing community immediately embraced Lefty's intriguing character and exceptional skills, and the MET prospered under his watch. During his days as a Miamian, he also wrote for the *Miami Herald* and helped Karl Wickstrom and Vic Dunaway during the launching years of *Florida Sportsman*.

Lefty ultimately moved back to Maryland in 1972 and became outdoor editor of the *Baltimore Sunpapers*, retaining the position until 1993. But retirement didn't even enter Lefty's mind as he embarked on new challenges. He has since fished in almost every state, all 10 provinces of Canada, and in many countries in Europe as well as throughout the South Pacific and Central and South America. As a result, Lefty knows the world of angling, and the world of angling knows him. His name still appears on numerous magazine mastheads, plus he's authored 30 books and produced many videos and DVDs; his personal appearances have numbered in the thousands.

He designed the Lefty's Deceiver pattern initially to fool striped bass, but it quickly gained notoriety as a fly suitable for most big-game fish. In 1991 the U.S. Postal Service paid tribute to his popularity by issuing a stamp with the Deceiver on it.

Besides being a world-class angler, Lefty is one of the finest outdoor photographers who ever lived. He's taught outdoor photography for the National Wildlife Society and was L.L.Bean's fly-fishing and photo consultant for several years. In 1989, Lefty performed a slide show on photography at the Florida Outdoor Writers Association's annual conference in Tallahassee, and it still ranks as the most informative I've ever seen. I took pages of notes on his suggestions and insights, and still refer to them now and then.

Speaking of his picture-taking prowess, Lefty is unsurpassed at maximizing the earning potential of images. He actually painted one side of his skiff yellow and the other side red. After catching a fish, he'd photograph it in several poses on each side of the boat; same fish, different backgrounds, multiple potential outlets.

The unusual color mix of his hull often drew notice, to be sure. "I once fished with a friend in Florida Bay and Lefty ran by us showing the yellow side of his skiff," said Bob Stearns, a noted outdoor writer based in Miami.

"We waved at each other and my friend asked who that was, so I told him. A few hours later, here comes Lefty from the opposite direction, but of course now the red side of his boat glared at us.

"My friend's eyes scrunched up, his mouth dropped open, he shook his head and said, 'What the hell?' stretching each word out about three times longer than normal. That wasn't the only time Lefty's boat got that kind of reaction, either."

John Randolph, former editor at *Fly Fisherman* magazine, once observed just how much Lefty enjoys imparting his photography knowledge to others.

"He always prefers to leap from bed before dawn to hit the water for early morning sidelight," Randolph said. "So one dawn we headed for Hayden Valley in Yellowstone Park and got there when the bison, elk and moose were lit by the sun with mist drifting from the Yellowstone and running in a smooth amber ribbon beyond.

"We had a good morning and stopped to snap pics of three large bull moose grazing in reedy shallows, their horns dripping water and back-lit by the sun. Two elderly ladies stood about 40 yards away, between us and the moose, impatiently fiddling with a point-and-shoot camera that they obviously could not work.

"Lefty immediately trotted over, introduced himself and began what became a half-hour lecture in photography and how to work their camera. The women were surprised and delighted, but my companion and I were impatient to move somewhere else before the low light disappeared. We finally hollered at Lefty to end his session and he reluctantly did so, but it shows how he cannot resist an opportunity to help others."

Lefty has racked up enough awards and honors for several lifetimes. He's been given the prestigious Lifetime Achievement Award by the North American Fly Tackle Trade Association, inducted into the International Game Fishing Association's Hall of Fame, the Fresh Water Fishing Hall of Fame, the Fly Fishing Hall of Fame, the Catskill Fly Fishing Center and Museum Fishing Hall of Fame, and on and on. He's also served as an advisor to Trout Unlimited and the Federation of Fly Fishers.

Perhaps the greatest role Lefty fulfilled involved his heavy contributions to the Salt Water Fly Rodders of America (SWFROA). In April 1965, a number of key individuals convened a meeting—dubbed the "Get-Together"—at Nansen's Restaurant in Toms River, New Jersey. The gathering was called to go over the buzz words, rules and record-keeping spadework that Mark Sosin had drafted. Sosin had previously received enormous input from many "names" in the world of fly-fishing such as Stu Apte, Joe Brooks, Hal Lyman, Vin Sparano, Frank Woolner and of course Lefty.

Talk had begun in the late 1950s about the need for a clearing house on saltwater fly-fishing regulations, an understanding that all could live with and operate from. It wasn't easy: Traditionalists wanted this, modernists wanted that, and one must have thought the U.S. Constitution was being debated. But through it all the men persevered, with Fred Schrier acting as chairman. An agreed-upon set of rules was formed, SWFROA chapters sprung up, and at last the fly-fishing community

On the same day he bagged the 'cuda, Lefty tamed this huge tarpon. Photo courtesy of the International Game Fish Association.

Lefty's famous Deceiver pattern on a U.S. postal stamp. Photo courtesy of the International Game Fish Association.

had a bible from which to base how people fished for saltwater species. More of the organizational meetings took place in the next few years to iron out the kinks.

Prior to that occurring, anarchy prevailed and circuitous debates took place. The SWFROA rules adopted by those such as Lefty in the mid-1960s still serve as the recognized regulations for saltwater fly fishing, with amendments and changes only seldom coming along to change what the "forefathers" conceived.

Lefty's advice and input is worth listening to because no one questions that the man knows what he's talking about. Even so, at times Lefty's good-natured advice might go a bit overboard. John Randolph recalled just such an incident, again taking place in the famed Yellowstone National Park.

"I fished one afternoon with Lefty and the *Fly Fisherman's* associate editor, Craig Woods, at Elk Meadows on the Madison in Yellowstone. Lefty was giving his normal instructions on tackle, knots and fishing techniques, including casting. The instruction went on for some three hours as the sun sank low and fish began to rise.

"We cast to them urgently but without success as the elk cows gnawed grass nearby and stared at us vacantly. Craig finally waded from the stream to where I sat while Lefty fished on.

"'I'm going to relieve myself,' Craig whispered, 'but don't tell Lefty. He'll try to tell me how to do it more efficiently!'"

Those who have the pleasure of getting to know Lefty soon come to appreciate his endless litany of jokes. According to fly-fishing icon Ed Jaworowski, Lefty's repertoire of one-liners seems inexhaustible. "I've known him 36 years, and in that time I've only told him one joke he hadn't previously heard," said Jaworowski.

"His renowned eating habits—'Never put more than three colors on a plate'—and his belief that a hamburger is perfectly cooked when it takes on the texture of a hockey puck gives chefs indigestion."

Al Pflueger Jr. has also taken note of Lefty's peculiar dietary predilections. "The man loves cheese sandwiches," Pflueger said with a laugh.

While Lefty's talents encompass photography, teaching, speaking, writing and designing tackle, not many people know that he was once also an exhibition shooter for a large firearms manufacturer. Lefty successfully multitasks on a grand scale, and Ed Jaworowski has seen it firsthand.

"Lefty possesses an incredible sense of organization that I find mind-boggling," said Jaworowski. "While showing me the cabinet where he stored monofilament line, without hesitation and without looking, he reached in, pulled out a bulk spool of line, held it up to me and said, 'Six-pound Trilene.' He repeated this several times with various weights and brands. He knew the location of every item in there and could instantly place his hand on it.

"I also saw a series of his tackle boxes—each labeled for a specific species—all packed and ready to go at a moment's notice. Likewise, he once showed me three travel bags pre-packed for a succession of upcoming trips. Upon returning from one, he simply dropped one bag and grabbed the next."

Lefty possesses over 20,000 35mm slides, a format that was the essence of outdoor photography for decades before the digital age. He can access any of the slides instantly due to his precise filing system; the same with just about any fishing or hunting topic you can imagine.

During another one of Jaworoski's visits to Lefty's home, his wife, Michele, asked about seasickness. "Lefty stood, took two steps from his desk and pulled a sheet of paper from a pile that summarized all the latest studies and remedies," said Jaworoski.

"We're forever amazed at his efficiency and ultra organization."

Lefty's world is also replete with homemade or modified gimmicks and gadgets to make fishing, photography and writing easier. Said Jaworoski: "Lefty doesn't merely think about building better mousetraps, he finishes every project. Most people come up with ideas but don't follow through."

Susan Cocking, outdoor writer for the *Miami Herald*, appreciated Lefty's thoughtfulness when she went on a fishing excursion with him soon after his induction into the IGFA Hall of Fame a few years ago. "Lefty, Capt. Steve Kantner and I went after snook on fly in the Tamiami Trail Canal," she recalled.

"That day I luckily out-fished him and I really ribbed him a lot about it. Instead of being put off like some people get, Lefty loved it and even sent me a fly rod as a memento of our day. I really appreciated his good sportsmanship."

Acts such as that reflect Lefty's mentoring from Joe Brooks. After all Brooks had done to launch his career, at one point Lefty asked Brooks how he could possibly repay him for all the years of help and insights.

Brooks smiled in his typically unassuming way and replied, "Just share with others what I've shared with you." Lefty has done just that, and then some.

19

Bill Curtis, b. 1925

MIAMI

Although retired from guiding, Bill Curtis can still be found most days working in the fly shop at Bass Pro Shops in Miami. On the walls hang pictures of Curtis posing with trophy fish and various anglers from times past. And we're talking a lot of time since he began guiding over a half-century ago.

Raised in Oklahoma, Curtis went on fishing trips with his uncle to New Mexico in 1934. He learned how to cast a fly rod at age nine on the San Juan River. Unlike most fidgety kids that age, Curtis remained focused and observed how fish reacted based on changing conditions as well as the proper way to hook and land them. Those experiences and memories popped into his mind often years later during the dangerous events of World War II.

Curtis flew reconnaissance missions over North Africa to help in the efforts to defeat Erwin Rommel, the formidable Desert Fox. At times his plane returned to the hanger riddled with AA holes, but that never rattled Curtis or tempered his eagerness for the next mission.

In 1948, Curtis moved to Miami and put his aerial photography skills to work as a profession at Pan American World Airways. "I was on contract for Pan Am, visiting all the places they flew to get pics for advertisements and their annual calendars," said Curtis.

However, his heart was leaning away from photography and more toward sport fishing, something he was enjoying with increasing regularity on his time off. Although Curtis went on many offshore trips, he preferred the shallower waters and flats of Biscayne Bay. He quickly

The Four Sportsmen (from left): Bill Curtis, Jerry Kirk, Ed Luise, and Stu Apte in 1957. Photo courtesy of Stu Apte and the International Game Fish Association.

came to cherish the special shoreline scenery and relative serenity compared to the rougher waters of offshore fishing.

"All the fly fishing I'd done up until coming to Miami was for trout in Minnesota, Colorado and California," he said. "I started going out on the Tamiami Trail Canal not far from Miami for bass and panfish. Then one day for the hell of it, I just kept driving west toward Everglades City and when I got there stopped at one of those wooden bridges.

"I couldn't believe my eyes at all the big snook under the bridge. Guys used to harpoon them, and at times you'd see the ones they missed swimming down the canal with gashes in their backs. When I saw all those snook, I figured out how to get at them with my fly rod. The action was particularly amazing in winter when the snook ran up the tidewaters into the canals."

Curtis helped tag snook for the University of Miami in 1958. "They had the very first research programs," Curtis said. "The tags were made of metal with numbers on them, and we'd attach the tags to the gills with Monel line. One day I tagged 28 snook and a friend tagged another

30. Cars were stopped on the Trail watching as we'd catch, tag and release all those fish."

With most of the snook averaging seven pounds, many went 15 or more in those days. Curtis took a 27-pound linesider but, according to him, "It stood as the Tamiami Trail record for only six weeks until Gene Crooks beat it with a 28-pounder."

"We also used to fish off Marco Island when you could drive up and down the beach," he recalled. "One of us would stand as the car moved along to spot schools of tarpon rolling within casting distance. That's when the area was completely undeveloped, with no hotels, houses, nothing at all to the end of the road."

Curtis started guiding in 1958 in Biscayne Bay. "People kept asking a friend of mine to take them out bonefishing," said Curtis. "He lived in Crandon Park on Key Biscayne and sometimes he'd ask me to take some of his customers on my boat. So many bonefish were around then. Gradually, as my guiding business built up, I slowed down on the photography work. Now and then I'd still do a few brochures for Miami Beach hotels, but gradually I became a full-time fishing guide.

"I'd been living close to the Miami airport in Virginia Gardens and didn't like it there, so I moved to Key Biscayne in 1958 since it was close to downtown Miami yet still fairly remote. My first house—two-bedrooms, one-bath—sold for only $9,500. Just that lot would be worth a million bucks today."

Bill Curtis will never forget the prolific bonefishing in Biscayne Bay in the 1960s and '70s. "A client of mine named Ron Hyde released 18 bones on fly in just one day, and even people who'd never caught any on fly could get six or seven. I didn't even have to go far from Crandon Park Marina; I'd just start poling at the first point and be in schools of bonefish no matter what the tide was doing."

Of the many celebrities Curtis fished over the years, the two most memorable are Don Johnson, star of the popular *Miami Vice* TV series at that time, and actor James Caan, who owned a condo on nearby Virginia Key.

"Don was nice, but he kept everyone at arm's length," said Curtis. "He liked being a celebrity. Jim was more open and like a regular guy. He loved to catch bones and I taught him how to fly fish."

He rejoiced in helping anglers catch bonefish, even on gray, cloudy days. Photo courtesy of the International Game Fish Association.

When Nixon, during his presidency, visited his residence on Key Biscayne—known then as the "Southern White House"—his press secretary, Ron Ziegler, would dash away from the compound and run around the bay with Curtis.

"I got Ron his first bonefish," said Curtis. "Same with Beebe Rebozo, who owned the first bank on Key Biscayne and was a close pal of Nixon's. Dignitaries visiting Nixon like Henry Kissinger would usually stay at the Key Biscayne Hotel."

Stu Apte, himself a greatly accomplished guide in the lower Keys and destined to be a prolific world-record holder, said he took "Wild and Woolly Willy" out for his first bonefish catch in Biscayne Bay.

"He was totally thrilled by the speed and strength of that fish," Apte said, "and as we know, he became one of the world's premier bonefish guides."

Curtis met Apte in the 1950s when the latter was on leave from the U.S. Navy. They'd been kibitzing in Mac's Tackle Shack in Miami, and it led to a friendship that has lasted to this day. They agreed to combine efforts in the big Metropolitan South Florida Fishing Tournament and also the Miami Beach Summer Fishing Tournament by taking turns poling each other—Apte poling Curtis for bonefish and vice versa for tarpon. As a result, each earned release trophies in the competitions.

"Back in those days, I was one of the few full-time guides covering Biscayne Bay," said Curtis. "Others of course guided here now and then, usually from the upper Keys or Ft. Lauderdale." One of Curtis' favorite fishing haunts is still shown on Miami-area charts as Curtis Point.

For all intents and purposes, Curtis was considered *the* authority from the 1950s through the '90s on bonefish, tarpon and permit around the Miami area. He's still sought out for advice and perspectives. His skiff became a common sight on any given day on the water. Curtis also enjoyed exploring other locations at times out of curiosity and adventure, including the Everglades, Palm Beach, Naples and the Ten Thousand Islands. It was on one of those trips with Apte that they ran into trouble.

"He ran a small skiff with about a 25-horsepower engine," Apte said. "We left for Chokoloskee and went inside through Turner River. We got so far up Turner River that we could see lights in the distance from trucks on the highway. And that's when his engine conked out."

They realized the danger of being in such a remote location; plus, it was getting colder by the minute. They threw a grapple-hook anchor ahead of the boat and slowly pulled themselves forward. "We did that all night long and by daybreak finally got near the mouth of Turner River until a boat towed us in," said Apte.

Curtis not only established himself as a great guide but also became an innovator. Of all his many improvements, the poling platform ranks at the top. "I tried standing on the motor cowling but could never really achieve good balance," he said. "I put a small stand over the engine by bolting it to the deck, and it worked pretty well. Other guides laughed at me, but before long all of them wanted to know how to build one."

Curtis helped pioneering skiff-builder Bob Hewes with designs of the Bonefisher flats boats. He also tested products for Ted Williams' tackle company. Curtis perfected the art of chumming for bonefish, which often produced fish even when sight-fishing conditions turned bad. He learned the best tides, current and bottom composition for optimum chumming, and pretty soon his anglers seldom returned to the dock without releases to their credit.

In the early days, Curtis would dice shrimp with a knife. In later years, he utilized a plastic vegetable chopper on his boat like the ones advertised on TV. It allegedly became comical to view Curtis from a distance as he balanced the contraption between his legs and repeatedly hit the top of the chopper with a fist.

In 1999, Curtis formed one of his greatest legacies, Bonefish & Tarpon Unlimited (now called Bonefish & Tarpon Trust) with businessman Tom Davidson. The non-profit organization based in Key Largo—for which I served as executive director for several years—now boasts an impressive coterie of research partners such as the current executive director, Dr. Aaron Adams. Its founding directors list reads like a Who's Who of the fishing industry, including Stu Apte, Billy Pate, Chico Fernandez, Dr. Guy Harvey, Lefty Kreh, Sandy Moret, Johnny Morris, Mark Sosin, Karl Wickstrom, Joan Salvato Wulff and dozens more. Activists by the score supported the work when the organization began and still do.

Even with all his impacts on sport fishing—including world records and appearances on a variety of TV fishing shows—his ego doesn't need attribution and massage. He acquires appreciation and respect quietly, one person at a time. Curtis does have detractors, however, because at times he can be very tough on his anglers. His wife, Adrienne, proved to be no exception when she hooked into a bonefish on her first outing with him. After the fish made its initial run, she began cranking the reel.

Curtis (standing far right) after a successful offshore trip in the formative years of the 1950s. Photo courtesy of the International Game Fish Association.

"Jerk on him harder," Bill yelled as he stopped the boat and moved toward her.

Adrienne, despite her diminutive frame, would have none of it. In an even louder level of volume, she turned to him and screeched, "Get to the back of the boat."

Bill did so immediately, and it was the first and last time he ever yelled at her when fishing. In fact, he forevermore treated women with much more tenderness than men.

With an impressive clientele built on consistently producing good catches of fish each trip, his manner sometimes didn't result in repeat business. Adrienne described the time Bill was fishing with a fellow from Nassau who claimed to be a lord. His son-in-law accompanied him, and the young man kept swinging his elbows to the side when casting, keeping him off balance and ruining cast after cast. Frustrated that the man wouldn't follow instructions, Bill took off his belt and wrapped it around the son-in-law's arms.

"They didn't like that," Adrienne said with a laugh. "And they never fished with Bill again."

But that was one of the exceptions to the rule. The late, famed broadcaster Curt Gowdy once told me about his first outing with Curtis. "I climbed aboard his boat *Grasshopper* in Miami, and from my very first cast to the last one, I felt totally exasperated. Bill was really tough, constantly giving me hell for this mistake or that.

"I went back home after that to Palm Beach and told my wife that I'll never fish with that SOB again.

"When she asked what I'd caught, I answered that we released four bonefish and two permit." At that point we sort of looked at each other blankly until she rhetorically asked, 'Curt, how often do you do that well on the flats?' The fact was that I seldom did, and a realization swept over me that Bill was simply trying to help me, to make me a better angler. Without any doubt, I improved a great deal after every trip I took with him."

Jeff Harkavy of Ft. Lauderdale, who's been instrumental in the development of Bonefish & Tarpon Trust and donates a lot of time on behalf of the International Game Fish Association, considers Curtis an unsung hero.

"He has a hardness to him coupled with a softness as well," observed Harkavy. "Like many captains, he needed to have things done a certain way on his boat, but at the end of the day, he does his job well and coaches anglers very effectively. Bill is certainly quick to call out a mistake if he thinks it will help on the next fishing situation, so he says what's on his mind and then moves on without attribution. It's not a matter of him proving he's the king of the mountain, as so often happens with other guides."

All of this is not to say Bill Curtis is a hard guy to get along with. Off the water his intensity lightens measurably and he's always the cordial conversationalist. Susan Cocking, outdoor writer for the *Miami Herald*, said that Bill once told her he values four things in life: "Friends, fighting, fishing and making love."

20

Joan Salvato Wulff, b. 1926

MIAMI

I walked amid a group of about 100 conference-goers to a large pond next to the International Game Fish Association's headquarters in Dania Beach, Florida. Joan Salvato Wulff paced the crowd slowly, the gallery exchanging small talk with her much the same as excited fans do with Jack Nicklaus, Michael Jordan, Dan Marino and other legends of sports.

I could only wonder if Joan would feel jaded doing yet another fly-casting exhibition. After all, who wouldn't be after thousands of them over the past 60 or so years?

As you probably can guess, that wasn't the case at all. Exuberant and articulate, she flipped 100-foot casts with muscle-memory ease, like an Indy driver instinctively shifting gears. You want distance into the wind? Joan showed how to do it. Having trouble roll casting, as an audience member admitted? She described a little trick that makes it easier.

After the exhibition, everyone clapped and murmured approvals. Joan smiled shyly, as if the first time she'd been the subject of applause. With such smooth style and sincere humbleness, she's simply impossible to dislike.

Joan has never failed to remember my name any of the times I've met her. Then again, the same goes for everyone she meets. Nothing escapes her ears or eyes, a skill acquired as a youngster in North Haledon, New Jersey.

At the age of 10, she borrowed her father's fly rod and made a bee-line for the nearby Oldham Pond, where the casting club met. Jimmy

Wulff showing her form in the 1952 National Casting Tournament in Flint, Michigan. Photo courtesy of Joan Salvato Wulff.

Salvato had brought his daughter with him here on occasion, and she'd also snuck down to the dock on her own. Joan watched the men working their fly rods, some of them fumbling but most very adept. Some styles were smooth and tight, others jerky and loopy.

Emulating what she thought were the better casting techniques, out went the fly—and half the rod too. The young girl gasped. She'd never attached the ferrules of a fly rod before, so she didn't know how loose they're often kept when the rod isn't in use. Joan ran home and a friend from next door came to her aid, fishing the rod tip out of the lake with a garden rake.

Her dad, when he got home and heard the story, did not become angry; instead, he was duly impressed. His daughter wanted to learn how to fly fish—what could be wrong with that? He not only permitted

Joan to take up the sport, he actively encouraged it. In those days, sons and daughters pretty much did what Dad said, period; if the old man was opposed to something, then that generally spelled the end of any such activity. The fact that her dad supported the whole idea wasn't just convenient, it was crucial in being able to go forward.

It didn't take long for the young girl's gifts of extraordinary coordination and timing to amaze her father. She accompanied him to the next gathering of the Paterson Casting Club, and from then on there was no holding her back.

Jimmy Salvato owned Paterson Rod & Gun, so the advantage to Joan was his involvement in the outdoor industry from the get-go. He raised hunting dogs, and their world consisted of fishing, hunting and puppies. Her mother, Alexina—born in Scotland and an Ellis Island immigrant during World War I—handled the era's traditional woman's role of raising the kids (Joan had two brothers) and taking care of the house. Dad taught the boys how to shoot a .22 rifle, but not Joan—after all, she was a girl.

"Being bypassed like that was something all females had to accept and handle back then," said Joan. "It wasn't so much Dad's fault as much as just the prevailing attitude with all families."

Still, Joan contained her envy and turned it into determination to succeed no matter her gender. In 1937, when very few females fly fished at all, Joan captured a local fly-casting contest. At age 12 she competed in regional tournaments while cultivating a similar level of interest in dancing. In fact, Joan was so good at the latter that she taught tap-dancing classes. The ingrained sense of timing needed to dance and fly fish spilled over to both pursuits.

"You need to coordinate all portions of your body," she was to later say. And indeed, you can't achieve a proper dancing balance using just the bottom half of your body; nor can you maximize fly-casting distance when involving only the top half of your body. According to Wulff: "It's timing . . . you cast from your fingertips to your toes."

Joan continued to hone her skills. At 16, she nailed the top honors at a Women's Dry Fly Accuracy event and went on to win 17 national casting titles between 1943 and 1960. These competitions, such as the international bait-casting contest in London in 1948, pitted her against

A simple jack crevalle caught on fly in the Florida Keys ignited a passion for flats fishing. Photo by Tom McNally, courtesy of Joan Salvato Wulff.

men as well as women, and not just with fly gear. Joan became the first woman to win the Fisherman's Distance Event in 1951, her cast of 131 feet defeating an otherwise all-men field.

Joan credits William Taylor with really taking her talents to a new level prior to 1947, when her success really gained steam. Taylor, the Paterson Casting Club's best caster, could effortlessly cast 150 feet. A rod builder, his timing was perfect, his form impeccable, and Joan desperately wanted to emulate that talent. Taylor constructed a light nine-foot bamboo rod for Joan that was very stiff. It allowed her to pick up the line faster and make a surer back cast: shooting forward, the fly zipping through the air like never before.

Joan lived in Florida in the early 1950s and again during much of the '60s, mostly in Miami and Coral Gables. She bought a condo in 1999 in Islamorada and still maintains it. Her first taste of Florida fishing occurred in 1950 near Tavernier in the Keys. Armed with a heavy bamboo rod, she caught only a jack. But just that one experience on the flats evoked something she hadn't felt in a long time: a hunting urge.

Fishing the flats involves a good measure of careful observation, stealth, stalking, taking your shots—just like afield. Joan departed with a whole new respect for flats fishing. Learning the skills needed to successfully hunt bonefish, permit, tarpon and the like kindled her psyche and stuck with her forevermore.

Joan recalled an event she fished in Marathon in the Florida Keys, something to give her a taste of saltwater competition. It was a bonefish tournament based out of "Ye Ole Feshin Hole" (sic) tackle shop.

"It was a spin-tackle tournament and I fished with Johnny and Wilma Brantner, the owners of the shop," said Joan. "Despite all my casting titles, nobody quite knew what to think of me as an angler. Luckily, I did well in the event and gained their respect."

Even so, the breaking down of preconceived notions about women fishing had already been slowly changing since Bonnie Smith, Frankee Albright and Beulah Cass—three sisters—took up guiding in the Florida Keys in the 1940s. But even that was looked upon by some as mainly just taking up the slack in the absence of men during the war. With so much stacked against her, Joan Salvato, who got married in 1954 to Walter Cummings after meeting him at the West Palm Beach Fishing Club, dropped the silly notion of making a living by doing anything associated with fishing.

She and her husband became part of the crew on a 56-foot schooner for 14 months, and thereafter she took a secretarial job for an insurance company in Granby, Connecticut. This lifestyle wasn't at all what Joan had dreamed about when she watched the fly casters in Paterson. But in 1959, her big break arrived.

The Garcia Corporation, based in Teaneck, New Jersey, recognized Joan's unique drawing power. She was attractive and shapely—yes, a sexist factor that likely played no small part in the decision to hire her. Joan could cast a fly rod better than just about any man. People liked

Plug casting the mangrove edges. Photo by Lefty Kreh, courtesy of Joan Salvato Wulff.

her, and Joan liked people. For $4,000 per year, Joan would work 100 days, doing seminars, attending trade shows and talking up Garcia. That was especially a good thing since she and Walter had their second child in 1962.

When Ted Williams made her an offer to join him at Sears as a spokesperson, Garcia sweetened her deal. Finally, Joan was making a living as a fly caster, something no one back in North Haledon or Paterson would have ever envisioned.

Also in 1962, Joan moved back to Florida full time. During this time she cultivated her joy of saltwater flats fishing and finally got a fly to a tarpon. She felt that special rush so often experienced during that initial experience with a silver king.

"During the fight I spotted a knot in my fly line and did something Lee Wulff had suggested to me years before when we'd met: Let off the pressure so the fish rests," she said. "That's exactly what I did, and the brief line slack enabled me to remove the knot. I later released that tarpon."

Speaking of Lee Wulff, in 1967, when Joan's union with Cummings was at a dead end, she married Wulff—a most interesting fellow in his own right. Born and raised in Alaska, somewhat embracing a Bohemian

A nice bass released near Tallahassee in 1993. Photo by Neil Marvin, courtesy of Joan Salvato Wulff.

philosophy that artists who have lived on the left bank of the Seine River in Paris tend to pick up, Wulff was much older than Joan. Nonetheless, their marriage and partnership led to the formation of a fly-fishing kingdom. Every bit a team, they were contracted by Garcia Corporation to represent the company worldwide for $30,000 per year—a considerable contract in those years.

In 1979 they formed the internationally acclaimed Wulff School of Fly Fishing on the Beeverkill River in New York's Catskill Mountains, and for 25 years they were unquestionably America's most famous fishing couple. Everyone knew the Wulffs and knew of their school, with their reputations at the top rung of the fishing circles and industry.

Capt. Duane Baker in Islamorada has been guiding Wulff off and on for the past 11 years. "She taught my son how to fly cast a few years ago," said Baker, "and I've seen her catch tarpon, bonefish and lots of other species as an angler on my boat. But Joan is way past the level of just being anxious to catch another fish—she's all about going out and having a great day."

Wulff released her largest bonefish, estimated at nine pounds, with Baker in 2005. "It was a single swimmer that wasn't mudding or tailing," Baker recalled. "She led it perfectly, the bone ate the fly and she played it just right."

Longtime Miami guide Bill Curtis knew Wulff before she married Lee. "Joan came down here with her dad and fished with me," said Curtis. "I knew he owned a tackle shop or such in Paterson, New Jersey, so he knew a lot about fishing and lures.

"Joan was super at casting. She could reach fish with a fly rod that most everyone else would pass up. Even 125 feet or more, the fish would be in her zone. You have no idea how nice that is to a guide in contrast to constantly putting people right on top of fish and they still can't reach them. She's a real joy to guide on the water not only because of her casting but because she knows what to do with a fish once it's on the line, too."

The encroaching years simply don't deter Joan Salvato Wulff. Although her rise in prominence represented a huge boon to greater female interest in fly fishing and fishing in general, she's been an innovator and teacher for anglers of both sexes. At age 78 she caught her largest-ever tarpon on fly, a 125-pounder on a 10-weight rod with Capt. Tim Klein in the Keys. She maintains a heavy schedule of appearances, still conducting fly-casting demonstrations and fishing all over the world. In 2007, Wulff was inducted into the International Game Fish Association's Hall of Fame.

"It's been a dream life for me," Wulff said. "All I've ever wanted to do is cast and dance, and that's exactly what I've done."

Renowned fishing writer Bob Stearns remembers well a fly-casting demonstration at the Miami Sportfishing Club before she married Lee Wulff. "At first we noticed how attractive she was, but then her casting simply blew everyone away," said Stearns. "One of the club members afterwards told me, 'You know, she can cast better with one hand than I can with two.'

"She's the first woman I ever met who could fish and cast with as much—and usually more—of a skill level than men, and all the while conducting herself with a lot of class."

Long live Joan Salvato Wulff.

21

Vic Dunaway, b. 1928

DUNNELLON

We can all name at least one person in our circle of friends who is forever upbeat, easy to be around and always likeable. After spending any measure of time with Vic Dunaway, that's exactly how you'd describe him.

Former Key West fishing guide Harlan Franklin, who went to Florida State University with Dunaway in the late 1940s and became lifelong friends with him, summed up his pal's demeanor. "Vic and I were walking the dock of a hotel in Apalachicola, checking out the boats, fish and fishermen. We paused at the cleaning table where a couple of Georgia visitors stood with three small jacks. One of them asked us if they're good to eat.

"Before I could say 'No,' Vic told them, 'If you know the right way to clean those kind of fish, certain parts of it are edible.' What happened next was pure Dunaway: He took their knife and proceeded to clean all three fish for two complete strangers. Now how many people would do that?"

Al Pflueger Jr., a man of taxidermy fame and a world-class angler, became close friends with Dunaway. The journalist and the tournament champion became a natural fit. They fished a lot together, with Dunaway often depicting their exploits and Pflueger's extreme skills in the *Miami Herald*. When Dunaway later became editor of *Florida Sportsman* in 1969, the two men organized seminars and teamed up to establish the immensely popular *Florida Sportsman Fishing Charts* for regions of the state.

This 28-pound cobia caught in 1960 on a wreck off Key West was the new fly-casting record at the time. Photo courtesy of Vic Dunaway.

"Nobody could tell stories funnier than him," said Pflueger. "Once we drove from Miami to Tampa and back—an eight-hour roundtrip—and he told joke after joke the entire way. Frankly, some of his jokes aren't all that funny, but the way he tells them makes you laugh anyway."

Dunaway grew up in the Panama Canal Zone as a military brat, later moving with the family to the Florida Panhandle, where the fishing bug consumed him. Dunaway obtained a degree at FSU and went on to work for newspapers in Georgia. The sprinkling of interesting fishing stories in his columns began to draw notice. His folksy and compelling writing style reached the attention of top brass at the *Miami Herald,* and Dunaway landed the prestigious job of fishing editor.

The combination in the 1960s of Jim Martenhoff as the *Herald's* boating editor and Dunaway covering the angling scene produced immensely popular outdoor pages that few other newspapers have achieved before or since.

Certainly, the high-profile status of the *Herald* as Florida's largest daily newspaper—covering a region bursting at the seams with fishing and boating interest—greatly elevated his podium. At the same time, Dunaway's to-the-point style enraptured anglers of all skill levels, thus ratcheting up the credibility of the *Herald* to the burgeoning sport-fishing industry. It was a perfect symbiosis for Dunaway that would play out again for him in the 1970s and '80s in the magazine trade.

While the *Miami Herald* had long served as a prominent outlet for the voices of recreational fishing and boating columnists—including notable predecessors like Erl Roman, Allen Corson, Jim Hardie, and, more recently, Susan Cocking—none of them gained the popularity of Dunaway. His columns, never self-aggrandizing, nonetheless cast him in the spotlight as an authority and spokesman.

In addition to the beneficial relationship he enjoyed with the *Herald,* Dunaway found that the emergence of television in the 1950s and '60s as the public's major entertainment and information source worked in his favor as well. To say Dunaway came along at a perfect confluence of all these mediums is an understatement. Public interest increased exponentially as TV episodes flashed the drama of tarpon and marlin battles directly into the living rooms of America. People who never before had even heard of such species suddenly became fans of their

Dunaway's 250-pound black marlin came aboard during an exploratory trip out of Club de Pesca, Pinas Bay, Panama. Photo courtesy of Vic Dunaway.

competitive nature as well as the anglers possessing the skills to best them. Fly fishermen in particular took on the persona of artists with their ultra-specialized gear and fancy casts. Competitions between fishing guides and the top outdoor journalists of the day aired on Curt Gowdy's *The American Sportsman,* and a series by Philip Wylie unfolded about the adventures of "Crunch and Des" aboard the *Poseidon.*

During this formative time, Dunaway's columns ventured well beyond mundane reports of recent catches and tournament results. He became a news breaker, the discoverer of fertile new fishing grounds, a teller of real sagas that turned his experiences into must reads for all anglers within the reach of the *Herald* and even beyond. It's no wonder that Dunaway's expertise as a newspaper columnist drew plenty of praise and awards in addition to a huge circle of contacts. Besides his fishing forays around Miami, Dunaway wrote about trips to the Everglades, the Tamiami Trail, the Ten Thousand Islands, Lake Okeechobee and the Florida Keys. He was the man.

Key West would become one of Dunaway's most remarkable fishing destinations. Prior to 1960, only a handful of people outside of Key West knew about the stupendous fishing resources of the area. It wasn't until Dunaway's depictions of his own successful trips there ended up in newsprint that Key West became a hot topic of interest at fishing clubs, marinas and tackle stores from Palm Beach to Miami.

As word got out, anglers began stampeding to Key West like the frenzy of a gold rush. Most returned with great tales of not only their own fishing exploits but also of the quaintness of the Southernmost City itself. The brouhaha continued to build and attract even more visitors wanting their share of the action and fun.

Dunaway's role in the recognition of Key West and the subsequent impact of this on its tourism didn't go without notice by the city's brass. On February 16, 1960—by proclamation of the mayor at the time, Delio Cobo—"Vic Dunaway Day" resulted in a parade, banquet and the awarding of a key to the city. Through all this, Dunaway maintained in his typically humble manner that the heightened interest in Key West would have happened anyway. That may be true, but there's no question that at the very least he fast-forwarded the process.

As the 1960s progressed and Dunaway's prestige kept increasing, another *Herald* writer working as an investigative reporter merged a passion for fishing with a business plan that would fill a niche.

Enter Karl Wickstrom, who ultimately left the *Herald* in the late 1960s to publish an in-flight magazine for National Airlines. That contract would provide the seed money to launch *Florida Sportsman* magazine.

Dunaway had been thinking of retiring from the newspaper business around this time as well, but only to write children's books. When Wickstrom—a fan of Dunaway's fishing columns—outlined the magazine's business model to him, it all made perfect sense. In the first place, the whole idea sounded plausible, and second, Dunaway thought

In June 1962, he bested this 577-pound bluefin tuna out of Cat Cay in the Bahamas. Photo courtesy of Vic Dunaway.

this could be a way to expand his fishing experiences and appeal to a wider audience.

Dunaway took the job as editor, and as 25 dramatic years unfolded, he and Wickstrom became the driving forces in molding *Florida Sportsman* into the veritable bible of the Sunshine State's freshwater and saltwater angling communities. In fact, the magazine quickly grew into the largest regional publication in the nation, typically brimming in the halcyon days with 300-plus pages each month and packed with contributions by the state's best outdoor writers and authorities.

I joined the staff of *Florida Sportsman* in 1993 as associate editor and later became managing editor. My hiring occurred several months before Dunaway opted in 1994 for a bit more peace and quiet. He'd remain as the publication's premier columnist and article writer, but he'd be free of all the tedious editing chores. He thus exited the overcrowded bustle of Miami in favor of a less hectic lifestyle upstate and the new title of senior editor.

While the timing of things negated our becoming close friends, I did get to hang out a bit with Dunaway prior to his departure. We enjoyed an editorial trip together to Cancun, and before coming aboard full time as an editor, I conducted a series of fishing seminars around the state in partnership with *Florida Sportsman*. Dunaway agreed to become the headline instructor at each location. As always, his humorous style and easy-to-follow delivery won over the audiences.

Just as Dunaway became a celebrity by way of his *Miami Herald* and *Florida Sportsman* gigs, he himself became the object of many interviews. On such occasions his wit captured center stage. I fondly remember such an occasion when Dunaway was a guest on a radio show I cohosted with Rick Berry in Key Largo in the early 1990s. Knowing that tackle manufacturers showered Dunaway with numerous unsolicited freebies in the hopes he'd refer to one of their models as his favorite, I asked his reel of choice.

"Any given brand," he deadpanned.

Wannabe writers also tugged at Dunaway's shirtsleeves for tips on how they could follow in his footsteps. With an impish grin he'd reply, "You need three things to succeed as an outdoors writer: A typewriter, a camera and a spouse who works."

Even when he writes about getting into a jam on a fishing trip, Dunaway always manages to end the story with a humorous twist. Take, for example, the time his engine broke down while he and a buddy fished a desolate shoreline in Florida's Ten Thousand Islands.

With no civilization within 30 miles and other boats few and far between, the situation seemed headed for disaster. As dusk approached, the men set up a lean-to and Dunaway caught a trout. He fashioned a campfire out of driftwood and they munched the fillets, washing them down with melted ice from the cooler. The balance of that sleepless night involved frantic hand fanning to stave off endless waves of frenzied mosquitoes.

As the sky lightened with the approaching dawn, the sound of an airplane turned despair into hope. Dunaway's friend quickly grabbed a piece of driftwood and scrawled three huge letters in the sand: H-E-P.

The plane flew overhead and kept going. Dunaway threw his hands up in disgust. "So much for getting help," he said, sighing. "They must just figure we think we're really cool." Fortunately the pilot circled back for another look, allowing Dunaway time for a quick rewrite and a rescue.

Karl Wickstrom's respect for Dunaway is boundless, particularly when it comes to his ability to tactfully handle even touchy family situations.

"Anglers would kid him sometimes about his eating most any species, but Vic got the last laugh by enjoying great dishes that others passed up.

"One day he came home with the shoulder section of an amberjack that many folks turned their noses up at. And Vic's daughter was in the I-hate-fish stage. 'Well, I'll fix veal parmagiana then,' he told her, secretly substituting a slab of AJ. Later, she announced, 'Dad, that's the best veal I've ever eaten.'"

Harlan Franklin claims to be one of the very few to have seen the glib Dunaway at a temporary loss for words. "We were fishing a hole in a creek north of Cape Sable," said Franklin. "Vic was sitting on the bow, me on the seat behind the console. I hooked a fish and pulled up a small jack that I held a few feet above the water. At that moment a four-foot blacktip shark shot up after the jack, but missed. The shark flew over

Vic Dunaway in 2008, at age 80. Photo courtesy of Vic Dunaway.

the console with its teeth popping and landed just past the other side of the boat with a huge splash. Vic and I were dumbfounded, neither of us finding words to fit our shock at that moment. When we finally did talk, we wondered what chaos would have ensued if the shark had landed in the boat with us."

Sue Cocking, the chief outdoor writer for the *Miami Herald* for the past 14 years, met Dunaway in 1986 in Key West right after he'd come out with his best-selling book *Baits, Rigs & Tackle*.

"He's easygoing and affable, but don't let that fool you," said Cocking. "When I first started working at the *Miami Herald*, my boss at the time spoke of Vic. He told me that when he gave the employment test to Vic that all employees at the *Herald* have to take, Vic scored higher than almost anyone who ever worked there."

Even anglers of legendary status often benefited from Dunaway's vast experience. Sam Griffin, the renowned guide and lure maker from Lake Okeechobee, received an unexpected tutorial on plastic worms.

"Vic joined me for a fishing trip on Lake O, and I opened my tackle box containing top-water lures and spoons," Griffin recalled. Dunaway nodded approvingly but showed Griffin a variety of soft-plastic lures.

"I just shook my head," said Griffin, "but Vic went on to catch several big bass, including a seven-pounder. A few days later a picture of it appeared with his column in the *Miami Herald*. You could see that dang plastic worm hanging out of its mouth, but thankfully not my face," Griffin said with a laugh.

I once shared lunch with Dunaway and a fellow who often advertised in *Florida Sportsman*. As editors, we never broached ad sales, thanks to Karl Wickstrom's wise edict about keeping the editorial process out of the sales arena. Nonetheless, our tablemate seemed intent on expressing why he hadn't been running ads recently, stating that "business has been so darn good we've got a huge backload of orders."

"That's great," said Dunaway with a foxy grin. "Then you need to run an ad telling people not to call you."

In keeping with true humorists, Dunaway's remarks often poke fun at the human nature of fellow anglers. For instance, he noted that waving frantically at passing boaters when your engine conks out frequently results in them pretending they don't see you and speeding off in another direction. Dunaway then offered two sure-fire remedies for this: "Put your hook in the anchor line and get a bend in the rod as if you've got a big one on, or lie on the deck so it appears no one is on the boat and wait until someone comes over to steal something."

Herb Allen, former fishing editor of the *Tampa Tribune*, told of a day when he and Dunaway headed back to the dock after fishing in the Gulf of Mexico. "As our boat passed a cul-de-sac teeming with rolling tarpon, we caught and released one silver king after the other for half an hour," said Allen. "Sometimes a poon would hit the fly and we'd miss the hook-up, and before stripping it back to the boat, another would nail it. It's the most magical moment of compacted action I've ever enjoyed."

Dunaway remembers many of those fantastic outings, but he's now content to just relax when fishing and not worry about the weight of his stringer or the number of releases. He still writes books occasionally and keeps up with *Florida Sportsman* articles from his hometown of Dunnellon. Life's slower than it was in those hectic 12-hour days as a newspaper and magazine icon, and that's just fine with him.

Karl Wickstrom took a measure of the essence of Dunaway, then and now. "Vic is the ultimate combination of all-around outdoors expertise and writing ability, pervaded by a sense of humor that has him ready to laugh at an instant's notice. With his know-how and ability mixed with an amazing talent at the typewriter, Vic had more reason than anyone to be a snob about himself, but he never blew his own horn. Others did it for him."

22

Stu Apte, b. 1930

ISLAMORADA

In my opinion, a better tarpon angler never lived. Before I met him, someone remarked that Stu Apte could put a 100-pound-plus tarpon to boat side in a matter of minutes. I didn't believe it, but that all changed the first time we went fishing. At one point Apte hooked into a really huge tarpon in the 130- to 140-pound class on 12-pound fly tippet. He played that fish like a boxer taking apart an opponent, moving here and there around the boat, leveraging the rod in rhythm to the tarpon's movement, changing pressure by the tiniest degrees to actually program the fish behavior, and wielding his down-and-dirty method to finish off the poon near the boat—and he was 58 years old at the time.

I looked at my watch and realized that 11 minutes had elapsed between the hook-up and the time the big tarpon began floating submissively on its side next to the boat; Apte patiently revived it until its tail waved us goodbye.

Since then I've seen Apte whip everything from bonefish to billfish on fly and light tackle, and he's like a lion slaying a lamb. No mercy, no let up, 100-percent concentration, ultimate pressure on the fish without breaking the tippet. He's a gifted tarpon tamer, pure and simple.

"There can be no stalemate in a fish fight," said Apte. "If the fish isn't taking out line, you need to be pumping and winding to within the very limit of your tackle and line."

Competitiveness has always been a hallmark of Apte's. Raised in Miami, his heroes didn't involve comic book characters or famous athletes but instead were fishing guides. He successfully fought a tarpon at the age of 12, and it sparked a profound energy in him. After attending the

This world-record silver king dragged Apte into the water twice on May 16, 1961. The 148 ½-pounder caught by Joe Brooks stood as a record for 10 years until Apte broke it himself. Photo courtesy of Stu Apte.

University of Miami, he became a jet fighter pilot in the U.S. Navy and later took the controls as well for Pan American Airlines.

The latter job gave him international access to virgin fishing waters, his trusty fly rods always stashed behind the cockpit for layovers. Apte started guiding in the late 1950s out of Little Torch Key on his skiff *Mom's Worry*. Within a few years, as his client list expanded and his reputation spread, it became a full-time pursuit.

Far from being content to merely guide, Apte became an innovator, devising his own tarpon flies—one of which graced the front of a U.S. postage stamp in 1991—and modifying knots to better suit fly leaders. His down-and-dirty technique for more quickly tiring a fish was adopted by other top anglers.

Giant tarpon became Apte's passion, and he led not only his clients to world records but himself as well. In 1961, Apte guided Joe Brooks to a world-record poon that at the time was the largest ever caught on fly. And once while fishing with Capt. Ralph Delph in Homosassa, Apte set two tarpon records the same day—one in the morning that he then bested that afternoon.

"In my early years, Ted Williams taught me how to pole a boat," said Apte. The student quickly became a leading pro. He could identify where and when fish could be found, how to best make the presentations to draw strikes and the proper techniques to land them as quickly as possible.

Although tarpon are clearly his forte, Apte cannot be considered only a flats master. Setting more than 44 world records—a conservative estimate to be sure—some of his non-tarpon marks include the two longest standing fly records: a 58-pound dolphin in 1964 and a 136-pound Pacific sailfish the following year, both on 12-pound tippet.

His 1976 book *Stu Apte's Fishing in the Florida Keys and Flamingo* remains a best seller among fishing titles. Apte also penned his memoirs, *Of Wind and Tides,* which detail his adventurous life as a naval aviator, Pan Am pilot and fishing guide. He continues to write articles, produce videos, appear on TV shows, design skiffs and develop fly-fishing gear.

Apte's strong-willed personality at times brought me to the point of wanting to strangle him. One day during a shoot for our video series

In the 1950s, Ted Williams tutored Apte in the ways of flats fishing, those lessons serving as a solid starting point for a successful guiding career. Photo courtesy of Stu Apte and Ted Williams Family Enterprises, Inc.

Saltwater Fly Fishing from A to Z, I brought along a batch of peanut butter-and-jelly sandwiches, with each in a plastic bag. We stashed them in a cooler in Capt. Ben Taylor's skiff rather than the camera boat in which I was riding.

On the run to Flamingo from Islamorada, I looked back and saw Apte munching on one of the sandwiches. At the time I thought nothing of it. About 20 minutes later as we staked out at our destination, I casually asked Apte to toss me a sandwich.

"No," he said, "we need to start looking for fish."

I blanched. I did a slow burn and after a silence repeated my request. He again refused.

"Hey, I *made* the damn sandwiches," I said, the smoke billowing out my ears.

"You do what the hell I tell you to do," snapped Apte, looking me straight in the eye.

I spouted a couple of words for him, and they weren't "Merry Christmas." At that stage, Apte couldn't hold back a grin any longer.

"You're sooo predictable," he said with a facetious grin. I knew I'd been had as he tossed me one of the plastic bags from the cooler.

We also share an ongoing personal joke. While in Mazatlan, Mexico, in 1990 for more footage in the video series, we took a cab back to our hotel after dinner the first night. In broken Spanish I asked the driver about a good place in town for a few drinks. Evidently, the fact that we enjoyed cocktails implied we might also have an interest in something else.

"My American friends," replied the cabbie, his teeth the size of piano keys, "I will introduce you to some *semi*-virgins. They are very special. By day they work as secretaries of banks and other *muy importante* businesses. At night they entertain my very select *amigos*."

At first we thought it to be a joke, but he was dead serious. After insisting on simply a return to our hotel, we couldn't stop referring to "semi-this" and "semi-that" for the rest of the trip. Even today when I call him, he's liable to say, "Hello, my semi-friend." If you should run into Apte, tell him you want to be his semi-friend and watch that big smile engulf his face.

Legendary flats guide Bill Curtis fished often with Apte in the late 1950s. "When Stu started guiding a year before I did, I loaned him my flats boat when he went to Little Torch Key. He had more of a bay-type boat, but I ran a little 15 ½-foot fiberglass skiff with a flat bottom. It was great around the flats, but once it got out in choppy water, you'd might as well unbutton your shirt and pants and take a crap when you got home."

Because of his many accomplishments and common title as a "legendary" angler, I wanted Apte to meet Richard Stanczyk, owner of Bud N' Mary's Marina in Islamorada and a long-standing friend. Stanczyk readily agreed and invited us on a bonefish trip. It was a windy day as we rocked and rolled while exploring a variety of flats in Florida Bay. It wasn't until many years later that Stanczyk would admit he was totally lost at one point.

"My plan involved running to Nine Mile Bank, but when we got there I realized we missed the tide," said Stanczyk. "The sky was gray and the mirroring made it nearly impossible to see bottom. I ran to Buchanan Bank but became totally disoriented. Being the first time I'd met and fished with Stu, I was nervous but didn't want to look like an idiot and say, 'I'm lost.' And—miraculously—that's when I spotted the fish."

On the opposite end of a long flat and against both the wind and current, Stanczyk poled like a madman toward the distant bonefish. Most guides don't even bother to look upwind, much less chase after them, but Stanczyk was afraid he wouldn't see anymore bones. He poled and poled, until suddenly the boat went over a sandy hump on the flat and got stuck. Out of the boat jumped Stanczyk, mightily pushing and pulling the skiff with Apte and me aboard until he could free the hull. Once accomplishing that, after considerable effort and with sweat drenching his face, he got back into the boat and climbed onto the platform for more relentless poling.

Stanczyk—no spring chicken at the time—finally moved us all the way to those fish so we could get a cast. Apte hooked up first and then I did the same, a nice double-header release.

Apte turned to Stanczyk, cocked his head slightly to the left as he sometimes does when stating something emphatic, and said, "Richard, you might not be the greatest bonefish guide in the world, but you're one of the hardest working I've ever seen."

Stanczyk, relieved and proud all at the same time, still vividly recalls the backhanded compliment.

Lamar Underwood, who served as editor-in-chief of both *Sports Afield* and *Outdoor Life* magazines, did not find it surprising when eventually his path crossed with Apte's. They never ended up fishing together, but from time to time over the decades they shared Happy Hour moments—and an unforgettable quail hunt.

"The trip was noteworthy because we didn't use dogs," said Underwood. "Instead, we charged up a hill in Arizona carrying over-under doubles, looking to flush what looked like a hundred quail flowing up

Posing for a TV segment, clockwise from top left: Al McClane, Joe Brooks (who caught the 120-pound tarpon), Stu Apte, and Jimmie Albright. Photo courtesy of Stu Apte.

the summit. We ran as if scaling San Juan Hill, and we finally reached the top, gasping like beached whales. The ridge-top exploded with birds, hurtling blue forms everywhere.

"We emptied our guns, watching the birds sail away toward nooks and crannies in the desert below the ridgeline. Stu beamed, as did I, both of us overcome by the excitement of the moment. He knew we'd just experienced something special together."

I can recount a good number of special moments with Apte as well. During the filming for our *Saltwater Fly Fishing from A to Z* videos, I caught my first fish on fly with him. We were aboard one of the *Star Fleet* boats out of Mazatlan on a steamy summer day with no clouds

A Costa Rica filming trip, featuring (from left) actor Jason Miller, who co-starred in *The Exorcist*; Curt Gowdy; camp owner Henry Norton; and Apte. Photo courtesy of Stu Apte.

in the sky, not even a whisp of breeze, and the sun just baking us. We soon raised a big Pacific sailfish in the trolling spread, and Stu teased the spindle beak behind the boat.

Just as we'd talked about and practiced, Apte screamed "neutral" and the Mexican captain took the boat out of gear. Apte yanked the mullet from the water and my blue-and-white foam popper hit right in front of the sailfish. He turned on it in textbook-perfect form and I set the hook several times with the 16-pound tippet.

The fish nearly pulled the rod from my hands. "Damn, Stu," I exclaimed. "Why couldn't I have started out on fly with a little jack or ladyfish?"

"Shut up and face your fish," he commanded, and I did exactly that. This wasn't the time for levity; it was time to fight. After 10 minutes I felt like a giant ice cube melting away in the Mexican sun, and the thought that I might toss my cookies over the side as the cameraman ran tape made me that much more appreciative of edited footage.

After several more runs and frantic pumping and winding, Stu coached me well enough that I could finally get the release. The crew guessed its weight at around 105 pounds. Hyperventilating like the out-of-shape wuss I was, I've little doubt that without Apte in my corner during that bout, the fish would've licked me.

Capt. Ralph Delph of Key West, who certainly ranks as one of the best guides ever, has witnessed Apte's angling prowess up close on many occasions.

"Stu totally amazes me," said Delph. "Some guys slow down with age, but he never does. Nobody I've ever known can fight and pressure a fish like Stu. He unquestionably attained the honor for many years of being the fly-fishing king of the tarpon world."

He's recently conquered something even greater than any big fish: cancer. Diagnosed with both lymphoma and leukemia about 10 years ago—either type considered fatal—the diseases are in total remission today. Most people undergoing the intense radiation and chemical treatments show the harsh effects, but Stuart C. Apte looks as vibrant as ever. It just goes to show how tough a competitor he really is.

23

Billy Pate, b. 1930

ISLAMORADA

I saw the excited gleam in his eyes at the dock at MacRae's Marina and will never forget it. Billy Pate was about to leave on yet another foray for tarpon off Homosassa. Each such day has brought the promise of another world record, the anticipation of battle with a triple-digit-size silver king. Into the skiff he went and down the Homosassa River he floated, all the while searching the shallow shoreline waters.

Pate jumped several poons that day weighing less than 100 pounds, but none stayed on the hook long. No matter—the next morning that same fire gripped him. It's been that way ever since he left his desk in the carpet-weaving business in South Carolina to fulfill his real passion: saltwater fly fishing. His family's financial success allowed him the wherewithal to travel the world and set records with a fly rod, and that's exactly what he did.

I didn't really know Pate that well until I served as executive director of Bonefish & Tarpon Unlimited (now called Bonefish & Tarpon Trust) for several years starting in 2000. Based out of Key Largo, the group sponsors tagging research on its namesake species, and Pate is one of the founding members. As the years unfolded and I worked more and more with Pate, we became good friends. I helped him learn the rudiments of the Internet, chatted occasionally on the phone with him about various personal and business matters, and came to appreciate his gentlemanly manner. His wife, Yana, is an absolute treasure—she formerly taught piano at the University of Kiev in the Ukraine—and she's a huge source of support for her hubby. It's wonderful that he's

Pate, with a
bent rod in
blue water and
his trademark
wide-brim
straw hat.
Photo courtesy
of Billy Pate.

found such a committed and loving partner as he hits the octogenarian age.

Billy Pate, one quickly discovers, is a likeable guy, and there's virtually nothing he likes talking about more than tarpon. Discuss the stock market and in minutes he switches the topic to tarpon; mention your favorite football team's latest foibles and that topic won't last long either. He's a tarpon man, tried and true, through and through. Which is understandable: His 188-pound tarpon caught off Homosassa, Florida, in 1982 stood as the world record on fly for over 20 years.

A feat even more remarkable than any of his world records took place in the mid-1980s, and it's something not likely to be duplicated by any mortal. He somehow managed to land a 173-pound tarpon completely by himself from start to finish. No one else maneuvered the boat or even helped him swing the huge fish onto the deck, though plenty of witnesses were on hand to substantiate the spectacle.

It so happened that Pate didn't have a guide that day but just didn't feel like staying home. So, he stood on the casting tower of his skiff using foot controls on the two electric motors. It's a bit tricky to do this, but he'd heard about fish being present in good numbers and, difficult or not, he wanted to see for himself what might be cruising the shallow near-shore waters.

Pate ran about five miles south of the river mouth, at which point he spotted a dozen silver kings swimming slowly toward him in the four-foot depths. He turned off the electrics and made a cast to the lead fish because that's often the largest in a pod. The poon garbaged the fly and he made several firm hook-sets. It immediately jumped completely out of the water and in turn Pate's heart practically did likewise out of his chest. At first glance the tarpon looked even bigger than the one he'd caught for his existing world record of 188 pounds.

It took off in a northerly direction and the rest of the school followed right behind. Pate turned on the electric motors in hot pursuit, putting as much pressure on the fish as he could on 16-pound-test tippet. Unfortunately, the tarpon headed directly toward a large group of skiffs, and a number of the anglers saw the fish and knew it to be a really big one.

Amazingly, the tarpon zigzagged through all the boats and jumped three times without any tangle-ups. The VHF radio in Pate's pocket came to life with chatter, but without a free hand available, he couldn't answer. He instead concentrated on battling the poon, following its mad dash as best he could with the electric motors.

Back it headed toward the gaggle of skiffs. Just when Pate suspected the tarpon would snarl in one of the fishing lines, it again turned out to sea for open water. Two hours later, Pate was still hooked up and trying to stay near the huge fish.

Another pose with a big tarpon. Pate, who has released thousands of tarpon of all sizes, only keeps probable world records. Photo courtesy of Billy Pate.

"I worried that my electrics might give out at some point," said Pate, "or the hook would pull. I also was heading directly into a stiff west wind that made it extremely difficult and tiring to stay on course while constantly manipulating the electric motors. It turned into quite a struggle."

His body aching, Pate finally caught a break. The tarpon swung back toward shore and away from any skiffs as the pod of fish broke up in the deeper water. With the wind now at his back, Pate felt a rush of confidence and strength. He gained line and moved close enough to behold the broad shoulders on this fish, a sight that excited him because it meant he just might indeed beat his own record. By this time, the tarpon had run back close to where they'd originally started hours before, and Pate's VHF radio went off again.

He quickly grabbed it with his left hand. "I'll come help you and gaff the fish," said a young guide nearby. "It sure looks big enough for a record."

Pate answered that he'd greatly appreciate it. At this stage, however, the tarpon still showed no intention of giving up. It wouldn't be until after another couple of shorter runs that the fish would finally tire and lie on its side. The guide moved his boat nearer, but in another burst of adrenaline, Pate grabbed a lip gaff and decided to handle the big tarpon himself despite the offer of help. He still thought it might be a potential world record; otherwise, Pate would have released it right then and there.

Pate moved the rod back as far as possible with his left hand, but he still couldn't reach the tarpon with the gaff. So, he took a calculated risk and lunged at the fish's open mouth. Amazingly, the gaff sank into its lip. As the tarpon started to go berserk, Pate let go of the rod and used both hands on the gaff.

He slid the massive tarpon to the side of the boat and tried to pull it in, but no way. Pate placed a foot against the gunnel for leverage and with all his might moved the fish's head out of the water. With their combined weight lowering the gunnel, Pate gave it one last heave and the mighty tarpon slid into the boat.

"I was completely exhausted but knew I couldn't rest even for a second," said Pate. "I grabbed the tape measure and read the girth as 45 and three-quarter inches, nearly three inches thicker than my 188-pound record. My only worry was that this fish looked to be a bit shorter in length.

"I wasn't sure what to do, so I summoned the guide who offered to help to jump into my skiff to retake the measurements."

From 1970–78, Pate caught six billfish species, including a billfish such as this—he was the first to do so. Photo courtesy of Billy Pate.

The man did so, coming up with the same 45 and three quarter inches and suggesting that Pate take the fish to the dock and weigh it. Pate called the dockmaster at MacRae's Marina to get the scales ready, and as he dashed for home, he looked at the fish on his deck and wondered how in the world he'd managed to land it unaided.

Pate arrived to a crowded dock, as the word had spread quickly in the close-knit fishing community of Homosassa. All eyes gazed at the weight scale as the glistening tarpon was hung. When it stopped at 173 pounds, everyone cheered while Pate's heart sank.

"Even though everyone said they were amazed that I hooked, fought and landed that giant tarpon by myself, I felt bad about keeping a fish that didn't turn out to be a world record," Pate said. "Even so, I'm still prouder of catching that tarpon than anything else I've ever done."

Two nice salmon taken from an Oregon stream. Photo courtesy of Billy Pate.

Pate would go on to do a lot of "elses" over the years. He started fishing South Carolina streams at the age of six. As a towheaded teen he received a fly outfit as a birthday present, and from that day on you'd seldom see him with anything other than a fly rod in hand. In the early 1960s, Pate caught a tarpon on fly and that began a lifetime love affair. Catching big fish on fly gear really captured his soul.

In 1970, Pate bested a 146-pound striped marlin off Ecuador, and after it became a record he realized that no one had yet taken a blue, black or white marlin on fly. Pate set his sights on doing so, and in the following years he did the trick on a white and black marlin as well as Atlantic and Pacific sailfish. He completed the list of six billfish in 1978 off Cuba with a blue marlin. In his travels to over 40 countries, Pate's also set records for bonefish, grouper, redfish, mako shark, jack crevalle and channel bass.

In the mid-1960s, Pate and Islamorada fishing guide George Hommell decided to open a "world-class" tackle shop that also booked exotic fishing trips around the globe, and soon thereafter, *World Wide Sportsman* successfully burst onto the scene. The store became the place to go for fly gear, clothing, advice and even for booking fishing trips. In 1995, they sold the company to Bass Pro Shops, and one of their mega-stores is an attraction in Islamorada.

Pate also worked with master craftsman Tibor "Ted" Juracsik to design top-quality fly reels that have borne Pate's name for over 30 years. The two met in the Florida Keys in 1970, at which time Pate bemoaned the constant problems he experienced with saltwater fly reels, including corrosion, inconsistent drag systems and their inability to last very long when a big fish like a tarpon or billfish was burning off line.

Juracsik went to work, and after several prototypes the Billy Pate Fly Reel hit the market. In 1976 the first much-acclaimed, anti-reverse reel bearing Pate's name became a big hit, establishing new levels of craftsmanship. The reels, engraved in script with Pate's name, became widely accepted in the industry and, more importantly, by legions of fly fishers around the globe. Made of pure bar stock aluminum and red, black and gold in color, they looked altogether handsome on a rod. With their success, Pate became more than just another world record–

seeker. Models include those designed for salmon, tarpon, marlin and freshwater trout.

"I'm darn proud of those reels," said Pate. "Ted and I worked really hard to put out something special, and it's safe to say we did so."

Pate produced many videos on fly fishing, some costing upwards of $100,000, what with the use of multiple cameras, expensive sound gear, helicopter shots and a lot of water time in order to complete the scripts. Titles include *Billy Pate's Fly Fishing for Billfish, Saltwater Fly Casting Secrets with Billy Pate, Fly Rodding for Tarpon,* and *Challenge of Giant Tarpon.*

He's also won a number of prestigious tournaments, such as the Gold Cup Invitational Tarpon Fly Championship and the International Billfish Fly Championship. Furthermore, he turned two innovations into industry standards: his harness system that helps prevent the angler or mate from being pulled into the briny when applying a fixed-head gaff and the practice of using eels as teaser baits for sailfish.

Susan Cocking, outdoor writer for the *Miami Herald,* wanted to go on a fishing trip with Pate due to his status as a tarpon fishing legend. "It was in the mid-1990s out of Hernando Beach," said Cocking. "You of course can't always count on catching fish you target on any given outing, but we got lucky. Billy's every cast on that windy day seemed to be right on the money, and he finally got a 90- to 100-pound silver king to take his fly. He brought it to boat side in only about 10 minutes, which really impressed me. More importantly, he was the perfect gentleman all day."

Billy Pate quite clearly epitomizes the world-class fly angler and true southern gentleman.

24

Jim Wilson, b. 1931

PANAMA CITY

One day I drove from Destin to meet Jim Wilson at a breakfast eatery about 15 miles to the east on U.S. 98. Arriving first, I found a table facing the door. Minutes later in walked Wilson, who would be the spitting image of Santa Claus himself if he were to sport a white beard and red suit.

Then again, I doubt Santa would receive much more notice in the Panama City region than Wilson, at least from adults. Even before joining me a number of exiting diners stopped him.

"We just wanted to say hello," said a lady holding hands with two small children. The kids, wide-eyed with mouths agape, acted as if meeting someone mythical only seen on TV, like Mickey or Donald. "I watch your show every day before leaving the house for work," a man in a business suit gushed.

While we sat at the table, I noted someone waving frantically to get Wilson's attention, which Wilson acknowledged with a nod and a smile. Another man walked by, saw the great man and lowered his head to whisper, "Hey Jim, what's my best bet if I go fishing this afternoon? I won't tell anyone else."

I couldn't believe all the ado. It wasn't on the level of Elvis or the Beatles, mind you, but the ardor went nonstop. I was impressed. Jim Wilson is a local celebrity, par excellence.

Wilson isn't unaffected by the attention, but I observed no signs of self-absorption either. In fact, I'm envious.

Wilson (right) on his first article assignment in 1947, a one-week canoe fishing trip. Photo courtesy of Jim Wilson.

"When you're on TV in Panama City for 25 years, people are going to recognize you," said Wilson, "kind of like the local TV weatherman or newscaster."

Wilson admits he enjoys it, mainly because he just likes people, which is obvious. In turn, people like Jim Wilson. His exuberance is infectious.

In 1985 he launched *Jim Wilson Outdoors* on WMBB-TV in Panama City. It was originally a daily live broadcast from 6 to 6:30 a.m., Monday through Friday—one of the first such formats in Florida. He still does the shows on a less frantic Saturday and Sunday basis.

News director Larche Hardy remembers the first day Wilson walked into his office at the TV station. "Jim pitched the idea of the show," he said. "I warmed up to him immediately and knew he'd be great on camera. What's impressed me the most about Jim is that he knows how to make a living and have a lot of fun. The rest of us just slug away at it, but he's found the right balance."

Buoyed by the public's acceptance of his entertaining TV delivery—his pet dog is a regular guest and he once came up with a hilarious "Gills Gone Wild" spoof—in 1988 Wilson started *Florida Outdoor News,* his own outdoor newspaper. It covered fishing, hunting and other outdoor events from Pensacola to Carrabelle. Over the course of the next several years, the paper grew from an eight-page black-and-white monthly tabloid with a circulation of 5,000 to a full-color edition of 32 pages and 20,000 copies. In 2001 he sold the paper to the *Panama City News Herald* but continued working for a couple of years as consulting editor.

Coming to understand Wilson's challenging upbringing evokes quite a measure of appreciation. For starters, his coming into this world when he did can only be termed bad timing. It must have been tough enough going through the Great Depression as a child, but being abandoned by your father on top of it really makes perseverance a long step. Jim Wilson, it seems, became no ordinary man because he was no ordinary kid.

Born in Galveston, Texas, in 1931, at age one he moved with his parents to Dallas. His dad promptly disappeared, walking out on his wife and son, leaving them homeless and destitute. A Catholic mission took them in until a relative gathered them up and drove to the home of

Rosa O'Rourke in Columbia, Mississippi. O'Rourke, Jim's 74-year-old great-grandmother, became their candle in the darkness.

Even with a roof over their heads, food was not a ready commodity and leisure activities only made sense if they involved no cents. Jim's mother became an office worker in a factory six days a week. But something rare for those times proved to be a crucial part of Jim Wilson's upbringing: a college-educated mother who appreciated the arts and music. She read to her child, instilled in him a desire to learn and ensured he found ready comfort at the fountain of knowledge: the library. Only a few blocks from home, the library became Wilson's haven, a refuge where written words between two hard covers served as a lifeline.

A special movie played in town in 1938 that also captured Wilson's interest. He vividly recalls joining others whose fate was bare cupboards but who thirsted for a taste of the good life, even if vicariously. A presentation of *I Married Adventure* flickered on a faded wall of the library, a narration of experiences by world travelers Martin and Osa Johnson. In the movie, the husband and wife team related the wonderful things they saw, heard and did on the mysterious continent of Africa. Transfixed, Wilson saw another world unfold before him that consisted of the great outdoors. It left him inspired.

"Something went off in my head," said Wilson. "I wanted my destiny to be built on what I wanted to do, not what I had to do to eke by."

Considering the hardships of life in his little corner of Mississippi, it's remarkable that Wilson never doubted his destiny. A few years later he got his hands on a book by the Johnsons with the same title as their film. He read it and re-read it. The book included a photo of the beautiful Osa and the dashing Martin bedecked in leather flying helmets. Oh, to be like them.

As World War II raged, 12-year-old Wilson acquired his first after-school job at the *Columbian Progress,* the local newspaper office. Wilson swept the floor, cleaned and ran errands. A beginning it was in the field of journalism. Now instead of just reading the written word, he learned how stories and reports were developed, which photographs matched best with articles and news items, and how the public reacted to media.

Wilson served in the U.S. Navy and Army and at times performed work for the Air Force. Photo courtesy of Jim Wilson.

A move to Gulfport, Mississippi, in June 1945 provided a complete change of venue. The Wilsons' house lay directly across from the Gulf of Mexico, giving the lad exposure to the beach. At the shoreline he could fish, catch crabs, watch seabirds and observe how tides affect the behavior of marine creatures. Strengthening his taste for the outdoors was Dr. Richard Stone, a family friend.

A psychiatrist by profession, Stone had realized that his real interests centered on natural history. He mentored Wilson and found the boy to be not only a willing student but always ready for more. Stone encouraged him, emphasizing that just catching fish and other creatures wasn't an end to itself. He taught Wilson the Latin names of species, the physiology of fish, a deeper understanding of how they foraged for food, how their fins and tails worked and other nuances a student of biology would know. Far from just providing book learning, Stone took Wilson and his mother on many fishing trips and outdoor adventures.

Even given the acquisition of advanced knowledge about fish in general, Wilson developed two itches that needed to be scratched: becoming adept as an angler and, like the Johnsons, entertaining others from those experiences. Wilson thus entered the stratosphere of "professional" journalism in 1947 when he sold his first photographs. It seems a hurricane had swept inland from the Gulf, and instead of taking shelter, he captured a visual story of the event. Wilson walked about gripping his trusty Argus A-2 camera, and the *Times Picayune* in New Orleans wanted all of his photos. Wow, hard cash, just for taking pictures.

From there Wilson advanced to an article with accompanying photos. He embarked on a week-long canoe trip with friend Harry Davis on the Leaf River. The 16-year-olds rowed from Hattiesburg to Poticaw on the Pascagoula River. Along the way they fished and scored easily each day with a good batch of catfish. As evening approached they eyed houses along the river mainly owned by black families, pulling onto the bank when their waving hands were met with friendly reception.

"They expressed surprise to see two white boys coming in from the river," said Wilson. "I'd offer the lady of the house a large catfish or two to cook for dinner and usually we'd be asked to join them."

Their sleeping gear consisted simply of musty World War II jungle hammocks. In the morning the boys usually joined their dinner hosts for ham and eggs and grits, and then off they'd float again down the river.

When Wilson graduated from Gulfport High in 1950, he entered Perkinston Junior College, which had a small but homey faculty and student body. His roommate turned out to be Fred Haise from Biloxi. Haise became editor of the school newspaper, *Bulldog Barks,* and Wilson anointed himself the outdoor editor. Now, instead of turning over his writings for someone else to pass judgment, he got to see what it was like on the other side of the ink jar. Haise went on to bigger things

Wilson's passion for photography resulted in his owning a camera shop. Here he's doing a scene for a film to be narrated by Lowell Thomas. Photo courtesy of Jim Wilson.

as well, becoming a U. S. Navy Air Cadet and an astronaut of Apollo 13 fame.

Following graduation from Perkinston, Wilson taught fourth grade at Gulf Coast Military Academy. He learned right along with his students, teaching outdoor activities such as horseback riding, canoeing and riflery. He also did a stint as a navy reservist until 1953, whereupon Wilson switched to the army and was assigned to the Army Security Agency.

The height of the Cold War gripped America, and the army recognized Wilson's fast-learning capability. They put him through their intensive language school to learn Russian fluently, after which point he was transferred to Fort Devens, Massachusetts, for Russian Radio Intercept training. Wilson's first assignment was to be the U.S. embassy in Vienna, Austria, but the army instead reconsidered and kept him at

Ft. Devens. Had he transferred, he'd have never met and married Ann Fletcher from Littleton, Massachusetts, in March 1955.

While stationed at Ft. Devens, Wilson began penning outdoor stories for the *Fort Devens Dispatch*. The columns led to requests from senior officers to take them fishing, which usually turned into a story with photos. His C.O.'s jockeyed for favor with Wilson, which resulted in a plum gig for a military man: A job consisting entirely of going fishing and writing about it.

Wilson wanted more, however, than to serve as a fishing guide to the military brass. He left the army and obtained a degree in Education from Boston University, working for the *Beacon* newspaper in Maynard, Massachusetts. Besides the outdoors he also covered politics. An early assignment involved attending a fund-raising event for then-presidential candidate John Kennedy.

Wilson's roots in the spy game still interwove with his journalistic pursuits. He left the newspaper and went to work for the Eastman Kodak Company at the New Boston Satellite Tracking Station. His job entailed operating a 35mm movie-film processing machine that used a new process so surveillance satellites could combine television with photography. From a distance of 150 miles, NASA could identify the makes of automobiles in the Pentagon parking lot. That technology soon evolved to where license plates on the autos could be read.

Now with a wife and family of four, the enterprising Wilson decided to strike out on his own. In 1963 he bought the Aldrich Camera Store in Laconia, New Hampshire. Wilson became familiar with a Bolex 16mm camera with a zoom lens—perfect for producing fishing and hunting films to air on the local TV affiliates. He covered a snowmobile race and met a fellow named Bill AuCoin who was entering a race car for Governor George Romney. AuCoin would later become president of the Florida Outdoor Writers Association (FOWA), as would Jim Wilson.

"Jim was a take-charge guy," said AuCoin, who now resides in St. Petersburg, Florida. "I watched him as a member of the New England Outdoor Writers Association and 30 years later as president of FOWA. He's the pivot that makes organizations run."

In the 1970s, Wilson toiled as a sales representative for Garcia Fishing Tackle and in 1980 joined Shakespeare Fishing Tackle, covering the same territory and setting sales records along the way. In 1983 he moved to Panama City to handle the Gulf Coast from the Big Bend to Mississippi for Southern Tackle Distributors of Miami. Wilson also became outdoor editor of the *Panama City News Herald* newspaper and joined the Florida Outdoor Writers Association. Wilson left Southern Tackle in 1985 for the start of his TV show and to be involved with *Take a Kid Fishing* in Panama City.

Wilson's presentation to schoolchildren includes showing his son climbing Mt. Everest (at the time was the youngest to ever do so) and quipping, "If you want to get high, here's the way to do it: Climb Mt. Everest."

A proud moment came in February 2007 when Willie Nelson arrived in Panama City for a concert. Wilson asked Nelson to autograph an unopened record album the country singer had recorded in 1965. Wilson said he wanted to raffle it off and give the proceeds to the family of a young U.S. Army sergeant named Joshua Cope from Panama City who had both legs blown off by an IED in Iraq. Willie Nelson not only autographed the record but also gave Wilson $1,000. Wilson and his wife sold raffle tickets at the concert and a parade at $5 each and then presented a check to Linda Cope, the young sergeant's mother, for $3,700.

Wilson's story would not be complete without mentioning the person who completes him, his wife, Patricia. They were married in December 1996 and he knew he'd finally found his own Osa Johnson. Fast approaching 80, he still produces his TV show and travels often with Pat.

Well wishers approach the local celeb and sometimes ask when he'll retire. Wilson smiles and replies, "Read the obituaries—I'll be fishing with my mother and grandmother at the Port St. Joe Cemetery."

Sosin's never more in his element than when he's working as an educator, especially with kids. Photo courtesy of Mark Sosin.

25

Mark Sosin, b. 1933

BOCA RATON

Rob Kramer, president of the International Game Fish Association, previously worked for Florida's marine fisheries. One of their projects involved angler outreach, and they decided to create some videos to educate people about how their fishing license money was being put to use.

"After thinking about whom would best be a recognizable face for the videos, we immediately thought of Mark Sosin," said Kramer. "So I contacted him and he agreed to host a series of these videos.

"We first got together with him in St. Petersburg, where the Florida Marine Research Institute is located. We began to put together scripts for the videos and decided the first one would concentrate on how researchers sometimes go out on boats and do net sets for fish counts to help create stock assessments. The first thing Mark noticed is that all the biologists were young people, and all the women biologists were piloting the boats and pulling nets. Meanwhile, the men simply stood around holding clipboards. This fascinated Mark, particularly with the women pulling and laboring with the nets, so from those experiences he coined the name 'Annette Puller.'

"Everywhere we went after that, Mark would refer to female marine biologists as Annette Pullers. On one occasion at an event, a fellow came up to Mark and me and began talking about the work of a biologist he knew. Mark interjected, 'Well then, you must know my friend Annette Puller.' The man nodded blankly and then kept on talking, but Mark and I shared a knowing grin and still do whenever the occasion presents itself."

You've undoubtedly seen Sosin as host of *Saltwater Journal*. The TV series has run 26 years and seems to get better with age. Then again, everything Mark Sosin puts his name to comes out as a professional product, whether a TV show or commercial, book, article, DVD, seminar, instructional video, lure or photograph.

Sosin even did a five-year stint covering the outdoors for CBS Radio in New York. I've never seen, read or heard anything he's produced that's less than top-notch, and I don't hand out that compliment lightly.

More than anything, the man's been an educator, and that's what he does best. His 3,000-plus articles in major magazines and newspapers, the 30 books, hundreds of TV episodes, and all else he's created target the same thing: helping people become better anglers. It's quite the noble motivation in our genre, despite my daughter once humbly boiling down my life's role as an outdoor communicator to "trying to figure out what fish like to eat."

I remember fishing with Sosin at a Bonefish & Tarpon Trust (BTT) tournament in Key Largo a few years back. While taking my rotation on the bow, I cast a red-and-black Johnny Rattler plug about 40 feet down a narrow mangrove-clustered creek. It zipped through a tiny gap between two branches and splashed down at the back of a deep pool—a perfect shot. Nothing nailed the plug, so I retrieved it.

"Do it again," Sosin said.

Another cast sent the plug in the exact same arc, again splitting the middle of the creek between the two branches like thread through a needle. The plug went *kerplunk* right where it'd landed before. Sosin looked like he'd been shot with a stun gun. After this retrieve the skiff drifted away from the creek and we continued fishing. Truth be told, I could never duplicate that feat again, but we'll let Sosin think I can.

His achievements and contributions are many: advisor to the International Game Fish Association (IGFA), director emeritus of The Billfish Foundation, president of the Outdoor Writer's Association of America, enshrinement in both the IGFA Fishing Hall of Fame and the Freshwater Fishing Hall of Fame. Sosin helped launch the Saltwater Fly Rodders of America in the 1960s along with Lefty Kreh, *Salt Water Sportsman* editor Frank Woolner, Fred Schrier and many others. In 1965, he wrote the original rules governing saltwater fly-rod catches.

Though he's a world-class angler, one of Sosin's favorite passions is fishing Florida's mangrove flats for redfish. Photo courtesy of Mark Sosin.

Those regulations largely govern the proper conduct, gear restrictions and do's and don'ts that exist today, proving how much thought and work went into the draft that Sosin was charged with producing.

Sosin's fished in all 50 states since his boyhood in New Jersey and in more than 45 countries outside the U.S. A graduate of the University of Pennsylvania's Wharton School, he knows the business end of the fishing industry better than just about anyone, and his list of contacts would amaze anyone. Rob Kramer told me that no matter whose name he brings up to Sosin—even if the man or woman lives in the most obscure and remote location in the world—Sosin either knows that person or someone who does.

Tom Greene, who's owned the huge Custom Rod & Reel tackle shop in Lighthouse Point, Florida, for over 35 years, has known Sosin all that time. "He often drops by my shop on a Saturday morning just to get away from the telephone and computer," said Greene. "He'll watch his TV show or talk about one he's working on with customers. He especially likes kids, and they immediately recognize him with that trademark flats hat and distinctive face. I get a big kick when someone tells Mark something like, 'Hey, I see you're really a nice guy, but you don't come across that way on TV.' I just look at Mark at grin."

Greene also surmised that because Sosin is so personable, people sometimes erroneously think he doesn't know all that he does about fishing. He believes that misimpression stems from his on-camera persona. "Of course Mark does understand all phases of fishing and his experiences are vast," Greene said. "But sometimes people don't realize that from his very first TV show, he's always tried to make his guests appear to be the experts, not him."

As with shows of any genre, what comes out on TV doesn't always reflect all that happened, thanks to the value of artful editing. Greene said that on one trip with Sosin to Venezuela, the show didn't come out quite as he would have expected.

"I caught seven sailfish that day," he recalled. "The blue diesel smoke behind the boat was so bad you couldn't see clearly at times to film, but by changing the angles, we finally got what was needed. I think Mark caught one or two sails during that time. When I finally saw the show air, it was filled with Mark catching fish after fish rather than me.

"When he next came into the store I asked, 'Hey, what happened to all my sails?'

"'You were lost on the cutting room floor,' he replied sheepishly."

Greene accompanied Sosin on another trip for a TV segment based in Costa Rica. "In the distance behind the stern, we watched in awe as blue marlin knocked tuna into the air," said Greene. "The skipper turned around and ran straight on top of the fish to get closer, but it just caused the marlin to sound. We got zero video of all that mayhem and weren't catching anything at all, so we decided to head toward the coastline to try and catch some roosterfish."

The skipper of the boat asked Sosin where he wanted him to go. Spotting a huge full rainbow on the horizon, Sosin pointed at one of the terminuses and said, "Go right there."

"We ran to a beach 10 or so miles away, right by an outcropping of rocks where the nearest end of the rainbow seemed to be touching," Greene said. "Right after arriving I hooked up a rooster on plug that

Sosin's prolific career as an outdoor journalist spans five decades and counting. Photo courtesy of the International Game Fish Association.

had to be over 50 pounds. We caught two or three others directly where that rainbow had shown on the rocks with just perfect filming conditions. The captain and crew thought Mark to be some sort of divine prophet. Then again, Mark did call that perfectly."

Harlan Franklin, a longtime guide in Key West before retiring to Sebastian, Florida, told me about a fishing tournament with Sosin as one of the celebrity anglers.

"I guided Mark and a dentist friend from Tallahassee named Dr. Jay Wilson," said Franklin. "I ran to the Marquesas and moved inside where it's calm. We spied a bunch of really big permit in the 30- to 35-pound class. Jay threw his lure and it ballooned in the wind, landing only about 20 feet from the boat and nowhere near the permit.

"Mark took his turn and did exactly the same thing. I again moved us into casting range and Jay messed up the cast, landing it well short of the school. Mark reloaded for another back-up cast and, you guessed it, he also let the wind catch his lure. After all that time, we could do nothing more than watch helplessly as the permit finally scattered. Mark turned to Jay and in jest said, 'You infected my casting.' We all got a good laugh."

Sue Cocking, outdoor writer for the *Miami Herald,* knows well the creative mind of Sosin and how it often leads to a humorous bent. "Some years back I was attending an outing in Bimini," Cocking said. "While having breakfast in a small café on Main Street in Alice Town, I could barely believe my eyes when who should walk in but Mark. He came through the door, spotted me and pulled up a chair at my table. After a bit of small talk he said, 'I've got to do something to jump-start my career. I've come up with an idea: I need to pretend to sexually harass someone. I wouldn't really do it, of course, but the rumor would go around and get me a lot of publicity.' We mused about the scenarios for several minutes, giggling like teenagers. That's what I like about Mark: He's always entertaining."

With so many global travels for his TV series as well as appearances and industry representations, Sosin often is accompanied by colleagues. At times that means bearing witness to unseemly behavior that, putting it delicately, can be described as glandular excess and over-appreciation for the local lager. I do know that the clear-headed nature of Sosin's character and his long-term marriage to wife Susan keeps him on the straight and narrow.

Tom Greene concurs. "We were in Venezuela years ago and after I fought about a 1,000-pound marlin and lost it right at the back of the boat, we later celebrated the grander battle by toasting a beer," said Greene. "Mark sipped a little too, but it's the only time I've seen him drink any alcohol in 25 years."

Let's go back for a moment to Sosin's piece de resistance, the long-running *Saltwater Journal* TV series. I always felt that the two best TV fishing shows, fresh- or saltwater, were *Saltwater Journal* and Flip Pallot's *Walker's Cay Chronicles.* The production quality was always excellent and the hosts very capable. Certainly in Sosin's case, he went out of the way to feature not only the fishing resources of his location but also the ambiance. This broadened the travel appeal as it showed the color, traditions and landmarks of the filming sites. He also tried to weave in reminders about our fragile ecosystems and the need to be mindful of our anchors, fishing line, hooks and release ethics. Like a baseball player concerned about image, Sosin certainly didn't want to talk the talk without walking the walk.

Dr. Guy Harvey, the noted artist and conservationist, admires Mark Sosin's career and certainly respects his considerable on-the-water days and unique experiences.

"One day I want him to show me how he caught a sailfish in Panama using a cigar for a bait," said Harvey.

Stay tuned, because if that trick hasn't already been aired, it will undoubtedly be featured on another episode of *Saltwater Journal*.

26

Karl Wickstrom, b. 1935

STUART

Karl Wickstrom used to watch his dad set type for a newspaper, letter by letter. The precise details did not escape his eyes, and the smell of printer's ink proved to be infused in his heritage. Little surprise, then, that he'd earn a degree in journalism at the University of Florida and jump right into the life of a scribe.

Wickstrom became a reporter at the *Orlando Sentinel* and from 1960–68 worked as the same for the *Miami Herald*. In 1966 he garnered the first-place award for investigative reporting from the Florida Associated Press, and as happens sooner or later in the hearts and minds of all entrepreneurs, Wickstrom knew that he'd take the wheel of his own publication when the right opportunity came along.

That opportunity stepped front and center in 1968. Wickstrom obtained the contract to publish *Aloft Magazine* for National Airlines, convincing their top brass to shed the self-promotion and hype so common in most other publications. It made good sense to all, and from that very start, Wickstrom would become known for his fierce protection of editorial integrity.

Long before the launch of *Aloft Magazine,* he noted the burgeoning interest in fishing, hunting and other outdoor pursuits nationwide and especially in Florida. He saw that some newspapers took into account their region's action, but little attention was paid elsewhere. A number of national magazines such as *Field & Stream* and *Outdoor Life* covered those topics, but only infrequent snippets appeared that involved Florida.

A nice-size yellowtail for the grill taken off Miami. Photo courtesy of the International Game Fish Association.

If the U.S. had become the fulcrum for the explosion of tackle shops, marinas, boats and rod/reel manufacturers, Wickstrom reasoned that Florida could be considered the filet mignon of the nation. A magazine did not exist that shone the spotlight solely on the fishing and hunting scenes from Pensacola to Jacksonville to Key West and back. Would it work? Would people buy it? Would advertisers come aboard? Wickstrom's business plan said yes, but what's on paper doesn't always pan out.

But we all know what happened. In 1969, the first bimonthly issue of *Florida and Tropic Sportsman* hit the shelves. It soon became simply *Florida Sportsman* and a monthly publication. A fellow named Vic Dunaway and another former newspaperman, Bill Hallstrom, agreed to throw their lot into the effort, and between them and Wickstrom it became a formidable team.

Over the years the publication won numerous magazine industry awards, earned the respect of even those with the top national titles and became passionately embraced by anglers and hunters. Advertisers soon recognized that to reach the Florida market, only one cost-effective venue was practical.

Nobody worked longer with Wickstrom—or achieved the same level of camaraderie with him—as Vic Dunaway. I therefore asked Vic to reflect on his many experiences with Wickstrom and to provide insights about the man for this book:

"Karl Wickstrom was not cast in the same mold as your average angler. He did not catch the fishing bug as a tow-headed youngster, but only became infected after he was solidly entrenched in adulthood, with a growing family, a background that included a stint as an investigative reporter for the *Miami Herald,* and a career switch that saw him become owner and publisher of a major airline's in-flight magazine.

"Even then, he did not do things quite the same way as a typical initiate into the world's greatest sport. Instead of merely pampering his new hobby by impulsively compiling a bunch of fishing tackle, he went farther than any angler before him.

"He started his own fishing magazine and, happily, he hired me to help him.

Wickstrom's involvement in conservation causes like the "Ban the Nets" amendment has made a big difference in Florida's fisheries. Photo courtesy of the International Game Fish Association.

"For a couple of issues, his new publication was called *Florida and Tropic Sportsman*. For the last 40 years, more or less, we have known it simply as *Florida Sportsman*.

"With that chore taken care of, Karl finally did start filling his tackle box. That box—as his fishing pals are well aware—contains but a bare minimum of lures. And only one model of those ever sees much use.

"To put it bluntly, Karl is a nut for top-water plug(s). I made the 's' optional because he has always depended on only one model of surface plug at a time—the one which, for some reason, he has decreed the reigning king of fishing lures. Of course, no monarch reigns forever, and so every few years Karl has seen fit to depose his previous pet plug in favor of a new one. I won't presume to name the entire dynasty, but a couple of his earliest one-and-onlys were the Ratlure and the Hula Popper, and the latest—to my knowledge—the Chug Bug.

"Since I most often depended on jigs when we fished together, I generally piled up bigger numbers than Karl, but, embarrassingly often, his relentless surface-pounding not only produced the biggest catch of the day but one that earned bragging rights for many days to come.

"As one example, I recall a day in Bimini when we set out in separate skiffs to fish for a couple of hours over the shallow, patchy bottom that lay just south of the harbor entrance. My jig produced a dozen small yellowtail and a couple of two-pound bar jack, all of which my Bahamian guide wanted to keep for his table.

"I did not object—partly because I would then be able to show off my catch back at the marina. Karl, I figured, would come in fishless, for the area seemed highly unlikely to harbor fish of any great size, and none of the little ones—such as the ones I caught—would be brave enough to attack his thunderous plug.

"As it turned out, I came within one cast of being correct. That was the one cast which landed his popper within hearing distance of a 15-pound mutton snapper. You can guess whose catch hogged all the glory at the dock. That snapper went on to adorn a cover of *Florida Sportsman.*

"An unexpected chance to gain revenge for many such instances came my way on another trip—this one to blue water off Miami. We had drifted live baits without success all morning and were headed back toward shore when we ran smack through a school of cobia accompanying a big ray. Do that with almost any other fish and you can kiss your chances good-bye, but by the time Karl decelerated and turned the boat around, those single-minded cobia had gone back to scuffling around their ray, paying us no mind at all.

"Since they were already rigged for live-baiting, Karl and the passenger who was with us both tossed live pinfish into the melee and hooked up instantly. I inspected the rod rack for something which might allow me to join the fray. The only weapon available was Karl's omnipresent spinning outfit with his plug of the day attached. I hesitated for only a

A redfish caught at night in Stuart on Wickstrom's favorite kind of lure—a top-water. Photo courtesy of Karl Wickstrom.

second. What the heck! Karl couldn't care; he was busy already. So out went the plug—almost straight into the waiting maw of a big cobia.

"Unfortunately, Karl's hook pulled out a few minutes later. He hurriedly wound in his slack line and turned to pick up his favorite outfit. My fish was sulking at the moment, as cobia are wont to do, so I had time to watch Karl's demeanor switch from surprised to mystified upon discovering that Old Faithful had somehow escaped its pinions.

"The moment when it finally dawned on him that I had not only appropriated his outfit but was using it to battle the biggest fish of the trip was probably the moment when I came closest to getting fired.

"But it was also a moment of payback."

One of the reasons writers and editors such as Vic Dunaway treasured their association with *Florida Sportsman* was Wickstrom's resolve to instill editorial integrity. Unlike Wickstrom with his hands-on background in journalism, many other publishers are in essence sales managers who often twist editorial copy to help please advertisers. But no pandering boat reviews were to be found in the pages of *Florida Sportsman*; editorial coverage wasn't packaged with advertising commitments and writers were never ordered to mention certain products.

Florida Sportsman grew in page count because the content was dedicated to one simple, timeless journalistic canon: Be true to readers. Capture the hearts and minds of readers and the eyeballs on the pages will inevitably result in more subscriptions, higher renewals and inevitably stronger advertising support. The formula worked. His ad pages more than doubled those of almost all rivals.

Wickstrom also utilized the magazine's popularity to promote causes beneficial to readers *and* resources. He succeeded in obtaining game fish status for redfish in the 1980s when commercial netting in Florida had nearly wiped them out. His magazine railed against the ill-fated Cross Florida Barge Canal. He spearheaded the highly successful "Ban the Nets" campaign that passed in 1994 as a state amendment by an unprecedented 72 percent of the vote.

The amendment effort could only be termed Herculean. During the early 1990s, neither the Florida legislature nor Governor Lawton Chiles wanted anything to do with the amendment. Instead, they insisted on promoting "talks" between the commercial netters and conservationists. Time after time, session after session, the talk turned out to be just that—all talk and no action by the netters. It was a futile expectation born out of either naiveté or a ploy to stall and prevent the issue from ever getting on the ballot.

Wickstrom smelled the rat and didn't bite. About a half million petition signatures were obtained despite the politicians—and accomplished for the first and only time in Florida history without the use of paid petition gatherers. While many entities got behind the "Ban the Nets" effort, it's safe to say that without Wickstrom's perseverance and driving force through *Florida Sportsman,* it likely would have never happened. As a result, gill nets were banned in Florida's waters and other limitations placed on wanton by-catch and habitat destruction from netting. In short order the relief to the resources gave rise to a rejuvenated fishery for many inshore saltwater species. I considered it an honor to produce the video for that campaign as well as to roll up my sleeves in the grassroots efforts, both before and after I was a *Florida Sportsman* staffer.

Wickstrom continues to keep an eye on commercial fishing excesses and to promote conservation issues. The magazine's messages are now buttressed by a *Florida Sportsman* TV series, popular books by Vic Dunaway and other editors, weekend fishing shows, a statewide radio network and an active Web site.

I strongly allied with Wickstrom—and still do—on the issue of federal fishery interests such as the National Oceanic and Atmospheric Administration creating no-fishing zones and pushing for endlessly more around Florida and all of our nation's coastlines.

"The closures create huge impacts for anglers without any significant benefits to the fishery," Wickstrom stated. Amen to that.

My years working with Karl and most of the others on staff in the mid-1990s were rewarding. He kept an extremely close eye on the costs, as all good business owners should. One day he'd comment about the extra pieces of paper used for an article draft and on the next he'd take the editors to a tackle shop and let us stock up on rods, reels and lures.

He caught me completely off-guard in my third year on staff when serving as managing editor. Karl stuck his head in my door and quietly asked me to come to his office. I could only wonder if I was about to hear a few terse words for some sort of egregious editing error, so you can imagine my astonishment when instead he handed me a check for $10,000. In addition to my editorial duties, I'd somehow found time to organize the first two Florida Sportsman Fishing Shows at the Dade County Youth Fair. We'd struck no agreement on further compensation for that—Karl simply paid me the extra bucks because he felt it was deserved. I saw him perform similar acts of generosity for others strictly out of his sense of fairness and from the goodness of his heart.

Like all of us, Wickstrom has his detractors. But on balance, his pluses far outweigh his minuses. In working for him I found his manner always measured and gentlemanly, with no raised voice or belittling; he exercised quiet authority. More importantly, his value to Florida's anglers and the state's resources continues to this day in his role as founder and editor-in-chief of *Florida Sportsman*.

27

~~~

Bob Stearns, b. 1935

MIAMI

Perhaps the name Bob Stearns isn't that familiar to you. However, if you've been an angler for any length of time and you like to read about your favorite pastime, it should be. His byline has appeared in most major magazines and he's been on mastheads as an editor. He's authored books, organized what was probably the largest fishing tournament on the planet, helped design the first commercially available flats boats and appeared on TV shows as a guest expert.

Never one to seek attention, however, Stearns keeps a relatively low profile while many of his colleagues seek the limelight. He's just not the type to measure his life in terms of how many autographs he's signed.

By sheer coincidence, he turned out to be my next-door neighbor in Miami when I lived there beginning at age 18 with my parents. I was attending the University of Miami (on a golf scholarship, of all things), which is also Stearns' alma mater. Also during that time, Stu Apte's house sat directly across a canal from ours, his golden retriever, Ginger, bounding around his fenced backyard. Lefty Kreh lived in the neighborhood too. We had quite an eclectic group in such close proximity.

I fished a lot with my dad and knew of Stearns' burgeoning outdoor writing career. We fished together just once—or, more appropriately, rode in his boat—when a group of us accompanied Bruce Babbitt, then the secretary of the interior, on a fishing trip in Biscayne Bay. Occasionally Dad went to Flamingo with Stearns to pursue redfish, cobia, snook and such. Stearns did surprise me one day by giving me a Daiwa spinning rod and reel—one of dozens stored in his garage—which far outclassed the cheapo stuff I used at the time.

Wading the flats for bonefish. Photo courtesy of Walt Stearns.

Since then I've gotten to know him and his wife, Shirley, very well. And way back in the mid-1980s, their son Walt worked for a sideline water sports business my Dad and I operated on the Rickenbacker Causeway to Key Biscayne—Walt's gone on to be a renowned photographer in his own right. So, Bob Stearns and I have some history.

Like many of us, he can be moody—at times I've found him to be quiet and introspective, at other times gregarious and very sharing. I once unexpectedly passed him—my next-door neighbor, mind you—in a hallway in Las Vegas at a tackle trade show. Although I swear our eyes met and I nodded, he looked away as if I were just another stranger and kept on walking. Running into him the next day, we stopped to idly chat for a while, so I just figured he was simply lost in thought the day before.

As worldly as he may be, I do know that there's nowhere else Bob Stearns would rather fish than in Florida, and he's been doing it about as well as anyone for 40-plus years. He's caught and released literally thousands of fish on fly. Even so, a series of catches in Central America in 1979 and 1982 rank as his most memorable accomplishments as well as serve as a turning point in his motivation to pursue world records.

In '79, fishing offshore of Costa Rica while based at a lodge just north of Flamingo, Stearns and crew utilized the bait-and-switch teasing method. He soon hooked into a really huge Pacific sailfish—so large he suspected it might be a world record on 16-pound fly tippet.

Stearns managed to whip that sailfish and the boat raced to the dock to weigh it. However, the scale hadn't been used previously for a world record, and International Game Fish Association (IGFA) rules stated that a known comparison weight would thus be necessary.

"Since I knew the precise weight of my wife, Shirley, she stepped onto the scale, and we could see it was exactly right," said Stearns. "The scale showed that the sailfish weighed 117 pounds, eight ounces, and I submitted it for a record.

"A few weeks later, I got a call from Elwood Harry, president of the IGFA, and he asked how I'd calibrated the scale," Stearns said. "I told him how it happened, and he laughed for 10 minutes straight—and I got the record."

The IGFA established an eight-pound tippet category a few years later and Stearns headed back to Costa Rica. He stayed at the same lodge and fished aboard the same boat with, yes, the same exact crew. He hooked sailfish after sailfish on the light tippet, but kept coming up empty. The next day in rough morning seas, the first fish hooked turned out to be a feisty 66-pound sail that Stearns boated in 30 minutes. It stood as the world record for many years, but at that stage he had an epiphany.

"My enthusiasm for establishing records began to wane," he said. "I didn't like making other anglers on the boat wait while I played a potential record—they came a long way to fish too. At the same time, I have no beef with those who charter their own trips to pursue world records or the angler who gets lucky."

As usually happens with world records, Stearns' were eventually bested. Even so, he'll always be proud of becoming the first to set the mark for Pacific sailfish on eight-pound tippet.

Stearns obviously knows what he's doing with a fly rod. He also possesses a detailed understanding of what makes a boat, from bow to the stern and beam to beam. He's a true pro as a journalist and an angler, aided by a background in meteorology and considerable on-the-water time in the U.S. Navy. He earned a B.S. in meteorology from Florida State University in 1958.

Eschewing the career of a "weatherman," the career path some of his fellow meteorology majors chose, Stearns spent six years on active duty as a naval weather officer and six more as a reservist, reaching the rank of lieutenant commander.

Stearns' knowledge of marine resources and how weather affects conditions is based on more than just his navy service and meteorology background. He worked as a research associate at the University of Miami's Rosenstiel School of Marine and Atmospheric Science (RS-MAS) from 1965 to 1973. During that time he participated in hurricane research projects aboard hurricane hunter aircraft—flying into the storms' eyes sometimes—and in biological field studies of marine vegetation in Biscayne Bay. It's pretty heady stuff, but plenty of valuable data for those visiting the flats of south Florida, the Keys and Flamingo.

Most saltwater experts often travel to do battle with freshwater foes too. Stearns proved his mettle with this 18-pound Pacific-coast steelhead. Photo courtesy of Bob Stearns.

Special Section: Marine Electronics '90

March 1990
$2.95

SaltWater
SPORTSMAN

Light-Tackle
Dolphin

Heavyweight
Salmon

Plentiful
Permit

Boat Reports:
Post 50
Seaplus 24

Precision
Downrigging

This picture became a magazine cover in 1990, with Bob's son Walt having the courage and technical know-how to snap the over/under shark release. Photo courtesy of Walt Stearns and *Salt Water Sportsman* magazine.

"More than anything, those experiences taught me how to learn," he said. "You really go to college to learn how to learn. As a lab rat for all those years, I got the most out of figuring out the right gear for the right job, how best to do sampling and so on. It's the same with fishing."

Beginning in 1969, Stearns began to apply his talents to writing. He'd started while at RSMAS to supplement his pay, doing so at the suggestion of neighbor Lefty Kreh.

"Lefty and I got to know each other and we fished together a lot," said Stearns. "At one point he said, 'Bob, you're crazy to be so knowledgeable about fishing and boating and not get paid—you ought to write for magazines.'

"I was already writing studies and papers anyway, so I told Shirley I'd make a stab at it in the outdoor magazine world and see how far it would take me," Stearns said. "She agreed and I turned down another RSMAS lab assignment to give it a shot. At the end of that year, I could see I was ahead of the game, and off I went."

In 1973, Stearns became one of the few to successfully make a living full-time as a freelance magazine writer and photographer in the fishing and boating industries. Most other contributing writers penned fishing articles strictly as a sideline, the meager pay never adding up enough to cover all the bills. Stearns, however, parlayed his early writing into more and more assignments, and to date he's published over 1,800 feature articles, cover photographs and regular columns. His work has been published in many popular titles, including *Boating, Sea, Yachting, Motor Boating & Sailing, Rudder, Motorboat, Field & Stream, Outdoor Life, Sports Afield, Fishing World, Florida Sportsman, Bass & Walleye Boats, Fishing World, Petersen's Fishing, Small Boat Journal, Saltwater Fly Fishing, Trailer Boats, Popular Science* and *Salt Water Sportsman* (for which he's still editor at large).

Some of his more significant magazine masthead titles over the years—to name just a few—include boat editor for *Florida Sportsman,* boating editor for *Outdoor Life,* and boating and saltwater fishing editor for *Field & Stream.*

Stearns published his first book in 1984, *The Fisherman's Boating Book,* and in 1991 he co-wrote with Erwin Bauer *The Saltwater Fisherman's*

Bible. More recently, in 2009 his book *The Homeowner's Hurricane Handbook* has had great appeal for all those living in the path of potential hurricanes. In addition to his writings, since 1974 Stearns has appeared on a number of top television fishing programs, such as *The Fisherman* series produced by Glen Lau and the *Outdoor Life* series. In 1987 he served as the host in a video production called *The Alaskan Angler*—Stearns has been making pilgrimages to Alaska for a month every summer for 30 years.

He's also been an industry consultant to companies like 3M, Aquasport, Carver, Dupont and Monark. "I've always tried to work with boat manufacturers toward the goal of improving safety and fuel efficiency," Stearns said. His advice to a number of tackle manufacturers resulted in improvements in fishing lines, lures, rods and reels.

Speaking of boat designing, a good measure of input from Stearns resulted in the interior design of Hewes Boats—the first production flats boats of the Hewes Bonefisher and Redfisher models that became a huge success.

"I bought one of my first engines from Bob Hewes back in the mid-'60s for a boat I'd built as a skiff," Stearns said. "I took him fishing in it a time or two and Lefty did the same in his aluminum boat. It was Lefty who first suggested that we study the design of the Wildcat, a 16-foot ski boat hull. I liked the ride of the hull, but it needed many changes.

"I drew up sketches with wide gunnels, rod storage, foredeck, center console, rear deck in back for poling—this was before platforms gained in popularity—and moving the gas tank to the aft end of the foredeck."

In 1969, the first production boat was named the Bonefisher and it worked out extremely well. Stearns ran hull number one for many years, later adding electric hydraulic trim tabs to it. Other design changes resulted in advanced models of the Bonefisher and the newer Redfisher made of Kevlar. The latter material stood up to just about any damage, and it was a bass-boat manufacturer in Tennessee who showed Hewes and Stearns the advantages of the much lighter yet stronger Kevlar. Hewes eventually sold out in 1989 to Maverick, based in Stuart, Florida.

"Had it not been for Bob Hewes taking our advice and putting designs into an actual boat, a production flats boat would have been delayed hitting the market," said Stearns. "Before Hewes got involved, all you saw on the flats were modified hulls and bass boats rather than vessels specifically for saltwater flats."

One might wonder how Stearns had any time left away from his keyboard and monitor, but somehow he still managed to serve as a director or advisor to groups such as the Recreational Fisheries Advisory Council of the Florida Department of Natural Resources, the Everglades Protection Association and the Florida Conservation Association. But that's far from all his contributions: From 1970 to 2003, Stearns was a director of the Metropolitan South Florida Fishing Tournament (MET) and took on the role of its president from 1982 to 1986.

For over 70 years, the MET was a public service organization that promoted south Florida tourism through sport fishing until it ceased operation in 2007. Upwards of 15,000 fish were entered in the MET each year by visitors to south Florida from all over the world; 85 percent of those fish were released alive. Keeping on top of all the details in running the MET took considerable organizational and management skills.

Considering that all his accomplishments stem from a career as a prolific writer, designer, researcher and organizer, it's easy to appreciate why Miamian Bob Stearns takes his place as one of the top journalists in Florida's boating and fishing history.

28

Sam Griffin, b. 1937

LAKE OKEECHOBEE

Born on a houseboat on Lake Okeechobee, Sam Griffin grew up surrounded by boats and bass fishermen. His family established Uncle Joe's Fish Camp on the south side of Lake O, eventually adding cabins and a restaurant to their boat rental operation as well.

Griffin guided in the summer months, and every weekend of the year he worked at the camp. After getting out of school in 1954, he continued with the family business and widened it to also guiding duck hunters.

"During that time, I really expanded my fishing education, thanks to George Brown," said Griffin. "The man had a glass eye and limited vision, but he was way ahead of his time with bass fishing. As far back as the 1940s, George would rest his knees on one side of the gunnel and drift in the current flow, kneeling and reeling. He could catch fish even when everyone else couldn't."

In the early days, lake water was so clear you could see a dime 10 feet below. Unfortunately, the nutrient levels changed, making the water murkier.

"We adapted as best we could to the water conditions," said Griffin. "We still caught lots of fish using gold or silver Johnson Minnows with # 11 pork chunks as sweeteners. Other good lures were frogs, darters, spoons made weedless with plastic eels, Dog Specials and on occasion the River Runt Crankbait. We chose lure colors based on the cloud cover."

Sam Griffin developed his own line of handmade, wooden top-water lures, including the Jerkin' Sam, Creek Popper, Lil' Richard, Florida

A largemouth caught on one of Sam Griffin's classic top-water lures. Photo courtesy of Robert Montgomery.

Shad, Pop 'N Joe, Moonshine Special, Fish Creek Darter, STP (for snook, tarpon and peacocks) and other models. His lures have drawn praise from not only Lake Okeechobee veterans but anglers everywhere.

Herb Allen, formerly the fishing editor for the *Tampa Tribune*, described Griffin this way: "Sammy made fantastic lures and became a top guide on Lake Okeechobee. He once got convinced to move to Mexico, but after a few months he couldn't shake the homesickness and back he came. That's a good thing, because he's a Lake O legend."

"Sam's lures really get the job done," remarked Larry Larsen, an author, freelance writer and well-known bass authority based in Lakeland, Florida.

"I fished with Sam in Venezuela and Lake O using his lures, and I quickly learned one of his pet peeves on the water," Larsen said. "Whenever the lure would get fowled during a cast, I'd slap the lure on the surface of the water to rid the grass. Sam hates that, and his displeasure would get quite animated.

"Years ago when Sam first came out with a half-ounce, three-inch top-water model—I think it was the Jerkin' Sam—I really liked it and asked him if he could make a larger version of it," Larsen said. "He agreed and produced one five inches long and three-quarter ounces. 'Here you go,' he told me. 'I'm sending six of them just for you.'

"But a couple of months later I learned he'd added that larger lure to his regular lineup, which was fine with me. Although I liked the bigger version he sent me, I wanted one even larger for the huge peacock bass in the Amazon River. Sam agreed, later sending six to me with a note that they're 'just for you and not for sale.'

"But like before, Sam had actually made 18 other models of my double-large lures and discovered that they worked extremely well. The irony is that I twice asked Sam to upsize from smaller plugs and he agreed to do so just for me, but each time he ended up going commercial with it. I'm happy it worked out that way for both of us."

Even so, it's not lures, rods or reels that Griffin feels has made the biggest difference in modern-day bass fishing.

"The main thing that's evolved is the invention of the electric trolling motor," said Griffin. "It really frees the angler from having to row, pole or otherwise propel the boat. It greatly increases your casting time and makes it easier to quietly sneak up on fish."

Sam Griffin is considered by all to be the fishing guru of Lake Okeechobee. At age seven he once made three casts and caught six bass on a Dog Special. Twenty years later he'd notch another remarkable achievement, catching 24 fish on 12 consecutive casts—on the 13th cast he caught "only" one.

On a memorable day when the 16-year-old Griffin guided a couple from Ohio, the wife made a nice cast to a spawning bed and soon reeled to the boat a 12 ½-pound bass. His own top mark stands at 11 $^7/_{10}$ pounds on a plastic crankbait. He's released so many five-pound-plus largemouths on Lake O that he can't even estimate the total.

Griffin favors monofilament line due to the stretch factor, and patience is paramount. "Jerk it twice and let it sit," he said, adding that those who fish more slowly will usually catch a greater number of fish than those who believe the number of casts is more important. He's also observed that with a prop bait, 95 percent of strikes occur when the bait comes to a stop.

Robert Montgomery, a senior writer for *Bassmaster* magazine, included in his book *Better Bass Fishing* a lot of quotes from Griffin.

Dave Burkhardt watches Griffin play a big one in Lake O. Photo courtesy of Robert Montgomery.

Now a resident of Moore Haven, Florida, Sam Griffin's name is forever linked to Lake Okeechobee. Photo courtesy of Robert Montgomery.

"He's the man to talk to about top-water fishing," said Montgomery. "He knows that when the barometer is rising, for example, fish are going to seek eddies and structures to take the pressure off them, so that's where to concentrate the casts.

"Sam also believes that lure colors mean more to fishermen than they do the fish," he said. "Sam field tests his wooden top-water baits without painting them and catches plenty of bass."

Being on the lake as much as he has, you'd expect Griffin to have experienced close calls with things that slither.

"Yes, I've had some close calls," Griffin confirmed. "Back in the late 1970s, a cottonmouth crawled into my boat and got under a life jacket behind the console. I carried a pushpole in those days and used it to kill the snake and hurl it overboard.

He remembered another snake scare during a fishing tournament. "We ran about 20 miles from Okeechobee at the northern part of the lake to the west side. We heard a splash next to the boat and turned to see if it might be a fish but instead saw a chicken snake slithering away.

"It seemed a bit strange, but we forgot about it until, a little later, my angler sees another darn snake, this time coming out of the bilge onto the deck. I'm wondering, What's going on? We then realized that the snakes were getting into the bilge while at my house on the trailer. I took care of the problem and never made that mistake again."

Snakes are not the biggest threat on Lake Okeechobee, however—the lake is famously home to thousands of alligators too. Griffin laughed about an incident involving two clients from Alabama.

"We were catching fish on top-water lures along the cattail and hyacinth banks on the north side of the lake. A big gator came along, probably a female just warding us off. I used the trolling motor to move away rather than kicking up the engine, and the fellows got really antsy when the gator at first was gaining on us. 'Hey,' one of them yelled, 'don't that big engine work?' The gator finally turned off but not before those 'Bama boys scrambled to the center of the boat."

Another sign Griffin respects when out on Lake O: summer thunder storms. When a kid, he hung around a bit too long as a storm approached. A cast resulted in the fishing line making an arc in the air due to all the static electricity.

"I thought it pretty odd," said Griffin. Then a lightning bolt struck nearby. *"That's* not odd," he remembers exclaiming before quickly vamoosing off the water.

Being familiar with practically every square foot of Lake Okeechobee, Griffin is often called upon to help search for people who go missing. "I've got unusually good night vision," he said. "That's been helpful in rescuing some who are lost or in trouble, but it became grisly on the two occasions when I spotted the bodies of anglers who'd lost their lives—not a nice sight for sure."

The respect Sam Griffin has garnered from those in the fishing industry continues to build. Dave Burkhardt, owner of Trik Fish, is quick to say that Griffin's the greatest top- water angler he's ever seen.

"One day that I vividly recall involved a trip with Sam on Lake O," he said. "I couldn't get a clean cast with my lure, snagging weeds on every retrieve. Meanwhile, Sam's lure came back to the boat time after time with nothing clinging to it.

"I finally asked how he managed to do that. Sam said to observe where the wind was coming from and how it affected the grasses at the surface. Breezes form distinct lanes, and Sam watched for the cleared lanes and maneuvered his lure through them."

Burkhardt summarized it best, saying, "It's simply a wonderful learning experience to share a front deck with him."

I hope one day to do the same.

29

Al Pflueger Jr., b. 1937

MIAMI

Albert Pflueger Jr. could easily boast of his list of accomplishments with a fishing rod, because it's nothing short of phenomenal. The soft-spoken master angler has probably notched more tournament victories and awards than any other angler who ever lived, not to mention countless club and world records. He could brag, but he won't. Heaping praise on himself just isn't Pflueger's style.

Pflueger (pronounced FLEW-gur), the youngest member to capture the title of "Master Angler" in the world-renowned Rod & Reel Club of Miami Beach, years ago authored the *Fisherman's Handbook*—still a best seller—and he even has an artificial reef named in his honor off Miami Beach.

Whenever he enters a tournament, the smart money says that the name Pflueger will be at the top of the leader board when the salt spray clears, and it matters not the type of tackle or whether the quarry is on the flats, reef or blue water.

But his natural talent reaches far beyond his angling ability. He's also won hundreds of trophies for such diverse activities as table tennis, swimming, powerboat racing and drag racing. He's also every bit as adept with a rifle or shotgun. In fact, to challenge Pflueger to a trap-shooting contest is an invitation to lose. Combine those natural athletic skills with the time and wherewithal to travel, and you have quite the worldly sportsman.

The Pflueger name itself is a well-known one throughout Florida and much of the world. It first came to prominence in 1926 when Al Pflueger Sr. opened a small taxidermy business in Hallandale. Up until

Four snook caught on plug, back in the days when you could keep that many.
Photo courtesy of Al Pflueger Jr.

then, stuffing a fish meant making a solid plaster form in the shape of the species, wrapping its skin around the form, and sewing it on. The result was a chunk of plaster with a fish's skin attached. Not only did it just somewhat resemble the real thing, it weighed a lot more than the original fish.

Pflueger revolutionized the entire taxidermy industry with a new process utilizing a hollow mold that fit the size and species as well as a gray, mud-like material he invented called Mache. The fish went into the mold and was lathered in Mache, reinforced with gauze and packed with sawdust. A wooden plate was inserted to accept the mounting bracket screws. After sewing up the fish, the process involved adding a primer and repairing or attaching fins as necessary. Finally, a craftsman painstakingly painted its natural colors. The process involved up to five months, passing through 14 departments that employed 150 workers. Not only did these new mounts look much more lifelike than ever before, they weighed a lot less than the actual fish. This allowed big mounts like billfish to be more easily shipped and hung on walls.

When Al senior passed away in 1962, his son took the reins of the company. The young Pflueger had already been active in the business and supplemented his precise knowledge of fish anatomy by scuba diving to learn their habits and natural colors. Pflueger would watch the habits of fish when baits and lures were present and how they reacted to strikes. He also took note of specifics about fighting behaviors. He learned far more about various species and their habits than even many fish biologists.

It wasn't long before he built a reputation as a crackerjack angler. But the young prodigy also built up the family's business, enlisting more regional agents to increase out-of-Florida mounts, and soon the bustling plant reached an acre in size and was employing over 200 workers. It was easily the largest taxidermy business in the world, and more than one million fish were ultimately mounted there. Famous clients sought them out, such as Errol Flynn, Ernest Hemingway, Herbert Hoover, John Kennedy, Richard Nixon, Ernest Borgnine, Dean Martin, William Conrad, Julius Boros, Curt Gowdy, Ted Williams and many others.

Miami guiding icon Bill Curtis still stays in touch with Pflueger. "Al used to charter me a lot," said Curtis. "Just the other day he came into the fly shop where I work at Bass Pro Shops. We talked about how I used to take him out and help him win the Miami Beach Rod & Reel Club competitions. I remember one year he beat out Jim Lopez for the club championship. We went out fishing and Al caught eight or nine bones that day on different tests of line with spin and plug and the same with different tippets for fly. It was really hard to beat Al at anything because he tried hard every minute."

Curtis and other guides used to do a lot of business with Pflueger Taxidermy. "In those days everything was skin mounted, and they did such a beautiful job that my clients never complained. I'd always use Pflueger Taxidermy, and knowing Al on a personal basis made a difference too. Unlike some other taxidermists around, you'd get your mounting commissions on time with no excuses or delays.

"Al had a truck going around to all the docks every day to pick up fish to be mounted," Curtis said. "Al eventually sold out to Shakespeare and they ran the whole operation right into the ground—they just didn't know how to run a company like that right."

Pflueger is now comfortably retired, having not only sold the taxidermy business but also parlayed his investments in real estate and other ventures. These wise moves produced ample time to do what he really cherishes: fishing. Add to that passion his deep thirst for knowing just exactly what makes fish tick and you can better understand what makes him tick as well.

In essence, Pflueger is the type of person you could drop blindfolded into any region of the world and in short order he would become the best angler around. And as anyone who has made the leap from one activity to another knows, the same characteristics that sweep a winner to the top of the heap in one arena usually spell success elsewhere. Whether it all comes down to an innate need to achieve or the absolute refusal to accept anything less than being the best, Al Pflueger is cut from that type of cloth.

Years back he sunk his teeth into hunting, and turkey hunting in particular. Pflueger credits the late Biff Lampton, former editor of *Florida Sportsman,* for giving him turkey fever. A couple of years before Lampton's unfortunate death in the mid-1990s due to a car accident, he took Pflueger to his hunting lease in the Fakahatchee Strand

A generation of fishing expertise, with Pflueger's mother and grandmother showing the results of a day on the water off Miami Beach. Photo courtesy of Al Pflueger Jr.

Preserve east of Naples. I know the place, because I've been there too. The moment Pflueger crouched in a blind and watched Lampton call in a big gobbler, he had an electric, cataclysmic reaction. Not surprisingly, Pflueger quickly became an expert himself at turkey hunting and later big-game hunting to boot.

"Al takes instruction well, after which he'll pick your brain and then spend 10 hours a day for as long as it takes to master the techniques," said Lee Lones of Miami, a longtime friend of Pflueger's. "When he gets into something, there's no stopping him."

The first time I saw Al Pflueger occurred on a fishing trip to Flamingo in Florida Bay. He stood on the bow of a flats skiff, his tall frame imposing against the gray sky and his eyes fastened on the flats. I saw an amazingly fast motion as he sent a fly about 50 feet with a cast as straight as a laser beam. It impressed me, particularly when a redfish grabbed the fly and Pflueger released it minutes later.

My next encounter took place at a kickoff for a Florida Keys fishing tournament. I'd arranged to produce a series of monthly seminars around the state with Karl Wickstrom that involved me doing the spadework and *Florida Sportsman* promoting it. I approached Pflueger to see if he'd participate as one of the regular headline speakers. As I talked, he looked down at me without expression, his eyes fixed on mine. After I finished delivering my pitch, Pflueger simply turned and walked away.

That's it. Nothing said.

I found Wickstrom in the crowd and told him about it. He laughed. "Don't be offended," said Wickstrom. "That's just Al."

As the years unfolded, Pflueger and I became good friends. I met him often at the *Florida Sportsman* office then in South Miami. He'd drop by to visit with Lampton and Wickstrom. At some point during a conversation involving hunting, Pflueger mentioned a .243 Remington for sale—a perfect Florida deer rifle for my 12-year-old son—and a .270 Weatherby magnum with a 3x9 Leupold scope that I wanted for an all-around big-game hunting rifle. From there our contact grew.

A remarkable aspect of Al's character is that he's indeed shy at first with new people but very gregarious with friends. His generosity also knows few boundaries, as he's helped many people anonymously in times of financial need and also organized fundraisers, such as one for Capt. Bob Lewis' successful but expensive heart-transplant operation.

I already mentioned that Pflueger doesn't like tooting his own horn because he really doesn't have to. Often when accomplished legends of fishing are on the water with someone, they'll go out of their way to loudly correct an angler or to provide unsolicited critiques as a way of showing off. Not Pflueger. We once stopped to catch pinfish for bait near a grassy marker in Florida Bay with several others on the boat. Noting I wasn't catching many pinfish, he leaned over and whispered so only I could hear: "Doug, drop your hook to the bottom." I did so and began catching lots of them. Like the greatest of the great, he doesn't mock others, bark or yell, belittle or pontificate. In other words, he's respectful of others' feelings.

Pflueger is right at home with any gear, including the spin rig that took this tripletail. Photo courtesy of Al Pflueger Jr.

Pflueger's never more tuned-in than when atop a casting platform on the flats. Photo courtesy of Al Pflueger Jr.

Capt. Ralph Delph of Key West has long admired Pflueger's skills, saying: "He's one of the first of the really top-drawer, all-around anglers. Al can handle any fish and any tackle. He has the time and money to do it, and he was always the one to beat in the tournaments or club standings. The best fishermen don't have to brag—the cream always rises to the top over the years."

Homosassa guide Earl Waters fished Pflueger for years and they remain good friends. Waters knows how determined he can be. "Back when Al used to smoke, I had to light up 11 cigarettes for him while he fought a tarpon for eight hours," said Waters. "He didn't rest that entire time and had blisters on both hands—he's relentless.

"What sets Al apart is his ability to read a fish and make that fish eat by manipulating the fly," he continued. "Al just pulled on their faces with brute strength and none of the down-and-dirty stuff or down-on-your-knees finesses and such—he had his own style."

Fly-fishing virtuoso Chico Fernandez of Miami fished with Pflueger on one unforgettable day in 1961 out of Flamingo. Aboard Pflueger's 13-foot Boston Whaler, they took an amazing 79 redfish on fly. The story goes that at the boat ramp that morning, someone walked over to ask about the function of the platform above the outboard engine—a new accessory on a skiff back then. Might it be a picnic table, the fellow guessed? Pflueger looked at Fernandez then back at the man and with a dead-serious face said, "Nope, it's a shading device to keep the hot sun off the engine." The man walked off with a knowing nod, and Pflueger and Fernandez held back any snickering until he was out of earshot.

One occasion when Pflueger did initiate a conversation with someone he'd just met, it completely backfired. He'd competed in a fishing event with The Splendid Splinter, one of the anglers in the field.

"I won the tournament and found myself seated next to the great Ted Williams at the awards banquet," said Pflueger. "I downed a couple of drinks and finally worked up some nerve. I turned to Ted with my thoughts on how the Red Sox had fared since his retirement. Ted nodded for about a minute as I talked and all of a sudden he cut me off cold. 'Look kid, you don't know shit about baseball—talk to me about fishing.' I felt like melting under the table and disappearing altogether."

Pflueger has no qualms about relating that encounter to friends because he's secure with his ability and character. And that's what makes Al so special. To find a finer friend and a greater angler would not be easy in either case.

30

Roland Martin, b. 1940

LAKE OKEECHOBEE

Media legend Bill Dance competed in a tournament in 1970 when Roland Martin was his roommate. It was late fall and the weather cold, rainy and icy.

"I knew if I had any chance to win this tournament, the one guy I had to beat was Roland," said Dance. "We'd share information and Roland told me everything he'd done that day in total honesty, and frankly sometimes too honestly.

"You come to trust the man's word no matter what. If Roland says a flea can pull a plow, you better hitch him up."

Dance at times liked to play practical jokes when rooming with Martin. "He liked socializing, and after a long day he'd go out in the evenings with some of the other fishermen," said Dance.

"He'd always invite me along but I'd usually stay in the room, so before leaving he'd ask what time we're getting up in the morning. I'd say 4:30 and with that he'd answer that he'd be back in 'just a little while.'

"We'd awake using a loud alarm clock, so before retiring for bed around 9 I'd set the clock for 3:30 instead of 4:30," Dance said, laughing giddily as he told the story.

"Roland would drag in around 12 or 1, go to bed, and sure enough, the clock would go off at 3:30. I'd reach over and turn it off and then tell Roland, 'Hey, it's 4:40, time to rise and shine.'

"He'd drag himself slowly out of bed and complain about being so darn sleepy. When he stepped into the shower, I'd change the alarm forward another hour. Roland would come back out and see me still in bed, figuring I was trying to get in a few minutes extra sleep. He'd start

Bass fishing isn't all Martin's good at—how many people have caught a
45-pound redfish? Photo courtesy of Roland Martin.

getting his stuff together, periodically warning me that I'd better get my sleepy self up or I'd miss the start time.

"As Roland left the room, he'd still be egging me to get up so I wouldn't be late. I'd sleep another 45 minutes. I did the same thing to him every night. In the morning, I'd glance at Roland's face at the dock and he'd be in a fog, like a cow staring at a new gate. By the third day his eyes were so swollen they looked like he'd plucked them out and played with them.

"He got even with me plenty of times, though," Dance said. "Once he put a snake in my bed—that kept me up all night. We're always having fun with each other, such as the time in a Carolina tournament when he was running a Johnson engine on his boat. I ran down to the marina when he wasn't there, removed the cowling off the engine and replaced it with an Evinrude from another boat. Since both were 150-horsepower OMC's, it fit perfectly.

"Roland takes off and is concentrating on where to go and doesn't notice it, but everyone else does. 'Hey Roland,' somebody yelled, 'when did you start running Evinrudes?' Roland turned around, frowned and exclaimed, 'I am going to kill Bill Dance.' It was a hoot."

Martin is a man of humor, and humor often finds him. Years ago he came to Islamorada to fish in a tournament, and rather than stay at a hotel, he decided to toss his bags in the new house he'd just bought down there. After the kickoff party for the event, Martin returned home, stripped down to his underpants to get comfortable and searched for the newspaper. Not seeing it, he walked outside to find it.

A gust of wind came up and slammed the door shut—he was locked out. All the windows were shut and locked too. Martin frantically began knocking on doors of nearby houses to ask if he could make a phone call. Imagine what those people must have thought to see their new neighbor standing before them in his underpants at 11 at night.

Fortunately, someone recognized him before a call went out to the police to catch a possible Fruit-of-the-Loom voyeur on the loose. It became quite the story as news of the mishap spread around Islamorada.

No one will laugh at Roland Martin's fishing ability, however. Sam Griffin, a lure maker and himself a legend around Lake Okeechobee,

Entertaining troops in Germany during the Iraq war. Photo courtesy of Roland Martin.

said, "There's everybody and there's Roland. He thinks like a fish. His brain is part fish. It's uncanny the way he can find fish."

That kind of talent gets noticed. Martin, who's launched a number of successful business enterprises, helped the fledgling Bass Anglers Sportsman Society (B.A.S.S.) do the same. In the late 1960s, he hopped aboard the company bus of B.A.S.S. founder Ray Scott. He encouraged bass aficionados to join the organization so their collective voices could be more effective. B.A.S.S. prospered in no small measure due to Martin's active support.

In 1970, Martin decided to try his hand at the bass tournaments. His impact was immediate, with a runner-up finish in his first event, a win in the next tournament and another second in his third. Not a bad start—second, first, second—in just three competitions, and something no one had accomplished up to that time. Martin went on to dominate the tournament circuit and became one of the men to beat.

A bass fishing jaunt with former judge Pete Messler of Oklahoma, who conduct-ed the marriage ceremony for Roland and wife Judy. Photo courtesy of Roland Martin.

He notched 19 B.A.S.S. wins and 20 seconds with nearly 100 top-10 finishes, 25 BASS Masters Classic appearances and a record nine Angler of the Year honors—the most in B.A.S.S. history. His TV shows span nearly 30 years, including 20 as host of the widely acclaimed *Fishing with Roland Martin*. With TV coverage showing his blond good looks and quick smile, Roland Martin enjoyed the type of celebrity never pre-viously achieved in freshwater fishing circles.

I was particularly astonished at the 19 titles, but the 20 second-place finishes is remarkable too. Martin knew that catching big bass required a professional dedication no different than what's needed for golf, base-ball or any other sport. Martin competed against other pros, not just any Joe Schmo or wannabe who could barely hit a bathtub with a lure from 10 feet away. He thus had to rise above even the expert level to become a consistent winner.

Roland Martin also became the first professional bass angler to see his name in three organizations' Halls of Fame: International Game Fish Association, Freshwater and Professional Bass. His achievements, victories, and honors go on and on, but you get the idea.

At times he's acted the pitchman for various lunker-bass-nabbin' products, including the "Rocket Fishing Rod" and even more notably, the "Helicopter Lure." The latter spun as it sank into a lake's water column, and some claimed that it worked like a charm in saltwater settings too for diverse species such as trout and sailfish.

"He truly believes that every time he makes a cast he's going to catch a fish," said Dance. "You do a TV show with him and he's just worried more about catching fish than the show.

"I've met a lot of fishermen, and Roland is the most versatile I've ever met," Dance added. "He can adapt to anything, all types of water, any depths, and he's just as good at moving water as still water—most anglers can't do that."

Martin made trolling motors a common utility in tournaments. His reliance on depth sounders resulted in the electronic gear becoming standard equipment on bass boats. He's also developed a water-clarity meter and come up with designs for rods, reels and lures that are still popular.

One of Martin's innovative discoveries involves a sophisticated patterning technique that helps determine where fish will congregate based on water conditions, bottom structure and other factors, such as depth.

Susan Cocking, outdoor writer for the *Miami Herald,* admired Martin's competitive spirit during an event in the mid-1990s.

"Even though it wasn't a big tournament, Roland simply wanted to win," she said. "At one point he spotted a promising area to make a cast just ahead of the boat. Not wanting to waste time with me coming back to sit in the cockpit, Roland asked me to lie down on the bow as he quickly rushed to the location. He made a perfect hole shot before another boat could possibly get there, and darned if he didn't pull a nice bass from it."

With his extensive knowledge of bass fishing, it didn't take long for Martin to become an outstanding saltwater angler as well. Veteran Miami fishing guide Bill Curtis took Roland Martin aboard his skiff *Grasshopper* and fished him in four of the Gold Cup Tarpon Tournaments held annually in Islamorada.

"We came in third one year," said Curtis. "He's an excellent all-around fisherman and great with a fly rod. He was so good he could throw his back cast farther than his forward cast, and on certain windy conditions, you're not going to get a fly to a fish without a good get-back cast maneuver.

"One thing he liked me to do that worked well involved getting the boat ahead of a school of tarpon," Curtis said. "We'd see which direction the fish were moving. I'd use the electric motors and move ahead of the school, stop the electrics and Roland would then cast as the school approached."

If Martin didn't get a fish to take, Curtis would again quietly run well around the school with his electrics and shut down a good distance ahead of their direction.

"In that way he'd get more hook-ups because it didn't spook the fish as much as so often happens when you chase after them from behind or the side," said Curtis.

Earl Waters, a well-known and longtime guide from Homosassa, had never met Martin until August of 1988, when he received a call from Glenn Lau. Lau, a noted filmmaker based in Ocala, Florida, told Waters he was shooting a commercial and wanted him to help out. Waters readily agreed, particularly when Lau said that Roland Martin would be part of the gig.

"Roland, Glenn, his crew and I met the day before to discuss the particulars of the shoot," Waters said. "I picked a suitable site location and later that afternoon took Roland out to make sure he knew where he needed to be in the morning. I got up a little early the next day to make sure I wasn't late, and as I approached the rendezvous spot, I found Glenn and his crew already present.

Glenn Lau had a job to get done and understandably felt antsy about Martin making it on time. "Glenn asked me if I'd seen Roland and I answered no, adding that if he'd left before me I would've seen him, so he must be behind me.

"Ten minutes later we started to worry, and Glenn wondered if maybe Roland made a wrong turn. I figured that if Roland did head up the wrong creek, he'd probably be in trouble by now due to all the hidden rocks. Glenn asked me to go check on him, so off I went wide open to a saltwater creek that turns fresh if you get far enough past the rocky areas."

As Waters approached the last possible turn up the headwaters of a tributary to the Homosassa River, he spotted him.

"My first thought when I saw Roland's trolling motor deployed was that he'd busted his outboard on the rocks," said Waters. "As I approached, however, he turned with rod in hand and said matter-of-factly, 'Son, are there any bass in here? This looks like an awesome place for fish to hold.'

"I reminded Roland that Glenn and crew were on site and needed us there. Roland just shrugged and replied with a huge smile, 'Hey, I got lost and figured I should just stay put and fish because you would be better able to find me than me find you.' Now how many people would just start casually fishing if lost up a tidal creek? Only one I know—Roland Martin."

My infrequent encounters with Roland Martin resulted in the same impression: He's a guy with an upbeat disposition and a ready handshake who's willing to go anywhere and try anything involving fishing. His mind is always at work, his enthusiasm literally pulsating. The man reflects an infectious optimism that's eternally appealing.

Chances are that if you see Martin in a boat coming from the other direction, he's going to be the first guy who waves hello; in a crowded cocktail party, he's going to be the first to introduce himself. I'd say that's no small part of why Roland Martin's been one of the most popular and successful figures in Florida's sport-fishing history.

31

~~~~~

Ralph Delph, b. 1940

KEY WEST

Come rain or shine, every Thursday for 15 years, Jim Anson drove from his home in Miami to Key West. Did he have business down there or family responsibilities? Nope, this man wanted to fish with Capt. Ralph Delph.

"When I first started with Ralph, I didn't even know how to open the bail of a reel—I'd never even caught a fish," said Anson.

"A couple of years later I'd won the Master Angler trophy in the Metropolitan South Florida Fishing Tournament (MET). I jokingly remarked to Ralph, 'Think of all the other people you've guided over the years who wouldn't put up with you.' Ralph would do a mock frown and say, 'True, most of the guys I chewed out never came back, and now you're the winner and they're the losers.' He was right—I ended up setting 31 world records with Ralph."

As a Green Beret, Anson learned to listen to people barking instructions. "I did exactly as Ralph told me and I've never regretted a moment of it." Anson went on to notch an additional 150 world records, and he now guides others to record catches.

Anson spoke of an occasion when they fished hard all day but nothing was biting. "We were about to call it quits when Ralph looked at me with a smile and said, 'Are you bleeding yet?'

"I knew what he meant. It does sound strange, but it seemed like whenever I got a small cut or injury, a fish would hit.

"So, I purposely nicked my thumb a little bit to draw blood," said Anson. "Incredibly, minutes later a huge fish pounced on my fly and made a long run. It turned out to be a world-record 83-pound cobia. Luckily,

Delph (left) led Stu Apte to huge successes off Homosassa in the 1980s. Photo courtesy of the International Game Fish Association.

A world-class angler as well as a world-class guide, Delph with a blackfin tuna.
Photo courtesy of Al Pflueger Jr.

we seldom struck out for an entire day, because I sure wasn't interested in making myself bleed."

The moment Anson decided to become an angler occurred in the jungle of Vietnam. Hunched over in the dark during a monsoon amid a dangerous Green Beret assignment, he wondered what he'd do if able to return to his native Miami in one piece. He'd never fished before, but tales from friends who did enjoy their time on the water battling game fish intrigued him. In that fleeting moment, Anson vowed right then and there that that would be his goal, to find out what the thrill was all about.

"When I got back the States, one of the first things I did was ask around about who would be the right person to teach me the ropes," he said. "You can guess who most of them recommended.

"I immediately liked Ralph's style," Anson said. "He pushes hard, but he's teaching you to be tougher than the fish."

Al Pflueger Jr., a master angler and of the famed taxidermy business he expanded with his father, has fished with hundreds of guides over the years.

"Ralph's one of the best I've ever known," Pflueger said with a nod. "He could take an average angler and tell him how to fight a fish successfully.

"Ralph knew exactly how much pressure his rods and line could take and how to tell someone what to do based on their skill level," Pflueger added. "He was simply way ahead of the curve in terms of guiding."

I interviewed Delph for the book from my residence in Clearwater, Florida, while he sat in his summer home in Gallatin Gateway, Montana. All through our conversation, Delph said he could peer out the window and watch his wife feeding two whitetail deer. What a wonderful—and vastly different—change of scenery from his winter digs in Key West.

Delph got his first taste of fishing in the summer of 1945 at the age of five. His grandfather took the youngster to the muddy bank of a creek in northern Kentucky. When his grandfather caught a carp, he attached it to Ralph's line when he wasn't looking. The bobber sank, Ralph excitedly reacted and set the hook, and the rod bending commenced. When he finally dragged it onto the bank, he screamed—in pain, not delight. The hook pulled out of the fish and lodged in his body, and ol' grandpa did a double-take when the boy let go an outburst of choice cuss words.

"Since that time I've learned to control my expletives, but not my enthusiasm for fishing," Delph said.

That same year his family moved to south Florida. He often fished with his father in a large variety of fresh and saltwater locations. Delph loved each outing and, when old enough, he began exploring on his own with a rod and reel. He learned how to fly fish and use a plug-casting rod. His strength, stamina and toughness overmatched just about any species he faced, no matter the tackle.

In the early 1960s, Delph often hung out at the "Tackle Box" shop owned by Mel Shipero. "He suggested we form a club to share ideas and experiences," said Delph, and that was the seed that started the Miami Sportfishing Club.

Delph's vocation during that time involved toiling as a contractor in the construction business in Miami, designing high rises. His escape mechanism involved jaunts whenever possible to fish the Gulf Stream, Biscayne Bay and surrounding waters. When the energy crisis of 1973 put the kibosh on the construction industry, it proved the perfect impetus for what Delph had already brewing on his mind: becoming a professional guide. Encouraging him even further was famed angler Joe Robinson and fly-fishing legend Stu Apte.

"When I first met Ralph Delph, he was a structural engineer and living near me in the Village of Kendale, a suburb of Miami," said Apte.

"We started fishing together and he often talked about hating his office job. I said, 'Ralph, you're such a great angler, why don't you get out of the engineering biz and become a fishing guide? Just go get your captain's license—I have no doubt you'll be a big success.' Ralph took the leap of faith, and it didn't take long for him to become one of the top inshore and offshore captains in the world."

Ralph Delph not only listened to his friends but followed his own instincts as well. A man of action, without any hemming and hawing, Delph promptly put his house up for sale and moved to Key West. Before long one of his initial associations in the Southernmost City was veteran guide Bob Montgomery.

Delph set standards in guiding that few others have ever approached.
Photo courtesy of Ralph Delph.

"Bob was one of the first to charter offshore in a center console boat," said Delph. "That type of setup made a lot of sense to me in terms of the anglers' maneuverability.

"At the time I ran a 20-foot open-sport fisherman that I named the *Vitamin Sea*. One day after the boat's single engine broke down at Half Moon Shoals about 40 miles west of Key West, I got towed back. That's a loooong way to get towed. I soon switched to a 25-foot SeaVee with a 15-hp kicker under the console for insurance. Believe, me, that kicker helped me putt-putt back to the dock more than a few times."

Over the years, Delph grew to enjoy the unique satisfaction of guiding anglers to success, which brought him the same sense of accomplishment as if he'd caught the fish himself.

"I think of clients like Jim Anson with a lot of pride," he said. "Our first and second trips together occurred in just horrendous conditions. We had small-craft warnings, the water was totally churned up and muddy everywhere, the air really cold and miserable, and Jim didn't catch a single fish on either occasion.

"After driving all that way from Miami and back, I figured I'd never hear from him. Heck, after experiences like that, very few people would go to that trouble and expense to try again. Instead, Jim hung in there and kept at it, and his resilience paid off big time over the years."

Delph's ascendancy to the highest levels of competitive fishing didn't happen overnight. In 1963 he began fishing against other top anglers in south Florida in the Miami Sportfishing Club. He won numerous club titles and division championships while up against great anglers such as Flip Pallot, Nat Ragland and John Emery.

He also ratcheted up his skills in the mammoth six-month-long MET tournament each year. Thousands of angler entries and tens of thousands of fish catches and releases were posted in the MET, and it involved nearly the entire sport-fishing and boating communities from Palm Beach to Ft. Myers to Key West.

In 1967, Delph won the Top Angler of the Year award and was designated Master Angler in the MET. In 1969, he duplicated that feat, becoming the only angler in the MET's 40-year history at the time to win the Master Angler award more than once.

Delph's rewarding experiences as a dueling angler greatly aided other MET anglers when his guiding career started. He knew the best tactics and strategies, what would likely win and which categories and line classes to target. To a competing angler, that level of guiding leadership would be tantamount to a soldier serving in Patton's army—you're probably on the winning team right off the bat.

Delph certainly lived up to the hype he was earning, and quite simply he was a guide who produced results for his clients. You can be the nicest guide in the world, but if you keep coming back to the dock empty-handed, your client list eventually disappears. Delph's wide variety of anglers—including a good many novices—took down one trophy and citation after another in the MET and other competitions. In 2004, Delph had won the Top Guide trophy in the MET for an incredible 28 out of 30 years, and we're talking about his being in a field of 200 or so professional guides.

Delph was always big on release tournaments, which the MET reverted to when most participants expressed the strong desire to conform to a catch-and-release ethic. In fact, Delph ultimately decided to fish only in release divisions of tournaments that featured weigh-ins for some species.

Although now retired from guiding, in 2005 the International Game Fish Association honored Ralph Delph with their Lifetime Achievement Award. The organization acknowledged his being the first person in history to have guided anglers to 100 IGFA world records, a mark he'd set many years prior as he amazingly eclipsed the 250 world records level.

Delph wonders about anglers becoming too specialized nowadays. "So many young anglers are single-faceted, such as being known just for fly fishing for bonefish or tarpon or some other particular species," he said.

"Back in our day, we really prided ourselves in being proficient with any tackle you could place in our hands and fishing for every game fish that might grab a lure, bait or fly."

Asked to recall any particular accomplishments among all of his the world records and experiences on the water, Delph mentioned when he and an angler took four bluefin tunas over 1,000 pounds off New England, including a 1,154-pound monster on standup gear. On another occasion while on an outing with an editor for *Outdoor Life* magazine, he captured a broadbill swordfish in Florida Bay—you read that right, a swordfish in shallow Florida Bay. And talk about toughness: At the age of 60, Delph bested a giant bluefin of 1,081 pounds in only 20 minutes.

Although Delph enjoys tangling with big bruisers, his personal favorite is trout fishing. "Every minute I can get away, I love to trout fish. And I don't care how big it is."

Delph took part in the explosion of fishing interest around Key West in the 1960s and '70s. Competitions spurred by the Tropical Anglers

Club, Miami Sportfishing Club, Miami Beach Rod & Reel Club, the Key West Fishing Tournament, MET and others had a ripple effect. Tales of great catches on flats, reefs, wrecks, channels and blue waters around Key West lit up the entire angling world. Soon writers arrived to flash the news to readers; TV and radio shows carried details of the fantastic catches made. It was an exciting era, and Ralph Delph was at the center of it.

While Ralph Delph usually came out the winner when combating tough game fish, some losing battles live on in his memory. One such fight actually involved a series of three bouts with Big John, a huge amberjack he discovered on a shallow wreck in the Quicksands region west of the Marquesas Keys. The AJ was so named because it reminded Delph of Jimmy Dean's famous song about Big John, "a big, big man"— this fish was extraordinarily huge to encounter not on a deep wreck but on a wreck in only 12 feet of water.

The Big John encounters started in December of 1976 with Jim Anson on his boat. The fishing drill in situations like this is basically for Delph to dangle a two- to three-pound live blue runner on a small hook—too small to actually catch a big fish—just a short distance from the hull in order to tease predator fish out and away from the wreck. His angler would then detach the release anchor while Delph kept the interest of whatever worthy gamesters were fired up from mouthing the runner. As the boat drifted away from the line-entangling wreck, Delph would command his angler to cast an offering in front of the targeted species that had risen as teased near the surface.

When Big John crashed the blue runner and leaped four feet out of the water, Delph and Anson couldn't believe their eyes.

"As I turned to Jim, I could see his eyes fixed to the foam on the water where the giant had just exploded," said Delph.

Delph set another blue runner and Big John crushed it too. Anson was ready for him this time and it struck his fly. "Jim almost got spooled, and then the line from the rod tip to the water went limp," Delph said. On two more occasions, the AJ took the flies and the results were bleak and unmistakable: Big John 3, Delph and Anson 0.

Another wreck duel with a 'cuda almost snuffed out the Delph family jewels. Barracuda often charge head-long into boats with those stilettolike teeth popping, sending the occupants scampering every which way.

"I was once pinned in the corner of the transom while a barracuda—its teeth chomping—was balanced on the gunnel of the boat," said Delph, er, off-handedly.

"Its head was mere inches from my groin. The fish performed a balancing act for longer than I wanted before falling onto the deck and flopping and slashing around. I performed the rapid tippety-toe two-step. After the 'cuda settled down and I had accounted for all my parts, the fish was returned to the water."

Considering their heritage, it's not surprising that Delph's sons Bill and Rob took up the calling of guiding. Their anglers too have won tournaments and notched more than 50 world records. The Delph name represents excellence in guiding, and it lives on while the proud papa looks on.

It's not only Delph's boys who have learned important lessons about life in general from him. "Ralph stays with you every second as a fish is being played, like a corner man in a prize fight—you learn to be resilient," said Anson. Anson's son received such an education one day while aboard the *Vitamin Sea*.

"Jim was 12 and fishing with us when he hooked into a big permit on an extremely hot day," said Anson. "Jim started getting sick from the heat and exertion. Ralph saw that and told him to keep at it anyway.

"Jim pleaded, 'I can't, I can't.' Ralph poured fresh water over his head to refresh him and then said not so quietly, 'I *can't* never wins; I *can* always wins.'

"Jim not only persisted but he finally caught that permit. He's never forgotten what Ralph said each time life's situations get tough. How more valuable can a person be than as an inspiration to others?"

32

Marsha Bierman, b. 1943

CORAL SPRINGS

When you meet Marsha Bierman, the first impression is of her unmistakable good looks: tall, long blond hair, sunny smile, athletic physique—definitely Hollywood material. The second impression recognizes her kindly disposition and soft heart. The final impression, if you're really lucky, is of her amid the furor of saltwater spray with a bent rod, standing firm to battle a powerful fish up to 10 times her weight.

I actually first met her husband, Lenny, in 1975. He was in charge of Marriott Security Systems, a division of the Marriott Corporation. Lenny ran the company and I served as director of investigations. Our mutual interest in fishing gave us common ground, particularly when I learned about his Rybovich boat named *Pacifier*. Just telling someone you own a Rybovich commands the same kind of respect in the fishing world as a Stradivarius to a musician.

On the *Pacifier* with Marsha, Lenny served as the nerve center for everything happening. He handled the wheel, directed the mate, decided where best to hunt. That's quite essential because a command person must be clearly defined on a vessel and his or her authority unquestioned in order to handle the mayhem when a hook-up occurs. Once Marsha learned the nuances of playing fish in concert with the boat and mate, she faced many giant adversaries one on one, her against the fish. She did so with skill and great aplomb as a tournament angler, but of course that didn't evolve overnight. The first spring and summer season that she went offshore with Lenny on the *Pacifier*, no one could have envisioned the pretty, classy woman as the next great

Marsha Bierman developed the optimum techniques for battling big fish on short-rod standup gear. Photo courtesy of Lenny and Marsha Bierman.

marlin conqueror. Neither did Marsha, for that matter, particularly when her on-the-water time essentially focused on being a sunbathing bow bunny. But as stories about great anglers go, all that was about to change.

With his wife as colleague and student, Lenny saw Marsha progress from a neophyte who spent her very first offshore trip barfing to a gifted, gritty and seasoned professional big-game fisher. He also taught her how to captain the vessel and maintain the diesel engines. Capt. Tommy Zsak of Ft. Lauderdale joined the duo on many trips around the globe, and together they honed a very special technique for Marsha that would challenge even the stoutest of men: catching big-game fish on short-rod standup gear. In other words, it involved playing marlin and tuna weighing hundreds of pounds—sometimes blues and blacks over a thousand—without ever spending any time sitting in a fighting chair.

"In a heavy chair bolted to the deck, the angler becomes part of the boat," said Marsha. "But you can't just stand and fight a 500-pound fish with your arm, leg and back muscles—the first few times I tried it that way in 1986, it put me in bed for days with bruises and pain."

Instead, she learned how to tilt her hips so the legs absorbed more of the fight than the weaker arm and back muscles. By experimenting with different angles and posture positions such as a pelvic tilt, the Biermans figured out how to achieve maximum leverage with less stress on the body. Marsha employed a custom-made back-support vest, a beefy 5 ½-foot rod instead of the standard seven-footer, and settled on reels holding a maximum of 50-pound test rather than the heavier 80- and 130-pound gear most chair-seated offshore hunters prefer.

Fishing with standup gear even with the best leverage techniques still requires considerable strength and stamina. And without finesse, good timing and teamwork, the effort would be for naught. The whole process of putting together the pieces began when they read an article about anglers out of San Diego using standup short rods. It included comments from Hal Chittum, who at the time owned an upscale retail store in Islamorada.

"We met with Hal, and he demonstrated the lifting power of the rods to us and convinced me to try them out on our upcoming trip to St.

Bierman celebrates in Bimini after her 100th blue marlin release in the Bahamas. Photo courtesy of Lenny and Marsha Bierman.

Thomas," Marsha said. They did so, with Marsha releasing blue marlin and obtaining a clearer understanding of what gear and methods she wanted to refine for her use. The pelvic tilt indeed achieved a back-flattening position that transferred pressure away from the lower back to the larger muscles of the buttocks and thighs. Lenny and Marsha hence spent just about every weekend on the water perfecting the standup technique.

The effort seemed like a good fit for a tackle manufacturer too. And so it was that Marsha signed a deal with Penn International. After tinkering and modifications, they all came up with the right rod that worked perfectly.

"The equipment really needs to be on the money so it fits each angler." said Marsha. "People approach standup fishing way too casually sometimes. Granted, it doesn't make much difference when matched against small fish, but when the big ones come along, any breakdown in the entire system becomes glaring; the unprepared angler will not be able to finish the fight."

Born a farmer's daughter in Delhi, New York, Marsha grew up on a dairy farm near the Catskill Mountains. She didn't even know how to swim, and it wasn't until a trip to Long Island with friends in college that she drew her first breath of salt air. After earning her college degree, Marsha worked for the New York Jets from 1964 to '66 as secretary to the coaching and scouting staffs under head coach Weeb Ewbank. Upon receiving and accepting an offer to join the Miami Dolphins in the same capacity, Marsha moved to Miami. She met Lenny when he was intent on dating her roommate, also a Dolphins secretary. Lenny took one look at Marsha, however, and was smitten. A year later they got hitched.

Marsha subsequently left the Dolphins and became a stock broker for 15 years. However, from 1986 to 2002, her resume would more aptly state: "Professional big-game angler." During those glory years, the Biermans and Tommy Zsak traveled the globe to present seminars, put in appearances for Penn and other sponsors, and target giant fish in unfamiliar waters, all the while employing and promoting Marsha's standup technique.

Zsak, who's known Marsha since 1975, often worked the bridge as captain unless they were on a charter boat with a crew. "Lenny and I switched off as captain and mate," said Zsak. "The mate's main job was to stand behind Marsha in case she suddenly lost a big fish due to the line breaking or hook pulling. When that happened—and it did now and then—she needed someone to break the fall."

Odd things sometimes occurred on international trips, and that certainly was the case on the trio's visit to the island of Mauritius in the Indian Ocean. "We were present during a celebration similar to our Easter," Zsak said. "We walked around and saw a procession of natives, with needles protruding from their cheeks and noses. One of the ceremonies involved laying infants on the road and stepping on them—I'm serious. Anyway, the people in the procession spotted Marsha and they stopped dead in their tracks to stare at her. Lenny and I didn't know if this might be a hostile situation or just curiosity. Luckily, it was the latter."

Marsha Bierman, though modest and not one to seek the limelight, nonetheless enjoyed meeting the public at fishing shows around the world. At times that resulted in humorous encounters.

"One year while working the booth at the Miami International Boat Show for Penn, a girl of about eight years of age and her father came

Bierman during her days as secretary for the Miami
Dolphins coaching and scouting coaches. The good looks
certainly didn't hurt her celebrity status in the fishing
industry. Photo courtesy of Lenny and Marsha Bierman.

over to talk with me," Marsha said. "The father mentioned that he'd
recently broken one of the Penn rod models I use and wondered if I'd
experienced the same problem. I replied, 'Not unless you button-hook
them.' I explained that the wedding of graphite and fiberglass produced
the best rods on the market, but if you bring the rod tip up too high
with the line running straight down, it could cause the rod to break due
to the severe angle.

"The father nodded approvingly, but then his daughter blurted out,
'Umm, what if you shut the garage door on the rod?' With a knowing

smile, I told her that that would probably do the trick. Meanwhile, her dad's face turned beet red. Out of the mouths of babes, the true fates of broken rods are often revealed."

Zsak believes that Marsha's stamina separated her from most other anglers—plus a "fruitful" discovery that spared her aching feet. "She'll stand in the cockpit fighting a fish for eight hours if necessary, never sitting down," said Zsak. "At times that put a lot of pressure on her feet, so Marsha started experimenting and found out that eating bananas took away her foot pain. She'd munch bananas and could stand firmly and fight fish long after most people would just wilt."

Of course, the irony is that many captains and guides swear a superstition about the bad luck of having bananas aboard the boat—to the point of discarding them overboard if they're found in a client's belongings. That certainly wasn't a belief held by Marsha.

Mike Leech, former president of the International Game Fish Association and a close friend of the Biermans,' also revealed some interesting tidbits about Marsha. "She doesn't eat fish, still doesn't know how to swim, and she always brings dog food along on trips. Whenever we visited places with stray dogs, it really made Marsha happy to feed every one of them."

Marsha will never forget one spring day while targeting white marlin off Venezuela's La Guaira Bank. "We fished with Capt. Luis Suarez on the *Marguilla,* a 46-foot Bertram solidly constructed of fiberglass," she said. "The first day out I caught a couple of blue marlin on 30-pound test, and we had just released the third when it charged the boat. Its bill drove completely through the hull just below the waterline, right up to the fish's eyes. Though badly wounded, the marlin backed out and swam away as if nothing had happened.

"We now had a two-inch-diameter hole in the boat, and worst of all it had penetrated the hydraulic steering line and taken out the steering. Suarez wanted to go in, but Lenny told him, 'No way, the fishing is too good—steer the boat with the gears.' Suarez agreed, and we caught another three blue marlin. He managed to fix the steering line by the next day, and we ended up releasing an incredible 15 blue marlin in just a few days."

The sheer number of fish Marsha has subdued is impressive. Of the more than 2,500 billfish captures to her credit, more than 350 of them consist of blue and black marlin. She's tagged and released all nine of the billfish species (three times over) and all three of the major tunas. These feats become magnified because they were achieved on nothing heavier than standup short rods and 50-pound line.

Some of her accomplishments include being the only person to capture 100 blue marlin off Bimini, the first woman to win the Bahamas Billfish Championship and the first angler to catch blue and black marlin granders on 50-pound standup short rods.

Leech vouches for Marsha's intensity when looking for fish offshore, but he says she's the same with any style of fishing. "My son and I tarpon fished with Marsha at Baker's Haulover in Miami," he said. "As we drifted in the current with live shrimp, all of us just kept our rods in holders with the drags loose. Not Marsha—she removed line from the tip and held it in her fingers so she could tell when her shrimp got nervous. It gave her that fraction-of-a-second advantage to be ready when a tarpon hit."

Over the years, news of Marsha's success on standup gear has appeared on TV and radio shows as well as in newspaper and magazine articles; throngs of tournament activists from around the world respect her unique ability. While she did in fact earn every accolade, a number of detractors at times made it clear that they doubted the veracity of the reports about her accomplishments.

"Marsha didn't brag on herself, instead letting those who went on her trips talk about the 800-pound this or 1,000-pound that that she'd released," said Leech. "She let everything go, even obvious world records, so without weigh-ins or pictures of Marsha standing along a conquered fish on a dock, people either believed it or they didn't. Sometimes with just Lenny and Tommy and Marsha involved with a big fish, there was not time for picture-taking. Most people did believe it, though, particularly those of us who knew that Marsha would never make anything up.

"Peter Wright, the great international offshore legend, approached me repeatedly at various events to say he didn't think Marsha had caught all those fish people claimed," Leech said. "He just went on and on about it every time he saw me.

"When I appointed Marsha as a representative for IGFA, Peter even called and really gave it to me. He was absolutely indignant and didn't think Marsha was for real."

Soon thereafter, Wright got to see for himself whether or not she was for real. In the mid-1990s when the bluefin tuna frenzy was taking place off Hatteras, North Carolina, Leech received a call from Lenny and Marsha. It so happened that a friend of theirs from New Jersey had invited them to fish aboard his boat off Hatteras. In turn, Leech was asked to come as well.

"It was cold, windy and the seas churning," recalled Leech. "We headed offshore and ran from wreck to wreck to see if the big schools of bluefins might be feeding.

"As luck would have it, Peter Wright was also fishing off Hatteras that day in his boat. Wright located a school of bluefins and called us and other boats on his VHF radio to join the action.

"Well, you can probably figure out what happened," said Leech. "We arrived at Wright's location and in minutes Marsha hooked into a really big bluefin. As the boat rose and fell in the huge swells, Marsha is standing in water a foot deep in the cockpit, relentlessly doing her standup work on the bluefin. As the salt mist engulfed her, I noted that Peter had moved his boat nearby to watch the action. I said to Marsha, 'Whatever you do, don't lose this fish.' Finally Marsha whipped that bluefin when the leader reached the rod tip, and it was released in full view of Peter. She went on to release two more that day when most other boats either ran in early because of the rough conditions or caught nothing. It was quite a statement she made without saying a word."

Later back at the dock, Wright walked over to congratulate her. Wright's opinion of Marsha's ability had just made a 180-degree turn, and they went on to become good friends.

"After that happened, whenever stories circulated about great catches and releases by Marsha on some far-flung trip, I never heard a peep out of Peter," Leech said.

No one else any longer doubts her accomplishments, either. Marsha Bierman securely takes her place as one of the legends of Florida—and international—big-game fishing.

33

Brian Lowman, b. 1948

NAVARRE

Dennis Lowman can attest to his brother's never-say-die attitude. "On a Sunday morning about 10 years ago, Brian and I went to Bailey's Bluff off New Port Richey," he said.

"We waded past the mangroves about 50 yards from the shoreline on a dead low tide. We started catching a few redfish and trout on light spin tackle as the tide quickly began to rise.

"Soon the water is waist deep, and although I'm six feet tall, Brian's got an extra four inches on me, so he can stay out there a bit longer. Just as we're about to go back to shore, he hooks a huge fish that we guessed must have been a giant red.

"He's now waist-deep and I'm hollering for him to get the heck out of the water too. Not Brian—he hung onto that fish without a backward step and with no thought of letting go.

"He finally feels the fish yielding and backs out of the surf. We were surprised to see a four-foot bonnethead shark thrashing on the line—possibly a world record—and that fish wasn't at all happy. Brian managed to get it off his line and luckily the shark took off without looking for a little revenge.

"I said, 'Okay, that's enough, it's time to go.' But Brian is so stoked he releases the shark and bounds back into the water. On the next cast, I'll be darn if he doesn't hook another big bonnethead.

"As he plays it, we start seeing more of them sliding this way and that through the water. I finally realized we'd been standing right smack dab in the middle of a school of sharks. We're lucky we got out of there without a disaster."

Lowman, at far left, after a Gulf foray aboard the party boat *Swoop* out of Destin Harbor with mates Chris Couvillion, Sara Mauney, and Ed Doubleday. Photo courtesy of Brian Lowman.

When you wade fish as much as Brian Lowman, unpredictable things like that will happen. Another instance of this occurred in the mid-1990s off Tarpon Springs in only three feet of water.

"I'm fishing with shrimp on 12-pound spin tackle and the largest redfish I've ever seen in this region—about a 50-pounder—sucked it into its crushers," said Lowman. "It took an hour and a half before I could lower my landing net, and its head was so wide it barely fit."

These days, Brian Lowman lives in the western portion of Florida's Panhandle. He might try to quietly go about his work without a lot of fanfare, but he certainly stands out from the crowd at six feet, four inches tall and 250 pounds.

Many guess he played linebacker or defensive end for some football team in his day. That would be a wrong assumption, however, because Lowman seldom found much time for anything in high school and college other than fishing—and that hasn't changed one iota.

"When Brian decides to do something, he puts everything into it and learns all there is to know about it," said Lyn Hager, his older sister, who now lives in Williston.

"He's also a reptile expert, and if you let him, he'll give an hour-long dissertation on this snake or that snake's life history."

The Lowman family grew up in the old southern tradition. Men sat in the front room smoking cigars and the women grouped together in the kitchen. They seldom enjoyed outdoor activities together as a family, but the big exception involved fishing. Hager distinctly remembers a lot of excursions in the Everglades.

"One year we lived in Immokalee because dad worked there at the time as a produce buyer," she said.

"Anytime we'd crave a tasty fish dinner or run out of money, he grabbed cane poles, loaded my mother and us kids in the car and off we'd go to sit on the edge of a nearby canal and catch bream.

"Dad stood near us with a .22 rifle, keeping an eye out so he could shoot moccasins, as there were always plenty of them around—the record for one stop was 26.

"We'd hook bream, Dad would clean 'em, and Mom would fry 'em right there on the river bank with a three-legged skillet. Delicious."

Born in Lakeland, Brian Lowman's parents moved around the state quite a bit before settling in Sanford in 1951. A fourth-generation Floridian, Lowman took up fishing at the age of four.

"I got a toy rod and reel for Christmas that year, and I loved it," he recalled. "Pretty soon I graduated to real tackle. Our family would make weekend trips to New Smyrna Beach, where my dad, brother and I fished while mom and my sisters sunbathed.

"I still recall fishing from the old wooden bridge to New Smyrna and how badly it would shake when cars drove over it. The noise didn't seem to affect the fish, as I suppose they were used to it."

In Sanford, the young Lowman was introduced to fly tying by a neighbor. He became entranced by all the accoutrements needed to precisely construct patterns. Lowman gathered the materials and tools needed to tie his own flies, and the activity literally had a calming effect on the boy—and still does to this day.

Even more, it electrified him to catch fish on his homemade flies,

Lowman cut his teeth on bass in his younger years before catching the saltwater bug. Photo courtesy of Brian Lowman.

especially for big bass. Watching a largemouth rising to a pattern he fashioned, striking it and then battling it was one of the biggest thrills and satisfactions of his life.

A subsequent move to Tampa put him onto the beaches and bays for trout, redfish and other saltwater species. As before, he experimented with his own flies, tied standard successful patterns and became a frequent on-the-water presence.

The Gulf seemed to have an unending supply of king and Spanish mackerel, grouper and amberjack. Particularly after the gill net ban in the mid-1990s, Lowman could wade the Gulf shoreline for hours and depend on lots of catches and releases.

The Florida Panhandle move in 1999 found him in the town of Navarre, about 25 miles east of Pensacola. From Pensacola Bay to Destin, Lowman pursued redfish, grouper, red snapper and other species with abandon. His favorite honey hole: Ft. Pickens at the entrance to Pensacola Bay, where he's released redfish up to 45 inches, king mackerel to 15 pounds, fat mangrove snapper and even keeper-size black grouper—all from shore.

Speaking of Ft. Pickens, a few years ago Lowman was fishing around a rock jetty for snapper when something odd caught his attention.

"An older man of about 70 or so approached me while carrying the largest king mackerel I've ever seen, probably close to 60 pounds," said Lowman.

"I'd put the man at about six feet, two inches tall, and the fish he was dragging shocked me. It was so big that its head was near his shoulders and the tail touching the sand.

"I asked what he'd caught it on and he replied, 'My feet.' I begged for an explanation and he repeated the same answer. Mystified, I just couldn't comprehend how in the world he or anyone else for that matter could manage to catch a fish of that size with his feet.

"As it turned out, he told me that a pinfish ate the shrimp he was fishing with, and as he reeled it to the beach, that giant kingfish skied on it. The man said, 'It flew directly out of the surf and landed on the beach, so I kicked it with one foot and then the other until it was dead.'

"All I could do was shake my head in disbelief. I mean, how often has someone kicked a fish to death that beached itself like that? Totally bizarre."

While many at Lowman's age—in his early 50s at that point—might start contemplating retirement, he instead volunteered his time at the Navarre Beach Fishing Pier. Two experiences at the pier made an indelible impression on Lowman.

"A young fellow wanted to catch a stingray, and I agreed to help him as long as he'd be willing to eat it," said Lowman. "He caught a huge 197-pounder on shark gear and it took three pier gaffs to get it up. We filleted it—the meat's in the wings with no bones—and he later told me it tasted fantastic.

He's always experimenting with new gear and techniques. Photo courtesy of Brian Lowman.

"The other incident involved two high school surfer boys," he said. "They came onto the pier, walked out 600 feet, climbed atop the rail and jumped off just as I came running up to try and stop them.

"The boys landed in a giant school of jellyfish—they got stung really badly and barely made it to shore. It could have turned out a lot worse, though."

Lowman's tried his hand at fishing from a kayak despite his considerable size, and one encounter made him especially glad it didn't tip over. "I hooked a spinner shark, its tail so high above the water that it was over my head. I let it go, of course."

A year after volunteering at the Navarre Pier, he was hired as a park ranger, which "instantly became a job of passion," he said. Lowman soon began teaching fishing courses and seminars, and he kicked off a weekly fishing column in the *Navarre Press*, which he still writes.

He's now a Biological Scientist I with the Florida Fish and Wildlife Conservation Commission. That puts him in the field much of each week surveying fishermen. Lowman rides aboard boats, meets people at docks and gathers as much accurate data as possible.

As a result of so much interaction with area anglers and guides, he's become known as "The Fish Guy." Even on his days off, you can guess what Lowman does.

"I don't consider myself a great fisherman as much as a promoter of fishing," he said modestly.

Kim Kloss, who was Lowman's boss at the Navarre Pier before a hurricane destroyed it, is a bit more expressive about his impact in the region.

"Brian's always willing to help people, no matter how busy he might be," she said. "He's knowledgeable about all aspects of fishing and knows how to motivate people, especially kids or those with physical challenges. Brian is one of those who makes a difference."

Kloss recalled instances where fishermen would have issues with pier employees when they refused to follow rules or do as asked.

"He could handle any problems at the pier, things like taking hooks out of people and pelicans, refereeing squabbles, quieting those displaying bad tempers and such. I knew that whenever Brian was on duty, he could be depended upon to be fair and use good judgment. I think his intimidating size was also a mitigating factor more than once," she said, laughing. "He's just a good ol' Cracker."

To any native Floridian, there's no higher compliment than that.

34

Guy Harvey, b. 1955

FT. LAUDERDALE

If you're reading this book many years after the publication date, few of the names herein will be familiar to you. That's only natural. An historical compendium is supposed to be evergreen and inspire a better appreciation for those Florida legends and pioneers of yesteryear. It's similar to how football fans often want to learn some interesting things about Knute Rockne, Red Grange, Johnny Unitas, Dan Marino and other greats preceding modern-day stars of the gridiron.

The names of people in the book you'll probably recognize right away include Ted Williams and Ernest Hemingway. I'm confident you'll have heard of Guy Harvey as well. His handiwork in art is timeless, and combined as it is with brand marketing in our Information Age, his work is nothing short of remarkable.

I've met Harvey at a limited number of functions over the years, yet he always remembers my name and does the same for the untold thousands of others with whom he comes face to face. That talent and concentration alone I admire, since usually I couldn't tell you someone's name three seconds after it's been said.

Herb Allen, former fishing editor for the *Tampa Tribune,* accurately framed Harvey's marketing prowess, saying: "Lots of great marine artists come and go, but the thing that sets Guy apart from the rest is his ability to market himself so well. He's obviously a top businessman in addition to his artistry and knowledge of fisheries."

Harvey acknowledges such. "I attribute the marketing success of my brand to hard work and having a good team of people in place," he said. "I work long hours; paint hard; attend a great many trade shows,

Have underwater camera, will travel. Observing live fish enhances the authenticity of his paintings. Photo courtesy of Guy Harvey.

consumer shows and tournaments; and do a lot of public appearances. I spent five years in the field shooting a TV series, and I write many articles each year about fishing and diving and conservation."

He's authored books and produced a TV series, he sponsors a research institute and a foundation, and his licensed line of apparel can be found in just about every clothing store you walk into. Needless to say, he's piled up numerous awards and honors for his many achievements and contributions.

Born on a British military base in Germany, Harvey's dad served in the British Army at the end of World War II with the forces occupying the Rhine. Thereafter they moved back to Jamaica, where his family roots can be traced back to 1664. Harvey relocated in 1999 to Grand Cayman, and for 11 years he owned a house in Ft. Lauderdale.

Both of Harvey's parents were keen anglers. Growing up in the late 1950s and '60s in Jamaica, he fished a lot with his family on their 26-foot dugout canoe on the south side of the island. The boat sported a large outboard engine, two bamboo outriggers and a rotating-seat stool for a fighting chair. It's where the young Guy Harvey developed an unquenchable inquisitiveness about the various species they caught. Enthralled, he'd hurry home to draw the sea creatures he saw and touched that day.

Bill Shedd—president of AFTCO Mfg., makers of the Bluewater clothing line licensed by Guy Harvey—is impressed with that curiosity. "At Tropic Star Lodge in Panama, we trolled live baits past Guy in his dive mask. He wanted to see the action of the baits going by and fish rising behind them.

"I could see his excitement and curiosity, especially later when he dived on a huge ball of sardines," Shedd related. "Jack crevalle were chasing the little sardines, and although I know Guy has done that before, it was still like a kid's first Christmas. That's a curiosity you can't pretend or manufacture."

Shedd also appreciates Harvey's intensity, an asset that shifts readiness into action. "Guy is on the deck all the time, his eyes on the baits all day," he said.

"Lots of even top anglers take breaks or even naps—not Guy. He's watching the spread while eating or talking. It's the same with his paintings. We once caught a white sea bass in the Pacific and Guy's looking at it intently, staring at the fish in different light, putting it back in the water, all the while making notes about the scales, fins, gills, mouth, color—everything."

Curt Gowdy recognized Harvey's attention to detail as well, referring to him as "the John Audubon of marine art." Harvey's gift for recreating sea life led him to become a professor. He studied marine biology at the University of Aberdeen in Scotland in 1977 and obtained a doctorate in fisheries management at the University of the West Indies. And so, the proper formal address for him is *Dr.* Guy Harvey.

Harvey's art exhibits in Jamaica became a hit, and in 1988 he gave

The young Guy Harvey, at right, spent much of his childhood fishing in Jamaica.
Photo courtesy of Guy Harvey.

up his professorship in order to paint full time. Scuba diving and underwater photography added to the young man's artistic renown, and he traveled the world to experience new habitats and marine life.

In 1986, Harvey became Jamaica's representative to the International Game Fish Association and in 1992 was appointed as a trustee. In '97 he sponsored the sinking of the "Guy Harvey Reef" in conjunction with the Pompano Beach Fishing Rodeo. He partnered with Nova South-

Dr. Guy Harvey, an artiste whose popularity is international. Photo courtesy of Guy Harvey.

eastern University in 1999 to create the Guy Harvey Research Institute (GHRI), and in '08 he started the Guy Harvey Ocean Foundation.

The goal of the GHRI centers on biological science research for a deeper understanding of the world's wild fish resources. The Institute provides advanced graduate training to U.S. and international students through the Nova Southeastern University Oceanographic Center in disciplines related to conservation. The proximity in Dania Beach to reefs and the ocean certainly adds to the convenience for the programs offered.

Meanwhile, the Guy Harvey Ocean Foundation brings together researchers, educators and philanthropists who aim to develop strategies for promoting conservation and supporting the next generation of marine scientists. Harvey enjoys using his name and influence in positive pursuits, and as successful as it's been to paint and brand-market shirts, he's not content to stop and bask in the glory or count his money.

Guy Harvey firmly believes that the most serious issue facing the future of our fisheries is human population growth. "All the other issues stem from this," he said.

"From the fishing perspective, any fishing technique or method of harvesting that is indiscriminate has had, and continues to have, a serious and unnecessary negative impact on marine resources. These methods include bottom trawling, shrimp trawling, long lining, gill netting, purse seining and the use of fish traps, particularly in coral reef habitat."

Harvey's most remarkable and fortunate angling achievement involved catching two blue marlin—each over 1,000 pounds—in a single day on July 27, 1997, off Madeira.

"I was fishing with Capt. Clay Hensley and mate Mike Latham on the *Freed 'Em*," he said. "We teased both fish to the boat and I pitched mackerel baits. I fought both fish on 80-pound tackle. The first took an hour and 20 minutes, but the best part is that I dived with the marlin and took some good underwater footage before she was released.

"We noticed that she had another leader coming from the left side of her mouth, so we knew she'd been through at least one battle before," said Harvey. "The second giant blue came up into the teaser spread not

The distinctive signature seems to be everywhere. Photo courtesy of AFTCO and Guy Harvey.

10 minutes after releasing the first one. This time, I cranked away for an hour and 45 minutes. We got it to the leader three times, tagged it, and I was going to dive with this fish but the leader parted."

I couldn't help but wonder if jumping into the drink with a variety of big fish might be fraught with danger.

"I'm very cautious and try to take no risks underwater, but a few exciting encounters while filming my TV shows do come to mind," he responded. "One involved a swordfish off Venezuela that charged me while I'm down at 80 feet.

"Another close one took place with a hooked sailfish in Mexico that attacked twice, and I had to fend it off with the camera. Still another occasion involved a 12-foot tiger shark that seemed intent on taking my camera away from me in the Bahamas. I've had many different species of shark bump my camera and then move away after realizing their mistake, but only a few of them have actually bitten the camera."

Although Harvey maintains his art studio in Grand Cayman, it's family trips with wife Gillian and children Jessica and Alex that make him the happiest.

Susan Cocking, outdoor writer for the *Miami Herald*, witnessed Harvey's dedication to family—even to family not his own, like her kin. "I flew down to the Cayman Islands during the Christmas break in 2001 with my family," said Cocking. "Guy took us on his boat to Stingray City and we had a fantastic time. He likes everyone around him to be happy and having fun.

"A couple of years ago I went on a research cruise with him out of Riviera Beach, and we tagged a nine-foot female tiger shark," Cocking added. "They sewed a tag right into the shark and off it swam. Guy is really involved in the study and conservation of our fisheries—he cares."

David Ritchie, editorial director for Bonnier Marine Group, has edited some of Harvey's books. He believes the key to Harvey's success lies in being driven. "Is Guy the most talented marine artist in the world? Some would say yes, others no. Beauty in art varies from individual to individual. However, talent is just the beginning for Guy. Many other characteristics that contribute to his success aren't subjective at all. I believe those who have worked hand in hand with him will all agree on one thing: No one puts in more time within his craft. He utilizes every moment of every day to produce something of significance."

As is the case with all those who reach the same level of success as Guy Harvey, Ritchie sees in him "an incredible and rare combination of talent, passion and good old-fashioned work ethic."

Appearances at boat shows and other public events can sometimes tempt embarrassing episodes, but Harvey is ahead of the curve on preventing those possible mishaps. Warren Resen, an outdoor writer from Greenacres, Florida, once attended a lecture given by Harvey. He observed a long line of people waiting for autographs, including a number of women in revealing attire.

"I jokingly asked him about any unusual body parts he'd been asked to sign over the years," said Resen. "With a playful brightening of his eyes, he replied, 'I don't do body parts or skin.' That shows you his maturity and a very polite upbringing."

Raleigh Werking, an internationally known light-tackle expert, seemed to particularly enjoy a story about a fishing trip he took with the artist several years ago in British Columbia for Harvey's *Portraits from the Deep* TV series.

"While wading and casting for king salmon, Guy got a strike and the fish headed downstream in a hurry with him in hot pursuit," said Werking.

"In the middle of it all, the reel jammed up and Guy took off running down the river in about two feet of water. I was right there with him stride for stride, camera rolling as he splashed water everywhere.

"Guy finally got the reel to work and landed the fish—his first king salmon and a really big one. I told Guy he should have been on the Jamaican track team."

Fleet of foot or not, Dr. Guy Harvey has made it to the mountaintop in his career and shows no signs of letting up.

35

Shaw Grigsby, b. 1956

GAINESVILLE

"I'll take Bass Fishing for 1,000, Alex."

"Here is the answer: He's won eight major tournaments, placed in the top 10 in 50 other events and is ranked fifth on the B.A.S.S. list of all-time money winners."

"Who is Shaw Grigsby Jr.?"

Correct. You might as well also throw in that Grigsby has been inducted into the "Legends of the Outdoors Hall of Fame." And let's not overlook his hit television show, *One More Cast with Shaw Grigsby,* and his book, *Bass Master Shaw Grigsby: Notes on Fishing and Life,* published by the National Geographic Society. Even that is quite an abbreviated, scrapbook version of a man who's spent over 35 years in competitive bass fishing—and has loved every minute of it.

"My best buddy in high school was Gerry Beavis, and nearly every day after our last class we'd grab the boat and go to Newnan's Lake, just outside of Gainesville," said Grigsby. "We didn't care about wearing our school clothes. We'd fish a couple of hours and catch 15 to 20 bass up to 10 pounds, with lots of threes and fours."

One day while on the lake, Beavis sat in front steering his boat and Grigsby crouched in the back. "While casting a plastic worm to the edge of a Cypress tree, I got hung up in a clump of bushes," Grigsby related. "As I'm shaking the line to try and free it, I heard this huge splash."

Grigsby turned around to find that his pal was nowhere to be seen. In his place, a massive swarm of wasps was making a, ahem, beeline straight toward Grigsby. The prospect of all those stingers sinking into his flesh didn't have much appeal.

Grigsby is understandably all smiles with this huge largemouth. Photo courtesy of Donald Strickland.

"I said a four-letter word and dove in," said Grigsby. "I could actually look up and see all those mad wasps hovering right the surface, mad as could be. I'd obviously shaken their nest, and we got the blame. Anyway, I took a quick gulp of air and went back down before they could get me. I swam underwater as far as I could from the boat."

When the wasps finally settled down and returned to their nest, Grigsby cautiously returned to the boat. There he found Beavis already sitting in front, dripping wet but otherwise looking totally unaffected.

"You never said a word to warn me," barked Grigsby.

His friend shrugged. "Hey, there was no time. I just fell out of the boat and swam off."

"I told him, 'You dog.' But the amazing thing is that neither of us got stung even once."

Grigsby got even, although it happened inadvertently. This time he steered the boat while Beavis relaxed in a netted chair in front.

"I wanted to say something to Gerry, so I crouched forward while leaving it in full throttle—a big mistake. That put too much weight forward, and the boat went under like a crankbait," Grigsby said laughingly. "We catapulted through the air as if shot out of a cannon. Luckily, we weren't hurt."

Shaw Grigsby once partnered with fellow pro angler and Gainesville resident Bernie Schultz. "We fished a little buddy tournament on the Withlacoochee River and won it," he said.

"Bernie hooked a big one of about eight pounds, and it dove into eelgrass and wrapped up the line. He didn't want to pull too hard or it would break the line. Since there were no rules against going overboard, I took off my clothes, looked around and saw a lady sitting in a chair on a dock near us.

"I asked, 'Hey, do you mind if I get naked?' She blushed and said, 'No, go right ahead.' So I stripped down to my underwear, dove overboard; the bass took one look at me and blew right out of the grass. And yes, Bernie caught it."

Schultz remembers that day clearly—who wouldn't?—and feels thankful for all he's learned from Grigsby. "Shaw was the first guy I ever drew in a bass tournament. At the time I was a new member to the Bassmasters of Gator Country, one of the strongest fishing clubs in the state. We were fishing a summer night tournament on Lake Kerr in the Ocala National Forest.

"The prospect of fishing my first organized tournament felt pretty intimidating to begin with, but I'll never forget Shaw's boat—an Allison Craft, which is basically a race boat with a trolling motor," said Schultz. "To get it on plane, Shaw's passengers had to crawl all the way to the bow. After what seemed like forever, the oversized prop would catch and off the boat would shoot like a rocket. That's what happened

Another tournament hook-up. Photo courtesy of the International Game Fish Association.

when I was aboard, and we moved so fast that even my fishing pliers blew right off the deck.

"Shaw couldn't have been a more perfect partner," he said. "He showed me what to tie on, what to expect, anything else that would help me. Shaw said that buzzbaits and Texas-rigged worms would be the best bet for doing well, and he was right. We each caught several fish in the first few minutes, and right at dusk I lost a giant on my buzzbait.

"Shaw suggested I put on a second trailer hook, and I'm thinking, 'Second trailer hook? Heck, I didn't even have a first one on.' Shaw helped me rig my buzzer with two trailer hooks just like his bait, and he proceeded to catch an unbelievable stringer of bass.

"Needless to say, he stomped my butt in my first tournament," Schultz reflected. "Although I didn't see it at the time, the lessons I learned that night proved invaluable. They've paid off countless times in my many years of tournament fishing.

"Although Shaw and I fished a lot of events after that, my memories of our first experience together on Lake Kerr pretty much describe Shaw to this day—a strong competitor, an outstanding teacher and just all-around great fishing partner."

Former *Tampa Tribune* fishing editor Herb Allen recognizes that competitiveness. "What really impresses me about Shaw Grigsby is his intensity. He's very focused and works hard at catching fish from start to finish, which certainly explains his successful competitive career on the bass circuits."

Phil Chapman, outdoor writer, guide and former Florida Fish and Wildlife Conservation Commission (FWC) biologist, sees Grigsby's character as an overriding factor. "Of all the high-profile angler personalities I've come in contact with, he's among the most genuine and personable of the bunch," remarked Chapman.

"He's never haughty; he's certainly well acclaimed and has always been on the cutting edge of evolving fishing technology. Shaw is versatile in both fresh and salt water and has some of the best sight-fishing eyes in the business. He gladly helped the FWC with several promotional efforts."

Eric Johnson, currently a biologist with the FWC, sees two factors that stand out about Grigsby. "Years back, I took part in the filming of one of his TV shows, and while off camera, Shaw looked over a punch-list of things to mention in an advertisement. When the camera light came on a few minutes later, it amazed me to hear him cover everything so thoroughly and eloquently on the first take. It showed what a true media professional he is.

"The other characteristic is Shaw's dedication. I can stand and cast all day long with the best of them, but like most people, I slow down a bit after eight or so hours. Not Shaw. He's casting incessantly long after everyone else is ready to call it a day. That type of commitment is certainly one of the factors as to why his competitive record is one of the best ever."

Shaw Grigsby attributes his success to receiving valuable insights from others willing to pass along their know-how. It's why he's acted in kind to fellow anglers and competitors during his career. An encounter when he was 16 years of age stuck with Grigsby through adulthood, a day of fishing that was to come full circle many years later.

"Gerry Beavis and I were catching drum in the Suwannee River, with big schools all around us and the fish running 30 to 70 pounds in size," said Grigsby. "We'd hook one up and then lose it, one after the other, and it really frustrated us. You could see the big fish boil and we'd follow along, more often than not missing the hook-up.

"We saw this one guy nearby just crushing them, whacking one huge drum after the other. He could see that we were struggling and meanwhile we wanted to know his secrets. The fellow came over in his boat and without us saying a word first, he said, 'It's real easy, let me show you.' He then proceeded to literally give us a clinic on how he could catch just about any drum he wanted.

"I finally asked who he was. 'Name is Doug Odom,' he replied. Being by then head over heels into everything that had to do with fishing, I recognized his name. I asked if he was the Doug Odom I'd read about in *Bassmaster* and winning this event and that. He answered, 'Yes sir,' and with that he parted.

"Nearly 30 years go by, and I'm doing a talk at a church in Sumter, South Carolina, at a wild-game supper. Someone approached me and

Grigsby is about to throttle forward to begin another bass-finding mission.
Photo courtesy of Polly Grigsby.

said that they had someone in the community who was also considered a professional fisherman. That happens often when people greet tournament anglers, with comments about so-and-so being a great fisherman and such, so imagine my shock when the reply came back as to who he was.

"'His name is Doug Odom,' the man said. 'He's a preacher.'

"I almost fainted," said Grigsby. "I asked if Doug Odom, by chance, was in the audience, and the fellow confirmed it. I got back behind the microphone and told the story about those young kids trying to catch drum and the guy who graciously helped us. I added that that act of generosity really made a mark in this young pro's career.

"Later that night I sought out Doug and we both agreed that one never knows how something like that is going to impact someone's future.

"His favorite saying was 'Watch your wake,' and to do the same thing in life. I always think of Doug Odom when I have a chance to help someone like he did with me and Gerry."

One of Grigsby's favorite and most notable competitors over the years is Doug Gilley from Winter Springs, Florida, who never let a little taste of whiskey stand in the way of competition.

"He used to win lots of tournaments in which I was also entered," Grigsby said. "One in particular really stands out. We fished an event that required us to meet at a specific place for the kickoff. Someone asked of Doug's whereabouts because his truck was in the parking lot.

"We opened the door of his truck and Doug fell out. He somehow staggered to his boat, drove it out in the middle of the lake and fell asleep. He woke up at 1 o'clock the next afternoon and fished until 3, and darned if he didn't catch enough fish to win the tournament anyway.

"He's just a funny, funny, great guy."

Not many people nowadays know this, but Grigsby had another interest besides fishing in his high school days: snakes.

"I once caught a diamond rattlesnake and about a four-foot cottonmouth," he said. "My biology teacher in school was Virginia Allen, Ross Allen's wife—he of Silver Springs fame. I took the snakes to school with the cottonmouth in an old-fashioned goldfish bowl contained inside an aquarium.

"We all watched as I put a bluegill in the bowl and the cottonmouth struck it and ate it. If a kid tried to bring venomous snakes to school these days, he'd be arrested."

With her hubby heading the Silver Springs Institute, Allen's class received a behind-the-scenes look from the side of the viewing glass the public never sees.

"I stood there with my back to one of the cages and I turned around to see a king cobra in full strike pose, no glass between us and only three feet away," Grigsby said.

"My knees went weak and I fell to ground. Ross Allen started laughing because he knew it wasn't aggressive at that point and just shooing me away, but I wasn't taking any chances."

Knowing his penchant for catching snakes without getting bitten, Virginia Allen did seek Grigsby's help once to catch not a snake but instead an alligator.

"She took me out of class and said we had to catch a gator submerged in a little creek that flowed right through the middle of the school grounds," said Grigsby. "She was worried a kid might get bitten, so I said, 'Hey, what about *me* getting bitten?' Anyway, I did have gators occasionally grab my lures and knew how to grab the small ones behind the head—those lures were too expensive to lose.

"So, all the kids and teachers watched as I waded the creek until I saw the gator submerged in three feet of water. I jumped atop it and grabbed the gator behind the head. It twisted and went nuts, but I had a death grip on him and didn't let go. We finally wrapped duct tape around its mouth, put it in a truck and later released it in the swamp. Everyone thought that was pretty cool."

Not much has changed since then, as fellow competitors still think Shaw Grigsby is a pretty cool guy. Whether pursuing bass—his first love—or his latest passion of tarpon on fly on the flats of the Florida Keys, he earns the respect of everyone he meets.

Pal Bernie Schultz regards his friend as one who doesn't know the meaning of the word quit. "He never gives up; he's on a mission when it comes to fishing. You can't help but admire a man like that."

36

More Fishing Legends and Pioneers

Thousands of outstanding guides, expert anglers, journalists and representatives of the fishing, tackle and boating industries have contributed mightily to the recreational fishing surge that continues in Florida.

While not singled out in the previous 35 chapters of the book, the following characters added here offer an additional array of impressive fishing legends. Unquestionably, many more deserve mention and would be included if this book consisted of unlimited pages. I'd welcome your comments regarding my choices and suggestions you may have at www.FloridasFishingLegends.com.

Allen, Jack "Bass"

An expert with popping flies for taking bass in the Everglades, this Ft. Lauderdale resident is part prophet, guide and historian.

Allyn, Rube

One of the most talented journalists on Florida's west coast, he helped found the Florida Outdoor Writers Association in 1946.

Bagley, Jim

He designed lures in the 1970s that took the nation by storm. Hand-carved from balsa wood with handsome finishes, each lure had an overwhelming appeal to anglers as well as to game fish.

Capt. Buddy Carey at the wheel with a full boatload of anglers on his *Sea Boots* out of Pier 5. Photo courtesy of the International Game Fish Association.

Brothers, Jack

Along with Cecil Keith and Jimmie Albright, Brothers is considered one of the triumvirate of flats guides in the formative 1950s in the Florida Keys.

Carey, Buddy

One of the greatest skippers to ever charter out of Miami's famed Pier 5 aboard his boat *Sea Boots*, he previously garnered sea experience while serving in the U.S. Coast Guard with the renowned Capt. Tommy Gifford.

Cass Brothers

This unique fishing family consists of six brothers, four of whom became fishing guides in the 1930s and '40s out of Miami's Pier 5: Sam,

Bonnie Smith, one of the amazing Cass sisters, knew how to catch bonefish on fly long before most male anglers even tried it. Here she lets husband Capt. Bill Smith handle the net. Photo courtesy of the Florida State Archives.

Archie, John and Harvey. They were among the first Florida charter captains to target bluefin tuna and marlin out of the Bahamas on their boat *Margrove*.

Cass Sisters

Even more remarkable than the Cass brothers were three sisters who guided in the Florida Keys. Bonnie "Bonefish" Cass married Capt. Bill Smith in the late 1930s; Bonnie's sister Frankee met a young guy she'd marry named Jimmie Albright in 1941; Beulah made up the third of the only known sister trio of fishing guides.

Cuddy, Lee

He set a world record for sailfish on fly and operated a successful tackle store at 79th Street and Biscayne Boulevard in Miami.

Dyer, Harry

A municipal judge, he was one of the first to recognize the tourism potential for the great sailfishing off Stuart. He also helped found the famed Stuart Sailfish Club in 1941.

Emery, John

Even though he died at the age of only 43, Emery influenced all those with whom he came in contact. He assisted in developing the first large-arbor fly reels as well as aluminum foots for pushpoles.

Fernandez, Chico

He's a brilliant fly fisher who arrived in Miami from Cuba in 1959. An active participant in the burgeoning south Florida angling community, his writings and seminars have made him famous.

Gaddis, "Gadabout"

Roscoe Vernon "Gadabout" Gaddis became one of the first fishing TV stars as *The Flying Fisherman* in the early 1960s. He also previously hosted a radio show in New York and worked as a Shakespeare tackle representative for over 30 years.

Gardner, John

One of the earliest of all known guides in Florida, Gardner began running charters in 1871 out of Ponce Park near what was then known as Mosquito Inlet (now Ponce Inlet).

Grant, Helen

This Palm Beach fishing whiz won numerous tournaments between 1950 and 1980, setting world records along the way and helping to change opinions about the ability of women to compete on an equal basis with men.

Greene, Tommy

A master of bridge fishing, this talented angler and rod builder has operated the popular Custom Rod and Reel shop out of Lighthouse Point for more than 30 years.

Gresh, Earl

A composer, boat racer, wood craftsman, editor and great lure maker during the Great Depression and beyond, he founded the St. Petersburg Rod and Gun Club.

Grey, Zane

Erl Roman, outdoor editor of the *Miami Herald* beginning in the 1930s, once wrote about Grey: "He had about as many friends and also as many enemies as any man I've ever known. Regardless of all that, he was a nut on salt water fishing and, in my books, one of the greatest that ever lived." Grey stayed quite often at the famed Long Key Fishing Camp, founded in 1906 at the northern end of Long Key in the Florida Keys.

Harrod, H. T.

One of the first to recognize fly fishing as a dependable guiding specialty, the Miamian led Col. L. S. Thompson of New Jersey to incidental catches of bonefish and tarpon on fly in 1926 off Long Key in the Florida Keys.

Harry, Elwood

A slight man but with great stature among his worldwide peers, he saw IGFA grow exponentially under his purview.

Hatch, Bill

A Miamian who became another of the masterful charter-boat skippers of his time. In 1915 he perfected the drop-back method for taking sailfish after getting the idea from Capt. Charlie Thompson.

Hayden, Charlie "Split-Tail"

In the early 1950s, he created split-tail versions of cut baits such as mullet to make them swim more naturally, resulting in more strikes by big gamesters like bluefin tuna.

Hewes, Bob

In 1969 the Miamian introduced the first production saltwater flats boat called the *Bonefisher;* the ensuing 16- and 18-foot models became instant successes throughout Florida and the nation.

Hommell, George

He's been a major contributor to the growth of the sport-fishing industry in the upper Keys from the 1950s to the present. He partnered with Billy Pate to start World Wide Sportsman in Islamorada before selling it to Bass Pro Shops.

Huff, Steve

This middle Keys light-tackle guide is renowned for working hard for every client, epitomizing the essence of excellence and commanding the respect of fellow captains.

Keith, Cecil

Along with Jimmie Albright and Jack Brothers, he was one of the top Florida Keys backcountry guides of the 1940s through the '70s, responsible for many of the earliest catches of 100-pound-plus tarpon.

Kelly, James "Jimmy"

He owned the popular fishing camp Eagle's Nest out of Solana near Punta Gorda from the 1940s through the '70s. The camp attracted a loyal following that included Sam Snead and General Omar Bradley.

LaBranche, George

In the late 1920s in Biscayne Bay, based from his house in Islamorada, he collaborated with Henry Howell on specialized tackle and methods for taking bonefish. At first insistent that bonefish could not be fooled by a fly, he became a proponent of the method after being proven wrong by Capt. Bill Smith.

Lau, Glenn

He's an award-winning filmmaker and outdoor journalist from Ocala. His underwater footage of bass behavior is considered some of the best ever taken.

Lerner, Michael

With his famous clothing stores setting him free financially, he and wife Helen traveled the globe to fish. He founded the International Game Fish Association in 1939, funded the Lerner Marine Lab in Bimini, and connected marine scientists with the angling community.

Lewis, Bob

Although not the first to come up with the technique of kite flying, Lewis broadened and perfected its use off Miami in the 1960s and beyond. One of the first successful heart-transplant recipients, he served as a Miami Beach motorcycle cop until landing a job running the boat of then-publisher of the *Miami Herald*, James Knight.

Lones, Tommy

He ranks as a top Key West skipper before and during the evolutionary "discovery" of Key West as a phenomenal fishing destination.

Madsen, Harry

A captain from the 1920s through the '30s, he's credited with being the man who first located the rich "sailfish grounds" just north of Palm Beach.

Martin, Roy

Once anointed by *Life* magazine as the "World's Greatest Angler," this former mayor of Panama City became a world-record holder and accomplished rod builder.

McChristain, Bob, Jr.

In 1946 he opened Captain Mac's Fishing Shack in Miami and became the first in Florida to retail spinning tackle.

Merritt, F. R. "Roy" and Ennis

One of the great custom yacht builders, Roy Merritt and wife Ennis started Merritt Boatworks in 1947 as a repair yard in Pompano Beach. In the mid 1950s, they switched to boat building and the family run business skyrocketed to success.

Moore, Edward

In the early 1900s, he ran a motor launch along the southern portion of Florida's Atlantic coast and also plied the virgin waters of the Bahamas.

Despite charging a premium ($35 per day) for charters, he was booked over 300 days every year.

Moret, Sandy

Considered one of the finest fly casters in the world, his Florida Keys Outfitters store in Islamorada is a must-visit for fly aficionados. Moret's fly-fishing school features marquee instructors such as Rick Ruoff, Steve Huff, Chico Fernandez, Flip Pallot, Craig Brewer, Diana Rudolph and others.

Pallot, Flip

His hit TV series in the 1990s, *Walker's Cay Chronicles,* set a high mark for production excellence. Over the years Pallot has ably filled the roles of guide, TV host, boat designer, journalist and accomplished fly angler.

Rast, Bob

Rast, whose talents and vigorous style raised the bar for charter-boat fishing off Stuart and Palm Beach, was the intrepid skipper of the *Rendezvous* for many years out of Sailfish Marina.

Reagan, Lefty

Along with Doc and Helen Robinson, this Key West skipper and his boat mate, Bob Marvin, helped develop the teasing method for taking billfish on fly aboard his boats *Cay Sal* and *Sea Raider.*

Rhode, Homer

He worked for the original Florida Game and Fresh Water Fish Commission and later plied the waters of Biscayne Bay, Tamiami Canal and waterways between Ochopee and Marco Island. He perfected a well-known loop knot named after him.

Capt. Lefty Reagan admiring a day's venture aboard the *Sea Raider* out of Key West. Reagan would become the skipper for Helen and Doc Robinson and help devise the effective teasing method for catching billfish on fly. Photo courtesy of Hackett and the Florida State Archives.

Roman, Erl

Outdoor editor of the *Miami Herald* for 17 years in the 1930s and '40s, Roman was among the first Florida outdoor journalists to champion fresh- and saltwater conservation issues.

Sanchez, Julio

He made a name for himself targeting big-game fish in the 1930s, inventing the foot rest for fighting chairs and setting many world records off Miami and the Bahamas on his boat *Willow D* with brother Emelio and Capt. Fred Lister.

Saunders, Edward "Bra"

A true pioneer of Key West charter captains, Saunders was one of the more prominent influences in developing Hemingway's fishing talents beginning in the 1930s.

Smith, Bouncer

Operating his *Bouncer's Dusky* open fisherman, he's considered among the best guides in south Florida and has represented recreational fishing interests on numerous fishery management boards and commissions over the years.

Snow, Harry, Sr., and Harry Snow Jr.

The accomplishments of this father-son team of fishing guides in the middle and upper Keys spans the early 1900s through the '70s.

Stanczyk, Richard

The owner of Bud 'N Mary's Marina on the southern tip of Islamorada, he's developed one of the top offshore and backcountry guiding services in the world. He's a versatile angler himself who has rejuvenated and revolutionized the broadbill fishery off the upper Keys.

Vernon, Harry

For 30 years, Capt. Harry owned a tackle store on the Miami River that's still going strong. He became the foremost saltwater fishing–supply dealer to Central and South America.

Longtime owner of Bud N' Mary's Marina in Islamorada, Richard Stanczyk cracked the code on how to take swordfish even by day. Photo courtesy of Ron Modra.

Vreeland, James "Pee Wee"

Builder of the "Kingfisher" boats in the 1930s in Ft. Lauderdale, Vreeland was a diminutive fellow with boundless ability and great enthusiasm for taking sailfish.

Waterman, Charley

The dean of Florida outdoors writers, Waterman's thousands of columns spanned 50 years and appeared in numerous major publications. His writing flowed with a simple, humorous and homespun style.

Wharton, Redwood

He opened the Inlet Harbor Fish Camp on the Halifax River in 1944 and led offshore excursions on his boat *Gay Wind*, which is now on display at the Ponce Inlet Lighthouse.

Wright, Peter

Growing up in Ft. Lauderdale, he graduated from the University of Miami with a degree in marine biology. This worldwide offshore expert has fished every season in Australia since 1968, and he's caught more marlin over 1,000 pounds than any captain or angler in history.

The famed dock Pier 5, which was destroyed in a hurricane in the 1960s and never rebuilt, served as headquarters for Miami offshore chartering greats like Tommy Gifford, Bill Hatch, Bill Fagen, and scores of others. Photo courtesy of Charles Barron and the Florida State Archives.

Acknowledgments

My favorite book is one my son gave me for Christmas a few years ago titled *Golf's Golden Age.* I looked high and low for something similar that specifically highlighted Florida's remarkable fishing heritage, but I couldn't find one. The closest I came was Nixon Smiley's pictorial books such as *Yesterday's Florida,* which provided great historical interest but only a smidgeon here and there about sport fishing.

With more world records than any other state or even any other country, Florida's fishing history deserves special bragging rights. When you figure that total annual fishing days equal a staggering 23 million and an economic injection of $7.7 billion—not to mention nearly 80,000 jobs—for the Sunshine State, a testament is in order honoring the phenomenal characters and personalities who have formed the backbone of this boom. And so, here it is.

A big thanks goes to those contributing advice, research assistance and suggested candidates for the book. A tip o' the hat to Tim O'Keefe—he gave me the impetus to write a book of value (or so I hope) to Florida's angling history. I salute John Byram for his patience and for putting up with my idiosyncrasies. Handshakes are also in order for Herb Allen, Rebecca Allen, Stu Apte, Dave Brown, Duane Baker, Dave Burkhardt, Phil Chapman, Susan Cocking, Mark Cooper, Bill Curtis, Vic Dunaway, Harlan Franklin, Russ and Beth Geyer, Tom Hambright, Jeff Harkavy, Eric Johnson, Rob Kramer, Larry Larsen, Mike Myatt, Robert Montgomery, Andy Newman, Rob O'Neal, Al Pflueger, Warren Resen, Walt Reynolds, Dave Ritchie, Pat Rybovich, Frank Sargeant, Bernie Schultz, Carol Shaughnessy, Bill Shedd, Mark Sosin, Richard Stanczyk, Walt Stearns, Wendy Tucker, Tom Twyford, Earl Waters, Raleigh

Werking, Karl Wickstrom, Jerry Wilkinson, Charlie Walker and of course all the subjects of the book still living who were generous with their time and resources.

I received familial encouragement from daughter Lynn and ex-wife Debbie, both of whom goaded me to complete this while still among the breathing. In particular, my wife Kelly—yes, she's "Kelly Kelly"—contributed mightily to the effort of organizing the huge volume of image files so essential to the historical flavor of this book. Branded into my psyche forevermore are her familiar words: "It's not enough resolution."

Another special high-five to my son Michael, who helped develop the original research files, assisted in hunting down sources and proofread every word. He also kept me supplied with Excedrin Migraine tablets for the times when my creative juices clogged and I felt like putting a foot through the computer monitor.

Much of the blurry-eyed research occurred in the venerable library of the International Game Fish Association (IGFA) in Dania Beach, Florida. Many of the images came from the IGFA as well, and without their substantial support this book would simply not have been possible. Gail Morchower and Darlene Raposa, IGFA librarian and assistant librarian, respectively, handled my endless requests with aplomb and cool. IGFA execs Mike Myatt and Rob Kramer provided encouragement and thoughtful suggestions. Tourism representatives throughout Florida also pitched in and some even did a little extra digging.

As to all the historians, staffers, quoted sources, living legends and families of pioneers past and present who have provided assistance, I do hope the result lives up to their expectations and does everyone proud.

Bibliography

Ames, Fisher, Jr. *By Reef and Trail*. Boston: Brown and Page, 1909.

Apte, Stu. *Of Wind and Tides*. Canada: self-published with Artbookbindery. com, 2008.

Bucuvalas, Tina, Peggy A. Bulger, and Stetson Kennedy. *South Florida Folklife*. Jackson: University Press of Mississippi, 1994.

Carter, Horace. *Tales & Truths*. Tabor City, N.C.: Atlantic Publishing, 1993.

Cory, Charles B. *Hunting and Fishing in Florida*. Boston: Arno and the New York Times Press, 1896.

Dimock, A. W. *The Book of the Tarpon*. New York: Macmillan, 1911.

Dimock, A. W., and Julian A. Dimock. *Florida Enchantments*. New York: Outing, 1908.

Endicott, Wendell. *Adventures with Rod and Harpoon along the Florida Keys*. New York: Strokes, 1925.

Gregg, William. *Where, When, and How to Catch Fish on the East Coast of Florida*. New York: Matthews-Northrup, 1902.

Hallock, Charles. *Camp Life in Florida: A Handbook for Sportsmen and Settlers*. New York: Forest and Stream Publishing, 1876.

Heilner, Van Campen. *Adventures in Angling*. Cincinnati: Stewart Kidd, 1922.

Henshall, James A. *Camping and Cruising in Florida*. Port Salerno, Fla.: Florida Classics, 1884.

Lawrence, H. Lea. *Prowling Papa's Waters*. Atlanta: Longstreet Press, 1992.

McLendon, James. *Papa: Hemingway in Key West*. Key West: The Langley Press, 1984.

Miller, Stewart. *Florida Fishing*. New York: Watt, 1931.

Montgomery, Robert U. *Better Bass Fishing*. Woodstock, Vt.: The Countryman Press, 2009.

Oppel, Frank, and Tony Meisel, eds. *Tales of Old Florida*. Secaucus, N.J.: Castle, 1987.

Pinckney, Frank S. *Tarpon or Silver King.* New York: Anglers, 1888.

Reiger, George. *Profiles in Saltwater Angling.* Englewood Cliffs, N.J.: Prentice Hall, 1973.

Roman, Erl. "Million for a Fin." Unpublished manuscript. Coral Gables, Fla.: c. 1960.

Shevlin, Thomas H. *Good Luck and Tight Lines.* New York: Town & Country, 1953.

Smiley, Nixon. *Yesterday's Florida.* Miami: E. A. Seemann Publishing, 1974.

Smiley, Nixon. *Yesterday's Miami.* Miami: E. A. Seemann Publishing, 1974.

Tebeau, Charlton W. *A History of Florida.* Coral Gables, Fla.: University of Miami Press, 1971.

Turner-Turner, J. *The Giant Fish of Florida.* London: Arthur Pearson, 1902.

Ward, Rowland. *The English Angler in Florida.* Micanopy, Fla.: Micanopy Publishing, 1898.

Windhorn, Stan, and Wright Langley. *Yesterday's Florida Keys.* Key West: The Langley Press, 1974.

Wylie, Philip. *Spare the Rod.* New York: Harold Ober Associates, 1940.

Yale, Leroy M., A. Foster Higgins, J. G. A. Creighton, Robert Grant, A. R. MacDonough, Alexander Cargill, and Charles Frederick Holder. *Angling.* New York: Scribner, 1896.

Index

Doug Kelly, a resident of Clearwater, Florida, is a long-term representative for the International Game Fish Association. He's served on the editorial staffs of several state and national magazines and as executive director for Florida-based Bonefish & Tarpon Trust as well as for the Florida Outdoor Writers Association. The author of hundreds of newspaper, magazine and Internet articles, Doug has also produced radio and TV shows about the outdoors as well as the award-winning *Saltwater Fly Fishing from A to Z* video series.

Doug's writing assignments still span the globe, and that perspective has given him an even greater appreciation for his home state's unparalleled fishing resources.

Turning the pages of *Florida's Fishing Legends and Pioneers* transports you through remarkable eras and lets you trace the amazing footsteps of important personalities, colorful characters and the talented experts who molded the remarkable history of sport fishing in the Sunshine State.

Comments about the book are welcome at www.FloridasFishing Legends.com

WILD FLORIDA
edited by M. Timothy O'Keefe

Books in this series are written for the many people who visit and/or
move to Florida to participate in our remarkable outdoors, an environ-
ment rich in birds, animals and activities, many exclusive to this state.
Books in the series will offer readers a variety of formats: Natural history guides, historical outdoor guides, guides to some of Florida's most
popular pastimes and activities, and memoirs of outdoors folk and their
unique lifestyles.

*30 Eco-trips in Florida: The Best Nature Excursions (and How to Leave Only
Your Footprints)*, by Holly Ambrose (2005)
Hiker's Guide to the Sunshine State, by Sandra Friend (2005)
Fishing Florida's Flats: A Guide to Bonefish, Tarpon, Permit, and Much More,
by Jan S. Maizler (2007)
50 Great Walks in Florida, by Lucy Beebe Tobias (2008)
*Hiking the Florida Trail: 1,100 Miles, 78 Days, Two Pairs of Boots, and One
Heck of an Adventure*, by Johnny Molloy (2008)
The Complete Florida Beach Guide, by Mary and Bill Burnham (2008)
The Saltwater Angler's Guide to Florida's Big Bend and Emerald Coast, by
Tommy L. Thompson (2009)
Secrets from Florida's Master Anglers, by Ron Presley (2009)
*Exploring Florida's Botanical Wonders: A Guide to Ancient Trees, Unique
Flora, and Wildflower Walks*, by Sandra Friend (2010)
Florida's Fishing Legends and Pioneers, by Doug Kelly (2011)